KT-465-302

EGO 6

MY BOOKS

★

Novels

RESPONSIBILITY
BLESSED ARE THE RICH
GEMEL IN LONDON

Belles-lettres

L. OF C. (LINES OF COMMUNICATION)
FANTASIES AND IMPROMPTUS
WHITE HORSE AND RED LION
ON AN ENGLISH SCREEN
AGATE'S FOLLY
THE COMMON TOUCH
KINGDOMS FOR HORSES
BAD MANNERS
EXPRESS AND ADMIRABLE
THURSDAYS AND FRIDAYS

Essays of the Theatre

BUZZ, BUZZ!
ALARUMS AND EXCURSIONS
AT HALF-PAST EIGHT
THE CONTEMPORARY THEATRE, 1923
THE CONTEMPORARY THEATRE, 1924
THE CONTEMPORARY THEATRE, 1925
THE CONTEMPORARY THEATRE, 1926
A SHORT VIEW OF THE ENGLISH STAGE
PLAYGOING
THEIR HOUR UPON THE STAGE
MY THEATRE TALKS
FIRST NIGHTS
MORE FIRST NIGHTS
THE AMAZING THEATRE
BRIEF CHRONICLES
THESE WERE ACTORS

Biography

RACHEL

Anthologies

THE ENGLISH DRAMATIC CRITICS, 1660–1932
SPEAK FOR ENGLAND
HERE'S RICHNESS!

Autobiography

EGO
EGO 2
EGO 3
EGO 4
EGO 5

Photo Hans Man

The Author

Fr.

EGO 6

ONCE MORE THE AUTOBIOGRAPHY
OF

JAMES AGATE

The *Oral History* has been my rope and my scaffold, my bed and my board, my wife and my floozy, my wound and the salt on it, my whiskey and my aspirin, and my rock and my salvation. It is the only thing that matters a damn to me. All else is dross.

JOSEPH FERDINAND GOULD

GEORGE G. HARRAP & CO. LTD.
LONDON TORONTO BOMBAY SYDNEY

TO

MY DOCTORS

ROBERT LEAVER, RALPH BAKER,

AND

NORMAN NEWMAN

FOR

THEIR CARE OF THE MACHINE

First published 1944
by GEORGE G. HARRAP & CO. LTD.
182 High Holborn, London, W.C.1

THIS BOOK IS PRODUCED IN
COMPLETE CONFORMITY WITH THE
AUTHORIZED ECONOMY STANDARDS

Composed in Scotch Roman type and printed by Morrison & Gibb, Ltd., London and Edinburgh
Made in Great Britain

ILLUSTRATIONS

1942

Aug. 3 *Monday.* I sometimes think I could have written good books if I had had the time. *L. of C.* was jotted down when I ought to have been concentrating on the Pay and Mess Book of an A.S.C. Divisional Train, *Buzz, Buzz!* when I ought to have been cooking forage accounts, and *Responsibility* when I should have been auditing those of brother officers. This sixth and possibly final volume of *Ego*—I can feel an October nip in the air—will be my thirty-seventh book, unless, of course, I publish some more while it is writing. This means thirty-seven slabs of stolen time. Every moment spent on *Ego* has been filched from the hours I should have been giving to this editor and that. George Meredith relinquished his job as publisher's reader because he could live by his novels. But since, all deductions made, my books have never brought me in even a hundred pounds a year, I must continue reviewing plays, films, novels. And then there is the old income-tax nuisance. My arrears tie me to the stake. Bear-like, I must fight the course.

And I am getting on. I grow old. I no longer care about appearances. In the days when I was horse-showing I was as well groomed as my little marvel Ego. Now I wear the same suit ten days running, and underlinen till its state is positively Johnsonian. I make a shave last three days, and can't be bothered with haircuts. When I go upstairs to make myself presentable and sally forth as in the long ago—all this takes a good hour, and in that hour I could have reviewed a play, a film, or a book. I feel that there is a certain unnaturalness about an old fogey smelling April and May. Is there not something grotesque and even revolting in the spectacle of the septuagenarian Goethe writing a Trilogy of Passion to the bouncing Ulrike von Levetzow?

Aug. 4 *Tuesday.* "Apportez le fatras, chérie," said She-Who-Must-Not-Be-Named to her companion Mme Normand whenever she could snatch a few moments for her *Art of the Theatre*. Larousse defines "fatras" as "amas confus de choses." The nearest English is "ragbag." But I prefer the French, and "fatras" it is going to be. I shall use this to denote odd thoughts which come into my mind apropos of anything and everything.

Fatras. As I write, Saint-Saëns on the wireless is grinding away at some monstrous piece of competence saying nothing with absolute perfection. So in the *Merry Wives* does Shakespeare toil at something in which he has no heart, but making a better job of it than any other Elizabethan who should have used brain, stomach, bowels, liver, spleen, and kidneys. Are the rapscallions but shadows of their former selves? Yes, but who else would have found such quips as are left them? Is Falstaff the man he was? No, but he can still talk about having his brains taken out and buttered and, moreover, given to the dog, and, to cap all, let it be for a New Year's gift! Ford seems to me to be a reasonable-sized figure to waste on a piece of hack-work, and Shakespeare was not bound to crib from Marlowe such a jewel as

By shallow rivers, to whose falls
Melodious birds sing madrigals . . .

or throw off such a gem of simplicity as William Page's Latin Lesson. And who but Shakespeare, having invented Shallow, could have gone on to conjure up that even emptier vessel, Slender, that "very potent piece of imbecility" as Hazlitt calls him? "He and his friend Sackerson and his book of songs and his love of Anne Page and his having nothing to say to her can never be forgotten." Yes, Slender is what happens when a man of supreme genius sets about a job of work to which he has had to be prompted, not to say prodded.

Aug. 5 *Wednesday.* Judging from certain quick-firing communications, the Income Tax people have started range-finding. Well, let 'em. When the war broke out I owed some £5000. The income tax went up, and my earnings showed an immediate decrease of £1500 a year, falling to £2000. Nevertheless I have, or rather Stanley Rubinstein has, paid off all my debts except £1500 still owing to the Revenue plus something for current tax.

Aug. 6 *Thursday.* During the last three days I have been laid low, or rather kept bolt upright, by a very painful attack of neuritis in the neck and shoulders, which has made me move in one piece. Michael Shepley says that I sit down and get up at the Café Royal like Banquo's Ghost at the banquet!

Aug. 7 *Friday.* The B.B.C. rings up to know whether I will travel to Bangor, stay the night there, and broadcast a talk with a Welsh factory girl. For wasting two days, and to make up for the bore of travelling, I am offered expenses and the fee of ten guineas, of which seven go to income tax. Really, there is a transcendentality of delirium—as Gilbert's Lady Jane would say—about these B.B.C. proposals which the earthy might easily mistake for imbecility.

Aug. 8 *Saturday.* Oh, that mine adversary had written a book! To my unutterable joy I find that my old enemy, G. W. Stonier, of the *New Statesman* (see *Ego* 5, p. 165), committed this indiscretion many years ago, and that I reviewed it. The book is called *The Shadow across the Page.* I cull:

> "God must be angry," said the child, "or the thunder wouldn't be so loud"; and she raised her hands in prayer like a lightning conductor.

Praying to be struck, I suppose! If I had raised my hands in prayer like Stonier's Awful Child, G. W. S. could not have delivered himself into them better.

Aug. 9 *Sunday.* Am writing this at some lodgings in Wellington Square, Oxford, after a week-end of riotous idleness. Came down with Edgar Lustgarten on Friday, too late for dinner at any of the hotels. But Joyce Lustgarten, who has more brains than her chic entitles her to, does wonderfully with stuff out of tins; the landlady, like most of her kind in this vile-mannered town, disallows any facilities for cooking, except for breakfast. Initiate Joyce and a highly dynamic young woman called Josephine Driver—a crooner in the Potato and Carrot Division of the Ministry of Food—into cut-throat bridge, at which Joyce wins. When the girls have gone to bed Edgar produces whiskey and invites me to listen to his reconstruction of the Marx Brothers films, *A Night at the Opera* and *Animal Crackers*. His gift for miming, his delighted apprehension of Groucho, whom he physically resembles in all but the moustache, his intense absorption in his own performance—these keep me up, a willing if slightly bemused listener, till round about three. By my bedside I find a bunch of pink roses, reading-lamp, matches, the *Love Poems* of John Donne, Proust's *Within a Budding Grove*, and Damon Runyon's *More than Somewhat*. Read, re-read, and read again the magnificent poem entitled "The Flea," and go to sleep wishing to-day's young poets could resolve their logic-chopping into a full-close as magnificent as Donne's

> Though parents grudge, and you, we're met,
> And cloistered in these living walls of jet.

Lunch yesterday was in a maisonette over a dairy in a back street. Two bedrooms turned into a restaurant by an elderly Austrian refugee—a well-known Viennese specialist—and his wife. A charming couple who will not let you think them pathetic. Beautiful cooking—soup, ragoût of beef, and a sweet. Half-a-crown a head. The cinema in the evening, dinner at the Mitre, more cut-throat. Edgar, again producing whiskey, gives me a lecture on the brilliance of Patrick Hastings—"the greatest advocate this century has produced"—and brushes aside my objection that distinguished lawyers and prominent statesmen should not let down their reputation by writing undistinguished plays. "Why, James, do you show horses?" The suggestion that my little Ego could even by implication be considered anything but a top-notcher sends me to bed. Not in a huff, but betimes. By the reading-lamp Pepys, *Ulysses*, and Bromfield's *The Strange Case of Miss Annie Spragg*.

Came down to breakfast this morning feeling well and fit. New-laid, lightly boiled egg—a thing I haven't tasted for a year. Ivor Brown in the *Observer* has this remarkable passage:

> The British Government, for the first time, is concerned with (and financing) the arts, not one but all of them, and

> not for purposes of propaganda only. This is a most remarkable break with the old tradition of Governmental isolation. It is up to the artist to realise the challenge which this implies. By their success now in providing recreation will their status in the future be determined.

Not by me. While accepting Ivor's definition of recreation as "renewal of mind and body and not just an hour's escape into dreamland," I shall still not give a Hamlet first-class status because he has succeeded in impressing yokels seeing Shakespeare for the first time. I am telling Joyce I can just force myself to believe in bringing Art to the masses because of the occasional receptive soul who might otherwise never establish contact with it, when Edgar looks up from Runyon's *Furthermore* and says like this : "Artistic education is no good at all. I am tired of that cant which wants to force on the working classes æsthetic uplift, a better taste in wall-papers, and symphony concerts. The working classes should be taught just enough writing to apply for a job and enough reading to know whether they've got it. And enough arithmetic not to be cheated in the shops. The exceptions who want anything better will go after it and get it. Abraham Lincoln, James !" I concur. I am tempted to agree seriously with one William Cameron, who wrote ironically : "Like bathrooms, it is the worker's function to make, not use, refrigerators." There lives more health in honest dirt, believe me, than in half the tubs. I hold that the effect of a bath of poetry on the dustman can only be to put him out of conceit with his job. I am talking about the British, to whom art is an extraneous thing, and not about, say, Russian workers, for whom art is something innate. "To speak of art as a recreation is to give it the highest social office," writes Ivor. I would much rather press into service half a dozen first-rate cricket elevens, football sides, teams of boxers and dart-players, and send them round the camps, naval schools, and aerodromes. As exponents of the British social idea they would be infinitely better than Shakespeare's plays or Shaw's harangues. Exceptions make bad rules, and equally the Bloomsbury poet caught up in the Services is not a good witness for the case Ivor is trying to establish. I believe in fostering that which is best in individual or nation, and not in forcing on him and them something alien, however admirable that thing may be in itself.

Again lunched at the little Austrian place. My hosts going off to secure some new rooms, I spent the afternoon listening to the B.B.C. and wondering why Ivor doesn't turn the heat on in that direction. Later two timid males held their breaths while Joyce descended to the basement and gave the landlady victorious notice. Proposing to celebrate this, we sallied forth. But proposing in this town is not getting. Oxford seems to be even more crowded than when I was here. The little Gloucester Arms, back-to-back with the Playhouse, whither I repaired every evening during the production of *Hedda Gabler*, was closed to-night through lack of beer. Stood four deep at the bar of the George for what seemed like twenty minutes, and couldn't get served. Why this shortage of liquor ? I can only explain it on the grounds of a rabid teetotalism on the part of the authorities, or the fear lest the soldiery passing through should take it into their heads to turn into a drunken, brutal, and licentious mob with an urge towards town councillors' wives. Was so angry that I rushed my hosts off to the Randolph and ordered the best in the hotel, which included grouse and champagne. EDGAR (*smiling*). "Well, James, I look back on the day's events, and I look at what is before us. And I say with Trimalchio, 'The day is nothing ; better to go straight from bed to board.' "

As soon as we get home Edgar makes a dive for the wireless. He turns it on, and we hear his friend Spike Hughes—Spike was my friend too before this broadcast—re-telling the story of Cinderella as it might happen in Harlem. Duke Ellington records. J. A. listens for some time, and then says, "What filth ! What foulness ! These swing people can't hit a note in the middle or stay on it. They make a noise like a cow in labour." EDGAR. "They don't want to hit a note in the middle. And I don't want them to. I dote on cows in labour." J. A. reaches for *More than Somewhat* and reads : " 'A torch song is a song which guys sing when they have the big burnt-up feeling inside themselves over a battle with their dolls.' " EDGAR. "Listen, James. I am quite unmusical. Your Brahms and your Hugo Wolf do nothing to me ; this caterwauling, as you call it, does. Why do you criticise something for which you have no feeling ? " J. A. "The average dance-band leader . . ." EDGAR (*interrupting*). "Ellington is not a dance-band leader in your sense. Neither is he average ; he is exceptional. Don't you realise that Lou This and Jake That live by cheapening and debasing your kind of music, whereas Duke invents his own kind, which is not a vulgarisation of anything?" The broadcast ended, Edgar switches the talk on to something else: "James, do you know the passage in Gorky in which he quotes the letter of Pliny to the Emperor Trajan?" No, James doesn't. "Well, here it is." Reads: "'It soon transpired that there were many Jews—this is usually the case when one begins to investigate a crime.'" J. A. "What's remarkable about that?" EDGAR. "Only that Pliny wrote 'Christians,' not 'Jews.'" Foreseeing serious discussion, I re-introduce the Marx Brothers, and under cover of Edgar's riotous analysis, with pantomime, of *Duck Soup*, collect my thoughts about the past two days. At midnight Edgar goes unexpectedly to bed, pouring me out what whiskey he thinks good for me after champagne, and telling me not to sit up late as we have to catch thc 8.40 in the morning. No books in the bedroom, presumably for the same reason. We have made an ideal trio. Edgar is a first-rate talker, I am a good listener when there's anybody to listen to, while Joyce has the quality of Runyon's Silk, the doll who knocks off a banker by the name of Israel Ib: "She seldom sticks in her oar, except maybe to ask a question. Naturally a doll who is willing to listen instead of wanting to gab herself is bound to be popular because if there is anything most citizens hate and despise it is a gabby doll."

Aug. 10 *Monday.* George Richards sends me an opening for a *Conte Macabre*:

> One late autumn evening as twilight was coming on I was walking in the lane at the back of my house, which I had then rented for a period of eighteen months. Looking up I noticed between the gables a small window which I had never seen from inside.

Aug. 11 *Tuesday.* They managed the trade-show of *Bambi* badly. First we had an M.o.I. film in which sailors of all the Allied nations gathered round a bar, clinked their canakins, and proceeded to reconstruct Europe on federal lines. Which I shall believe possible when Churchill tells me he is seeing eye to eye with De Valera and Gandhi. Next a long and boring film about bird-life, and then something longer and only slightly less boring about bees, accompanied by Mendelssohn's music played at half-speed. After which a selection of music reminding me of that Swiss Cottage shop-window which every day for months has offered me the choice of Addinsell's Warsaw Concerto, a song called *Jealousy* with Hutch's photograph, and something entitled *Booglie Wooglie Piggy*. The news followed, and as by this time one hour and twenty-five minutes had elapsed it may be gathered that I was not in the mood for Bambi, Namby, Pamby, or even a thriller about Helen Lambie. *Enfin Bambi vint*, and while we were being told who was responsible for the film's plumbing, etc., Leo Pavia, a frenzied Disney fan, took occasion to say, " You know, James, Disney is not only a magician ; he is a preacher without pulpit. He is the Crome of the screen. He can be as macabre as Hieronymus Bosch and as elegant as Corot. He is an inspiration, an exhilaration, and a sublimation of earthly experience." Before I had time to growl, " He's a blind spot with me," I found myself in an enchanted and enchanting world. Wholly admirable was Bambi's sire, not so much Landseer's Monarch of the Glen as a portrait of the Prince Regent in his early days. " The First Stag in Europe," said Leo. So much for three-quarters of the film. In the last quarter my admiration turned to positive dislike. For here Disney introduced his love-interest, foolish because humanised. To anybody with knowledge of farming, the stallion travelling the country road and serving his quantum of mares as unemotionally as the postman delivers letters is a more decent spectacle than this preposterous peeka-booing.

Aug. 13 *Thursday.* Terence Rattigan's *Flare Path* turned out to be a glib drama in the Emlyn Williams vein. A core of nothing in particular, with fascinating surrounds. Pretending to centre in a wife torn between a husband broken in body and a lover broken in mind, the play was really about a Polish airman who fell into ' the drink,' the airman's slang for the sea. Was reminded of that early sketch of Harry Tate in which Tate junior was told off to feed the new dog. Ten seconds later Junior made headlong re-entry, his clothes torn to ribbons. " Has the dog bitten you, my boy ? " queried Tate *père*. " Yes,

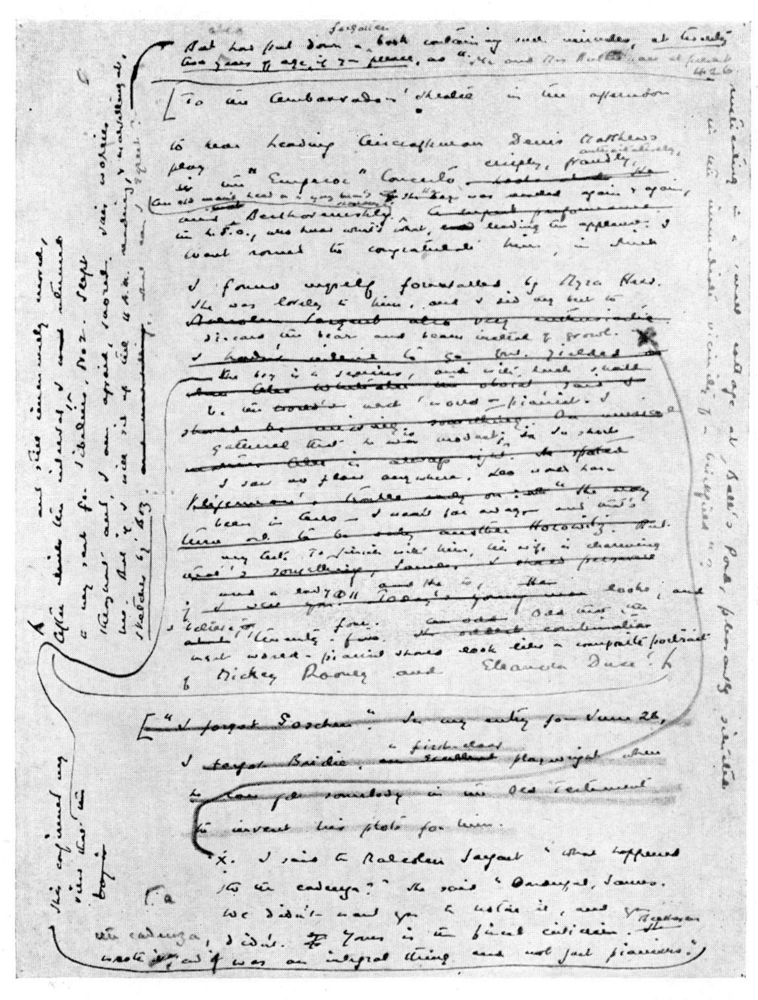

To the Ambassadors' Theatre in the afternoon

to hear Leading Aircraftsman Denis Matthews play

the "Emperor" Concerto

I went round to congratulate him,

I found myself forestalled by Myra Hess.

Mickey Rooney and Eleanora Duse!

X. I said to Malcolm Sargent 'What happened to the cadenza?'

Author's MS.

(*See p.* 212)

Photo Pictorial Press

The Author with Alexis Kligerman

thank you, papa ! " said Tate *fils*. Terry should have called his play *In the Drink ; or, Yes, Thank You, Jerry !*

Letter from Stanley Rubinstein :

5 & 6 Raymond Buildings
Gray's Inn
*London, W.C.*1
12*th August*, 1942

DEAR JIMMIE,

It is my duty to warn you that I have this morning received a letter from the Solicitor of Inland Revenue in Llandudno demanding payment of £2344 11*s*. 0*d*. within ten days, failing which proceedings will be instituted.

I have written in reply inviting an interview in London.

Yours,
STANLEY RUBINSTEIN

It looks as though the present instalment of *Ego* should be called *In the Soup ; or, Yes, Thank You, Stanley !*

Aug. 14 *Friday*. Some time ago I heard a young man playing the piano in the foyer of the "Q" Theatre. And playing it very well. Jack de Leon introducing us, he turned out to be Alexis Kligerman, a Russian Pole. I asked him to call on me with the object of seeing whether something better couldn't be arranged for him. De Leon very keen about this too. He came to tea this afternoon, and Leo at once recognised him as the young man he wrote me about. (See *Ego* 5, p. 68.) He asked what he should play ? I said, " We'll e'en to't like French falconers, fly at any thing we see," little thinking he would fly at Beethoven's Opus 111, which he played with great fire and delicacy. The Chopin Barcarolle was a little too much like a Cossack defending the passage of the Don. Wound up with the Rigoletto-Fantasie of Liszt, which he played with as much virtuosity as anyone living. The young man is twenty-two, tall, good-looking in the Slav way, and with a modest demeanour which, as soon as he sits down at the piano, changes to something commanding. I feel the urge to help as I did with Tait and Allott. (See *Ego*.) Perhaps because he will be a change from the hordes of mediocrities who pester me with their lack of talent. As I write the last word the post brings me Blackwood's

Lady's Magazine for one hundred years ago. Opening at random I read :

> The Paris journals are raving about a young pianist of the name of Dreyschock, who is described as uniting the qualities of Liszt and Thalberg. He was first heard at a soirée at M. Erard's, where the *élite* of the Parisian artistes were assembled to hear him ; and his performance received the utmost admiration.

Grove indicates that Dreyschock was the most famous virtuoso of his day—the man of whom J. B. Cramer said, " He has no left hand : he has two right hands." A good omen for Kligerman.

Aug. 15 *Saturday.* " I have nothing with this answer, Hamlet ; these words are not mine." I have nothing with these modern poets ; their words are certainly not mine. Some little time ago I quoted in the *Express* some lines from Keidrych Rhys's *Letter to Lord Beaverbrook* :

> Yes, I hope I am your solitary agent in the country parishes
> but in the erect cemented sunlight what can one do
> except take waterspout off too-too-weighted shoulders
> unless unless . . .

and asked what they meant. This morning I receive a letter from the author, who writes :

> " Solitary agent in the country parishes." This is a dig at W. H. Auden. Auden's verse always sees the countryside as dead-beaten, defeated.
>
> " Erect cemented sunlight." Seeing a pastoral scene as it is—farmyards are sometimes concreted, you know—giving an idea of the farmer's lot in actuality, not a distorted Georgian version. Even D. H. Lawrence romanticises about beasts at times.
>
> " Waterspout weight." The effort of pumping water into the milk-cooling tank which is felt in the shoulders.
>
> " Unless unless. . . ." Hinting at an agrarian revolution on the land : contrasting change by worth-while people with the bitter revengeful complex of the lazy and work-shy.

But does Rhys really think that a jury of normally intelligent people, sitting for hours with wet cloths round their heads, would be able to guess these things ? Or even a jury of brother poets ? If to approximate to a crossword puzzle is the test of poetry, then

" Torquemada " is the greatest poet since the last war. On the opposite page in *The Van Pool*, the little volume from which the Beaverbrook quotation is taken, is a poem entitled *Week-end in South Gower*, from which I quote the fourth and fifth verses—supposing ' verses ' to be the word :

Now the stiff climb, some duck-necked oyster-catchers,
Recall a poet's hæmorrhage at base ; talk bosh.
Watch specks move up towards sightseers' crags, so we, late
Just before tea-time dare go, and I, a wind-in-jawbone man,

Like madman, busy, pass over our mutual heathgrass,
Mark rock on trees, small ponies at their toilet,
The housetops round Pennard Castle, that single sentinel.
Appetites for evening palate when croquet is played.

Again, I lack the clue. I can understand a young man of fifteen taking, say, twenty years to attune his ears to the new poetry. If he succeeds he has the expectation of half a lifetime's enjoyment of it ; if he fails he has wasted twenty years at a time of life when he can perhaps spare them. At my age the case is altered. So I shall continue to repeat to myself :

Now dance the lights on lawn and lea,
The flocks are whiter down the vale,
And milkier every milky sail
On winding stream or distant sea.

I suppose hardly a week goes by in which Tennyson's picture does not come into my mind. " And milkier every milky sail " lies on my spirit like Schumann's F sharp Romance. Whereas Rhys's line about the duck-necked oyster-catchers and the poet's hæmorrhage affect me like Berg or Bloch or Bartók. My difficulty is the recognition that only a *poet* could write this stuff, bad though I think it is. Here is another bit from *Week-end* :

Soon, down, by level and deep shades
Powerful sea birds arch over ; out, a gale bellies ;
Thrives on sleep, for the house is perched on a cliff,
A summer suntrap steep to a pencilled bay and
Faraway fawn and chop : a jackdaw is clenched
In a nerve window—not real any more but no fake.

" A summer suntrap steep to a pencilled bay " is pure Tennyson. But I have nothing with the fawn, the chop, and the jackdaw !

Fatras. I have always held intuitively that Theodore Watts-Dunton was an ass. And now I know it. Turning up the article on Wycherley in the *Enc. Brit.*, I find that he wrote:

> The barbarism of the society depicted in these plays was, in the true sense of the word, far deeper and more brutal than any barbarism that has ever existed in these islands within the historic period. If civilisation has any meaning at all for the soul of man, the Englishmen of Chaucer's time, the Anglo-Saxons of the Heptarchy, nay, those half-naked heroes, who in the dawn of English history clustered along the southern coast to defend it from the invasion of Cæsar, were far more civilised than that " race gangrenée "—the treacherous rakes, mercenary slaves, and brazen strumpets of the court of Charles II, who did their best to substitute for the human passion of love (a passion which was known perhaps even to palæolithic man) the promiscuous intercourse of the beasts of the field.

Aug. 17 *Monday.* Truth is stranger even than Gertrude Stein's fiction. I base this statement on the following sent me to-day by an old gentleman of seventy-five:

> Here is a letter I copied about 30 years ago. It was written by a mother from somewhere in Somerset to her daughter (a fellow-servant of my sister's), and who was leaving her place at Corsham, Wilts. The letter was undated and is as follows, copied exactly as written.
>
> " Dear Annie, Just a few lines hoping to find you quite well as it leaves us at present mind and sure to come not for father to come up or if he do there will be a row and mind and sure to come by the earlyist train you can and mother is not very well and mind and sure to come and mother will be at Yatton station to meat you and send and tell us what train you think you can come by and mind and sure to come not for father to come up or else there will be a row mind and sure to come and here is a stamp for you to send back again mind and sure to come and you got to come Saturday that is the 7 of March mind and sure to come not for father to come up there or else there will be a row mind and sure to come and if you dont father will fetch you Monday without fail and if he do there will be a row mind and sure to come and mind and sure to send back by the return of post be sure to come on home Saturday when you do leave your place or else it will be late at night till we do get home and it will be dark so mind and

sure to come home not for father to come up for mother dont want father to come up or else there will be a row mind and sure to come home or else father will be sure to come and there will be a row if he do mind and sure to come mind and sure to come no more this time from your loving father and mother."

Aug. 18 *Tuesday.* Am toying with the idea of bankruptcy. My model, when this happens, will be Shakespeare's Antony :

> Fall not a tear, I say ; one of them rates
> All that is won and lost : give me a kiss ;
> Even this repays me.

I shall embrace the five volumes of my Diary, made out of the stuff which made me bankrupt. " Fall not a tear," I shall say. " Even these repay me."

Fatras. Cowley on Great Men :

> Let's begin with him by Break of Day : For by that time he's besieged by two or three hundred Suitors ; and the Hall and Antechambers (all the Outworks) possess'd by the Enemy, as soon as his Chamber opens they are ready to break into that, or to corrupt the Guards for Entrance. This is so essential a Part of Greatness, that whoever is without it, looks like a fallen Favourite, like a Person disgrac'd, and condemn'd to do what he please all the Morning. There are some who rather than want this, are contented to have their Rooms fill'd up every Day with murmuring and cursing Creditors, and to charge bravely through a body of them to get to their Coach.

Aug. 20 *Thursday.* Ralph Straus's excellent book on Sala sent me to the shelf where I have kept G. A. S.'s *Living London.* Sala was a wittier, wiser, and better-informed journalist than any of our gossip-writers to-day. Even so, he could go absurdly wrong. From his notice of *The Silver King* written after that first night at the Princess's, November 16, 1882 :

> The dramatists who maintain they can teach sobriety by showing us a Coupeau deformed and dwarfed with drink and degraded with the most hideous form of delirium ; virtue by the exhibition of a Nana left to die alone, half eaten away by the ravages of smallpox, and screaming for a drop of cold water to moisten her parched lips ; charity and pity by a

photographic illustration of the slums and the stews, the godless and the degraded, the bestial and the brutal ; humour by the conception of a man monkey mumbling his affection for the girl who has protected and nursed him—have perhaps a certain specious plausibility in their arguments. Is it amusing to gaze on corruption and to muse on horrors ?

The passage was written nine years before Clement Scott's famous outburst on Ibsen's *Ghosts*. This sort of critical nonsense never dies ; it crops up in every generation. I shouldn't be in the least surprised to find any one of our younger critics writing the same sort of rubbish about the Restoration dramatists.

Aug. 21 *Friday*. Wired to Kligerman, the young pianist, telling him to come round, the point being that I am taking him to-night to Gwen Chenhalls's, where he is to play to Basil Cameron. He, Leo Pavia, and I went into committee about what he should give them. His idea was to start with the Chopin B minor Scherzo. But Leo vetoed this because of the cantabile in the middle. Then we decided on one of the Liszt-Chopin Chants Polonais for an opening, to be followed by the Bach-Tausig Toccata and Fugue. And, of course, the Liszt Rigoletto-Fantasie to show what he can do pianistically. The boy is full of confidence about to-night ; it is I who am nervous. When he had gone I said of the scherzo that his performance was too much like musical gate-crashing. And Leo said, " I wish he could *sing* a little more. His forte is excellent ; but his piano is just as though some one had told him to keep quiet. That scherzo was written in the eighteen-thirties and should epitomise contemporary French romanticism. The middle part is de Musset's *Nuit de Mai* in sound."

3 A.M. Kligerman has just left here after two hours of talk, mostly by me. Gwen was impressed, but I could see that K.'s lack of romanticism upset Basil, who, at dinner, had talked a great deal about Pachmann and how much superior he was to Paderewski. Something must be done about that cantabile, and at once. The noisy bits are fine. I asked Gwen if we weren't making too much row. She said, " There's only one other man in the house. I've warned him, and he says we can all bang on thirty pianos without waking him. It's Lord Lovat. He's tired after Dieppe, I expect."

Fatras. A correspondent avers that in a novel by Ouida he has discovered this passage : " Entering her palatial music-room filled with all kinds of instruments, Eloise sat down at a spinet incrusted with lapis lazuli and silver, and flooded the room with the rich, voluptuous strains of Wagner's *Tristan and Isolde.*"

Aug. 22 *Saturday.* A few raindrops from George Richards's weekly downpour :

> When I die it will be a great load off my body. Of one thing I am convinced ; the thing for anyone who has not merely fluted on the woodwind of life's orchestra but had a few wallops on the cymbals, drums, and tympani is not to feign a hypocritical humility and quietude at the last, but to pass out in a frank blaze of Satanism, with a baptism of Witches' milk, a sacrificing of the neither-he-nor-she goat Baphomet, and an initiation, together with the celebration in its entire arcane obscenity of the Black Mass, into the secret Bogomile Brotherhood. For if a man at his final dissolution cannot be frankly and avowedly dissolute, when can he be ?

Aug. 23 *Sunday.* Spent an hour looking at the remarkable photographs, more than a hundred, of English lakes and Welsh mountains in Arthur Gardner's *Britain's Mountain Heritage.* It brought back all my holidays. One of the things which enraged me when I was a boy was the doctrine that the working classes should be content with the station in life in which it had pleased the ruling system of economics to place them. Every Easter the *Manchester Guardian* would come out with a leading article telling workers who could not afford a jaunt to the country to sit in their bits of back gardens and contemplate a hyacinth, their own or a neighbour's. Later in the year half a dozen rides on the top of the tram would be recommended as an excellent substitute for summer holidays. The most nauseating thing was the pretence that the substitute was as good as the reality. To-day it has to be ; we are ersatz-minded whether we like it or not.

Aug. 24 *Monday.* Leo sitting silent for some time, I asked him what was the matter. " I am inventing a musical quiz." Five minutes later he handed me the following, together with the answers ; he had done it without leaving his chair.

MUSICAL QUIZ

1. Who pushed her way into the pit on the first night of a musical piece shouting, " Make way, I am the authoress " ? Who composed the music, and what was the name of the piece ?
2. Who shouted out during the first night of an opera, " I would give six francs for an E string " ? And why ?
3. What monarch said to a famous composer, " Too many notes, my dear X," and what did the composer reply ? What was the opera ?
4. Who, having listened to an entire opera, congratulated the composer on a successful canon in the second act ? Name composer and opera.
5. What famous composer said of a less famous one that he had less counterpoint than his cook ?
6. Who said to a hostess at a party, " In case I have forgotten to be rude to anybody, please make my apologies " ?

ANSWERS

1. Helmina von Chezy. Schubert. *Rosamunde.*
2. Grétry at a performance of Méhul's *Uthal.* The composer used no fiddles throughout this opera.
3. The Emperor Joseph II of Austria to Mozart. " Not one too many, your Majesty." *Le Nozze di Figaro.*
4. Mendelssohn to Wagner. *Tannhäuser.*
5. Handel of Gluck.
6. Brahms.

I like the Brahms story ; his rudeness was rather like mine. Leo told me another anecdote about B., which Eduard Hanslick told him in Vienna. A young composer comes to Brahms with a symphony. " Is this your first ? " asks B. after glancing at the MS. " No, Herr Doktor," answers the young man. " I have already composed two symphonies, four string quartets, and six piano sonatas." " So ? " says Brahms. " Then go home, compose four more symphonies, eight more string quartets, and twelve more piano sonatas ; then perhaps you will come to me with a little song which might be hearable [*mit einem kleinen Lied, welches sich hören lassen kann*]."

Aug. 25 *Tuesday.* Spent the day wrestling with an overseas wireless talk. Subject, a dialogue between me and the ghost of Edmund Kean. Time, 13½ minutes. Am instructed that listeners must not be presumed to know anything about this actor. At my suggestion they have engaged Valentine Dyall to play Kean. He has a beautiful voice of great sonority.

Aug. 27 *Thursday.* Charming incident. Some time ago I reviewed in the *Express* a good little work by Joseph Lewis on the art of conducting. A miner in Llanelly asked me to send him a copy and enclosed a postal order. I sent the book and returned the P.O. This afternoon I receive a basket of tomatoes and cucumbers with the note : " The cucumber was the favourite fruit of the Emperor Tiberius."

Aug. 28 *Friday.* A heat wave having declared itself, I sally forth in the white rig-out I keep for these occasions. In Regent Street a blowsy harridan says, "Give us a bob, ducky." I shake my head, and she screams after me, " What! Can't spare a bob for a poor old bitch down on her luck? Then you didn't oughter be wearing them flannels, you dirty butterfly!"

Aug. 30 *Sunday.* I look forward to my Sunday papers, which invariably yield one nugget of exquisite nonsense. The better the paper the more precious the gold. William Glock is the latest recruit to the ranks of those who can only praise one thing at the expense of another. Because the English " have hardly produced a symphony or a string quartet or a piano sonata of the first class," English composers are urged to go back to the manner of Byrd and Wilbye and Weelkes, who, it appears, were " capable of universality."

> When I hear of Benjamin Britten carrying a bundle of excellent new vocal works under his arm I am delighted ; and I would give all three movements of Rubbra's serious and unimaginative Fourth Symphony for one of his better madrigals. . . . I am not pretending that a great and mature music will result merely from a change of front. We shall not outdo the spirituality of Byrd's five-part *Agnus Dei* or the planetary motion of Bach's 50th Cantata, simply by returning to a vocal style. The new music, indeed, will have to have its special sanction and purpose. All one can do is to watch developments and cast a baleful glance on virtuosi, symphony orchestras, and the enemy at large.

There you have it. Because Glock likes madrigals Walton must stop writing symphonies.

Aug. 31 *Monday.* Reply to one Nicholas Moore, who asks if he may dedicate a sonnet-series to me:

10 *Fairfax Road, N.W.*6
Aug. 31, 1942

DEAR NICHOLAS MOORE,

Go ahead, dear boy!

But you must not say I have pronounced Winston Churchill to be a poet unless you qualify the statement as I qualified it. I once heard Humbert Wolfe define poetry as "the maximum of matter in the minimum of space." I wrote that if this definition be accepted then Churchill's *Great Contemporaries* shows him to be a poet.

Ever since I was fifteen I have comforted myself in moments of depression by murmuring

> There is sweet music here that softer falls
> Than petals from blown roses on the grass,
> Or night-dews on still waters between walls
> Of shadowy granite, in a gleaming pass;

But it seems that for fifty years I have been wrong. Starting from next week, when I shall be sixty-five, I propose to go about the house chanting your

> His pen,
> Hired for its keep, strangely discovers too
> That Churchill is a poet. O how strange
> That time, fate, God and all should so arrange
> It that he is Prime Minister to-day.
> It must be nice for Agate.

It must be nice for Moore to be the author of

> It that he is Prime Minister to-day.

J'en chortle! as somebody said in another connection.

Yours sincerely,
JAMES AGATE

Sept. 1 *Tuesday.* Met Keidrych Rhys at the Café Royal. A large, shock-haired, intelligent, and witty soldier. The Traddles sort. Haversack full of Welsh poems. He said about another of the unintelligible brood: "My dear sir, like all the others, he is merely a leak from Dylan Thomas's petrol-tank."

Sept. 2 *Wednesday.* Lunching at the Savage to-day were Gerald Moore, the accompanist, and Ralph Hill, the musical critic of the *Radio Times*. Seizing occasion by the forelock I hauled them off to the Villa Volpone, collecting on the way young Kligerman, whom I found at his mother's flat surrounded by relics of Russian grandeur and practising at a superb, though I guess borrowed, Bösendorfer in a dressing-gown, and wearing socks with a great deal of toe coming out of very little sock. Knowing him to be fairly safe with the Bach Toccata and Fugue and the Liszt Rigoletto-Fantasie, I turned him on to these, also the Beethoven Op. 111. I could see the boy was nervous, because he hurried the tempi and took everything too fast, with the result that the fugato in the middle of the Beethoven first movement was a mere scramble. Just as he reached safety with the recapitulation Leo entered, his india-rubber face divided into three sections—disgust at not being advised of the party, delight in meeting his old friends Gerald and Ralph, and horror at the Beethoven. Up to this point my visitors had had nothing but praise for the young man's technique. But they preserved an ominous silence about his musicianship. Remembering my cautionary remarks at lunch, Ralph said he would like to hear the Chopin Barcarolle, which Leo and I at once vetoed. Gerald supported Ralph, and as the boy is naïve enough to think he can play it, we gave in. As we foresaw, the result was even worse than last time, and after he had finished there was a dreadful silence. A blight having fallen on the gathering, Leo, after much pressure, allowed himself to be pushed to the piano, where he improvised a paraphrase on Strauss waltz themes quite exquisitely. He had hardly played a dozen bars when Gerald whispered to me, " This is the first real piano-playing we've heard this afternoon." And then the two sat up and told poor Alexis exactly where he got off. How virtuosi were ten a penny, how he lacked phrasing, how his touch had almost no singing tone. To smooth matters over somebody started an argument about cadenzas, and Leo concocted something perfectly beautiful to Beethoven's second concerto ; he holds the view, with which Ralph agreed, that every pianist ought to improvise his own. Then I told them some of my vintage yarns, and after a glass of whiskey from my depleted cellar the company broke up. I point out to Alexis that our visitors have spent four hours in listening to his playing. " Yes," says Alexis with his rueful Slav smile, " but not young Kligerman it is they discover, but old Pavia." I told this to Jock afterwards, and he said, " Well, Leo is about due for a second infant prodigyhood." While Leo was showing the guests to the door the boy said, "I now go shoot myself." "Nonsense," I retorted, "you're going to take a few lessons from old Pavia." "But I should be delighted," says Alexis, somewhat to my surprise and certainly to my delight. And lo and behold, they went at it for an hour and twenty minutes like hammer and tongs, pushing each other off the piano-stool, Leo showing him how certain cantabile passages should be played, backed up by the unanswerable Chopin-Fontana-Leschetizky tradition. And at the end of the time we discovered not only that the boy could produce a singing tone, but that on his own confession he had deliberately under-cultivated this branch of pianoforte playing, because he had been taught to think of nothing but the fireworks. Later we adjourned to the pub at Swiss Cottage, after which Leo left amidst blessings from Alexis, and I took the latter to the Café Royal, and finally to his mother's, where I left a wiser, sadder, and much less sober musician in the making. It was very late when I got home, but before I went to bed I wrote to Myra Hess a long letter about A. K., telling her that she must engage him for the National Gallery concerts.

Sept. 3 *Thursday.* "The President of the Immortals, in Æschylean phrase, had ended his sport with Tess." "Come, children, let us shut up the box and the puppets, for our play is played out." Let who will prate of Hardy's and Thackeray's famous endings. My vote goes to the more modern "He went to live at Wolverhampton and died of cirrhosis of the liver."

Sept. 4 *Friday.* Let women write on subjects they know about. I do not want to read some Wimbledon spinster's views on the amours of a Spanish bull-fighter any more than I want to hear from a Swedish miss about the love-life of an Arsenal centre-forward. The play to-night was all about British saboteurs in France, at the end of which a glamorous authoress came forward. Afterwards to the Café Royal, where at the next table sat two young American airmen arrived in England the same day. One of them leaned over to me and said, "Say, buddy, d'ya think we could take a coupla women to our hotel ?" I asked what hotel they were staying at, and he mentioned one of the most respectable hostelries in London. I told him they could not possibly do such a thing. "Aw," says airman No. 2, "don't get us wrong. We don't mean a coupla women each!" Perhaps some young woman would like to write a war play about American airmen?

Sept. 5 Saturday. Letter from Myra Hess's secretary saying that her employer remarked, "Alas! Once I give an audition I am lost." But going on to say that if Basil Cameron and I think the young man is ready to play at the National Gallery concerts Myra will give his name to the Committee. I have, of course, sent the necessary certificates not only from Basil but also from Gerald Moore and Ralph Hill—as flat a piece of burglary as ever I committed. Thus begins the Battle of Kligerman. Actually there are two battles: one between K. and the impresarios, the other between the elders of the Villa Volpone and the youngling Slav at Compayne Gardens. The second battle is, of course, over the great problem: Can We Knock Some Musical Understanding Into Him? We had another skirmish yesterday afternoon when the Achilles heel was shown once again, this time in the cantabile of the Grieg Concerto, first movement. It was as though some fine actor had broken off in the middle of "O what a rogue and peasant slave am I," recited "Mary had a little lamb" like a schoolgirl, and then finished the soliloquy in style. During the morning I had been reading some of the Soviet poet, Mayakovsky, including the poem called *Brother Writers*:

> Gentlemen poets,
> have you not tired
> of pages,
> palaces,
> love
> and lilac blooms?
> If such as you
> are the creators,
> then I spit upon all art.
> I'd rather open a shop,
> or go on the Stock Exchange
> and bulge my sides with fat wallets.
> In a tavern rear
> I'll spew up my soul
> in a drunken song.

If this is Kligerman's point of view all well and good; then let him carry on with nothing but Revolutionary studies and Soviet sonatas. What Leo and I are determined that he shall not do is to play the old repertoire badly, which would be like Mayakovsky attempting the Tennysonian idiom and failing to pull it off. Liszt put the matter in a nutshell when he said to a pupil, "First you must become a virtuoso: then you can begin playing the piano." A great thing in K.'s favour is that, whatever he may think, he has sufficient mastery over himself to take correction very well, the most he does in the way of protest being to shake his head like a young horse in trouble with his bit.

Sept. 6 *Sunday.* Our Ernest, discussing "Greatness in Music," puts a question to me as reader. After telling me that much of the hold the great composers of the past have over me is due to ethical convictions similar to mine he goes on:

> But suppose the day comes, as it may well do, when the general ethical complexion of the last few European centuries is as alien to the new humanity as that of ancient Greece is, in many respects, to us. When that day arrives, will not listeners to the Mass in D or the Choral Symphony or *Parsifal* find it as difficult to get inside the skins of the men who wrote this kind of music, and of the men for whom it was written, as we of to-day sometimes find it hard to get inside the skins of the heroes of Homer or the characters of Greek drama? Will what we now regard as "greatness" in music be so regarded then?

But of course it will, *cher collègue.* I dislike Chinese music, not because I disapprove of ethical convictions which permit of systematised torture, but because it makes what, to my ears, is a hideous noise. The trouble, dear Ernest, is not in our composers but in our musicologists making difficulties where none exist, in the fact that you have ceased to listen with anything except your mind. So long as you can trace what psychological processes have led to a particular succession of notes you don't care how hideously that succession sounds. At least your writings give no indication to the contrary. Considered as musical algebra the atonalist stuff is doubtless very good. But I don't go to the Albert Hall to hear algebra. I don't care what it was in Shakespeare's make-up that caused him to write *Hamlet.* Nor do I think I should understand *Hamlet* any better if its author had left behind him an hour-to-hour diary of his mental processes while he was writing it.

> Oh! while I live, let me not be admitted to an actor's dressing-room. Let me not see how Cato painted, or how Cæsar combed! Let me not meet the prompt-boys in the passage, nor see the half-lighted candles stuck against the bare walls, nor hear the creaking of machines, or the fiddlers laughing; nor see a Columbine practising a pirouette in sober sadness, nor Mr Grimaldi's face drop from mirth to sudden melancholy as he passes the side-scene, as if a shadow crossed it, nor witness the long-chinned generation of the pantomime sit twirling their thumbs, nor overlook the fellow who holds the candle for the moon in the scene between Lorenzo and Jessica! Spare me this insight into secrets I am not bound to know. The stage is not a mistress that we are sworn to undress.

Like Hazlitt, let me not pry behind any work of art, whether it be music or drama. Preserve me from asking how much Gibbon was indebted to his hydrocele for the weight of his prose. The fact that I am not an ancient Greek does not prevent me from recognising greatness in Sophocles.

Sept. 7 *Monday.* On Sunday at the Café Royal I ran into D. A. Clarke-Smith, the Esterhazy in my Dreyfus play. He is now a captain and Director of Entertainments, Southern Command. Part of his job is to run concerts, and he is going to run Kligerman and to begin running him at once. He was most sympathetic and helpful. As I write, pandemonium is being let loose in the next room over the A flat Polonaise, K. playing and Leo objurgating—great fun, but makes writing difficult. (At this point Alice comes up from downstairs, and will we all help in giving Rob, the dog, a dose of castor-oil?) Actually Leo is enormously pleased with the improvement in K. We are dividing the job into two—Leo doing the musical half and leaving me the managerial part, which I shall do damned well. Yesterday I wrote to Clarke-Smith confirming our talk:

> 10 *Fairfax Road, N.W.*6
> *Sept.* 6*th* '42
>
> DEAR CLARKIE,
>
> This is to announce that Kligerman and I are coming down to Aldershot on Sunday next whether the Command wants us or not. We shall come down by an early train in the morning.

If you want him to play with orchestra it must be the Grieg Concerto. If you want him without orchestra I suggest the Chopin Polonaise in A flat followed by the Liszt Rigoletto-Fantasie. The middle part of the Polonaise, as you know, gives a picture of the Polish Army marching to freedom in 1830, and if I introduce Kligerman it will give me a chance to say something neat about the Polish Army marching to freedom once again. You can either build up the young man beforehand by arrangement with the musical director, or you can spring him as a surprise.

Now, Clarkie, I am going to hang on to this with all the persistence that is in me. I am quite willing that K. should be your discovery. Indeed this is only fair, since you will be the first person to give him a chance, which fact will be duly recorded in *Ego* 6.

Yours ever,
JIMMIE

P.S. And Most Important. In case there should be any difficulty in getting to Aldershot please send me a permit for two. We are coming, even if we have to disguise ourselves as Fifth Columnists !

The telephone rang this morning just after ten o'clock. It was Clarkie saying K. is to appear at the Theatre Royal, Aldershot, next Sunday (three guineas plus expenses.) Last turn before the interval and third turn after. The star places. I have bargained for no dress-suit ; the young man is a Russian Pole, and Russian Poles in war-time don't have dress-suits. The thing to do now is to keep K. cheerful : he is apt to relapse into a fit of Slav melancholia on, or even without, the slightest provocation. Leo is very good at preventing this. For instance, after K. had played us a fascinating concert-arrangement of Viennese waltzes by Alfred Grünfeld, Leo said, " How well I remember that old Jew ! He was the best *pianiste de salon* of his time and a tremendous Society favourite in the old Imperial days in Vienna. There was a fearful scandal about a Princess Bilinsky and Alfred. The Princess was on her deathbed and was about to receive Extreme Unction from the officiating Archbishop when she whispered, ' I want Alfred Grünfeld.' And after a pause, ' I want him to play some waltzes.' Every one was horrified, but her Highness's word was law, Alfred was sent for, and he sat down in the adjoining salon and played. And the piece he played, dear Alexis, was the one you have just performed. The Princess died happy, beating time with her hand." I suspect Leo of having invented the whole story.

All the same, I must go carefully in the matter of K., or I shall become a bore. Yesterday at the Savage I mentioned him again to Basil Cameron, and I saw a glazed look come into his eye. I must realise that to a conductor even an established pianist is a piece of furniture no more important than the stool he sits on; that to an impresario the only soloist of interest is one who brings money into the hall, not the unknown artist who empties it. No. I see I shall have to go slowly. The only reason anybody listens to me on the subject of K. is because they think I have the Press behind me. I haven't, but they think so. Managers look upon me as Miss Missouri Martin's customers looked upon Waldo Winchester in the Damon Runyon story. " A guy who may produce trouble, even if he is a sucker, on account of being connected with a newspaper."

Sept. 8 *Tuesday.* A sergeant air-gunner writes: " I don't suppose you have spent eighteen months in a desert. Or sat in a gun-turret for four hundred and fifty hours, eight hours at a stretch. Or been shot down and wounded. If you had, perhaps you would take a more kindly view of the enclosed poem." I have replied: " No, I shouldn't. Your poem, badly rhymed and worse scanned, did its job when it took your mind off the desert and the gun-turret. Having done this, it became waste paper."

Against this, a Home Guard corporal sends me something which, whatever its value as poetry, has more lilt than Keidrych Rhys and Co. are masters of.

THE INTROVERT

This morning a youngster smiled at me
And I felt so bloody glad,
It seemed like a privilege just to be
In the same world with the lad.

He gave me a fair and equal smile
And a nod as clean as could be:
It heightened my self-respect for a while
That he thought that much of me.

If I could have given him nod for nod
In the same kind of open style,
I might have struck him as much less odd
And stuck in his mind for a while.

But I gave him a kind of congested jerk
And a look that was less than square:
And I passed along on my way to work
With my head in the bloody air.

Sept. 9 *Wednesday.* Sixty-five. Telegram from Jock, 'phone message from my ex-houseboy, Charlie, all the way from St Asaph, the vocal score of *Tristan* from Leo. To-day, like another, I permit myself "A Backward Glance o'er Travel'd Roads." Exactly how good a dramatic critic have I been? It is always said that I stick too little to the play and players, am too discursive, and use quotation to show off. Well, there are people who, reading of "the sweet influences of Pleiades," would accuse Job of showing off his astronomy. No more of that. I have always stuck to the point when it was worth sticking to; when not, then not.

Sept. 10 *Thursday.* George Richards sends me the following:

Advance extract from *The Surrealist's Who's Who* (the editor will be grateful for emendations and corrections, which should reach him not later than June 4, 1983).

JAMES AGATE. *b.* 1858 of Sudanese stock. Was baptized six times. First became generally known with a volume of poems (1902) under the title of *Chains of Cleanliness: a Treatise in Verse on Lavatory Cisterns from the Earliest Ages down to the Present Time.* Invented the mouse-trap. In 1930 joined the League of Nations as chief delegate for Boston Spa, but was refused a seat on the Council owing to being in arrears with his contributions. After losing thirty-one by-elections was finally returned unopposed for Little Pregnancy, which seat he held far too long. Invented the corn-plaster, the stomach-pump, and the skeleton pad. Owned four yachts, two amphibious racehorses, and half the Aleutian Islands. Invented the hair-net. 1950 *m.* Priscilla, the elder daughter of Lord Halibut (*q.v.*). Awarded the freedom of Houndsditch 1960, in which year he opened the skating-pool at Balham and two swimming-rinks at Stoke Mandeville. Inventor of the safety-match. His thirty-odd volumes of memoirs (*Lumbago* I, II, III, etc.) have been banned or burned in all countries except Nazi Germany. Created first Baron Sciatica 1965. Appointed Regius Professor and Reader in Scatology at the University of Bokhara in 1970. Invented the Gothic Arch. Had a profound belief in the close relation between Buddhism and artificial teeth. *Hobby* : sex-perversion in Siamese cats. *Clubs :* Cannibals', Oodle's, Pork Chop. *Address :* The Trenches, Gidea Park (Summer : The Tudor Ruins, Tadpole-in-the-Strippet, Berks). Insane since 1980.

Sept. 11 *Friday.* " I am not valiant neither." I ought not to lose my temper with every puny whipster who dislikes my brand of dramatic criticism. I am told this morning that " The *only* objects of dramatic criticism should be to tell the reader whether a play is good or bad, whether the acting is good or bad, and the reasons for these conclusions. A. B. Walkley, I think, set the fashion of loading his criticisms with quotations—mainly in other languages—and used most of his space in shouting ' See what a clever fellow I am ! ' " Now what are the facts ? I have before me Shaw's notice of *Little Eyolf*. This contains allusions to Dickens's Artful Dodger, Grant Allen, Byron, Walter Scott, Thackeray, George Eliot, Fielding, Ibsen, Wagner, Sarah Grand, Shakespeare, Bernhardt, Irving, Duse, Leader, Rembrandt, Isaye, Sarasate, Joachim, the two de Reszkes, Calvé, Emma Eames, Lugné Poë, Arthur Roberts, and the London, Brighton, and South Coast Railway. I turn to Archer and find in an article about a farce called *Lord Tom Noddy* references to Swift, Chamfort, Gautier, and Wordsworth. To Walkley, who, in a notice of that night's production of *The Doctor's Dilemma*, dragged in, as they say, Brieux, Molière, Labiche, Charles Lamb, Dumas *fils*, Montaigne, and the Emperor Nero. To Montague, who, writing of the Christmas pantomime of *Sinbad the Sailor*, drew his illustrations from Ouida, Thomas à Kempis, Kipling, Molière, Meredith, and Riccoboni. Clement Scott ? Shaw has rightly said of him that he was " not a great dramatic critic but a great dramatic reporter." Readers who look to the *Sunday Times* to provide them with a reporter's notice are taking their custom to the wrong shop.

Sept. 13 *Sunday.* To Aldershot with neuritis and Kligerman. The piano procured with so much care by Clarke-Smith turned out to have a fine bass but little or no treble. The concert being got up by the Royal Armoured Corps, the programme was sprinkled with troopers and N.C.O.'s who sang, twanged guitars, thrummed ukuleles, and so forth. " Will you have a spotlight or not ? " asked the stage manager. K. said he would leave the lighting to the electrician. This is where I should have stepped in. I might have expected that stab of murderous spotlight ; what I could not foresee was that when K. got to the octaves in the Chopin Polonaise he would be centre and focus of a scheme of coloured lighting which would have stopped a fountain. But it did not stop K., who, sizing up the audience, let them have everything Chopin, he, and the poor piano had got. Even the band tiptoed into the wings to listen, which is quite unlike a band. The Rigoletto-Fantasie in the second half was a better choice and went very well. We had only ten minutes in which to catch the train, but in those ten minutes the bandmaster of the R.A.M.C. had invited K. to play a concerto in the near future, proposals were made for a full recital, and the manager of the local music-hall offered him a week's engagement. To-night satisfied me in two respects—the boy's nerves and temper. I now know that he is not one of your namby-pamby intellectuals who can play only when everything is going right. Everything that could go wrong externally did so to-night, and the effect on K. was to give him more fire than ever. Probably this is because he is a Slav, and Slavs play equally well in a palace or a brothel. I told him over our whiskey that the affair had been a great success, but that he must immediately forget it because to-morrow he is to take the first serious step in his musical career, that of playing before Howard Ferguson of the National Gallery Concerts Committee.

Sept. 14 *Monday.* K. played very well on Ferguson's excellent but not too manageable Steinway. The Bach Toccata and Fugue, followed by some minor Chopin. Took a minute or two to settle down, after which he was all right. I think Ferguson liked his playing. Anyhow, he asked me to send him K.'s repertoire and to suggest a programme. He told the boy to avoid things which are played too often, like the Barcarolle, and to leave the later Beethoven to the well-known pianists who want to keep that bit of fat for themselves. Hinted that an early Beethoven Sonata followed by three of the lesser-known Chopin or Liszt Studies might do the trick. Came home and spent the afternoon in a three-cornered wrangle with K. and Leo, who, now that we have got the boy virtually on to the platform at the National Gallery, wants to shove him off with a programme of elusive works which even the highbrows wouldn't stand for. Finally we reached a compromise. But not until I had taken the floor and Trafalgar Square'd K. as blisteringly as I could. Something like this :

" My dear Alexis : There is a quotation from Shakespeare which is so hackneyed that I shouldn't dare to use it in any of my articles. (*J. A. recites the lines from* " *Julius Cæsar* " *about the tide in the affairs of men.*) Every English schoolboy knows these lines, but you, Alexis, being a Slav, may not know them. They bear directly on your engagement at the National Gallery, for this is the turn of your tide. You must not miss it, Alexis. Remember, you are not a great pianist making assault upon a London which is waiting for you ; you are just an unknown pianist begging admission at the doors. (*Alexis grunts.*) Now you must realise that there may be some critics of importance at your concert. You are a virtuoso, and as such belong to what they call the 'virtuosic brood.' Some of them do accept pianism, it is true ; but they only do so when it is a question of some rendering of, say, a theme of Tallis by members of the Dolmetsch family and performed on instruments not later than 1600. You might get the *Times* critic ; who, when William Murdoch died last week, told us that he had far too much mind to be a solo pianist. And, by the way, he wasn't talking complete nonsense. Now, the National Gallery people have no interest whatever in you, either as virtuoso or musician. In so far as you exist at all, you are part of their scheme, which is to educate musical taste among the London masses. If you can help, all well and good. As Howard Ferguson hinted to you to-day, they want some early Beethoven ; if you can fill the bill with that you will be a success with them.

" Now please listen carefully, my dear boy. I want you to understand clearly that it is not young Kligerman that they want ; it is young Beethoven. And they don't want young

Beethoven seen through the eyes of young Kligerman ; they want young Beethoven seen through their eyes. In other words, as they want London's masses to see him. If you can give them this, good. It is the price you pay for getting your foot in the magic circle. But a dreadful trap awaits you. Perhaps Leo will tell you what he thinks of your early Beethoven. I make no bones about saying that I think it appalling, and I have listened to you playing early Beethoven for over an hour. Let me give you an analogy taken from the world of horses. In a racehorse, as perhaps you know, all that matters is how quickly the animal can get from one place to another ; what he looks like during the process doesn't matter. But with a show harness horse what matters is the majesty, the rhythm, shall I say, the poetry of his motion ; how long he takes in covering the ground is of very little account. Do you see this ? Now do you understand the trap I speak of ? You take your Beethoven at a terrific lick because it is in your blood to feel your Beethoven that way. Personally I think you are wrong, but I know you and therefore don't impute a wrong motive. But the musical critics, who don't know you, will assume that you are using Beethoven as a medium for showing off. And that will be the beginning, and, I fear, the end of Alexis Kligerman."

There was a silence, and then Leo, who likes to play Eusebius to my Florestan, said quietly, " I think you ought to be told, Alexis, that if you are going in for the early Beethoven Sonatas you ought to accustom yourself to getting a bird's-eye view of each movement as a whole, just as if you were looking at some building from the air. I am afraid you still only consider a piece passage by passage ; in that way there will never be any sense of continuity, you will be like those old actors who recited their parts without knowing or bothering to know what the others had said before or were going to say afterwards. . . . I think James is right about your playing too fast. I can understand that ; it has something to do with your Slavonic temperament. But don't give way to it in early Beethoven. There was nothing Slavonic there ; only German solidity, French elegance, and Italian lyricism exquisitely blended. When you begin your Opus 10, your *Pastorale*, your *Pathétique* . . . leave your Slav ego outside on the mat. Be Western. We are placid, unhysterical people in the West, you know ; we don't tear a passion to tatters.

Tradition must not be despised, either. If you can bear to hear James read to you how Kean played Othello, how Phelps played Prospero, or Irving Hamlet, then you must listen to people who can tell you how von Bülow, Rubinstein, Stavenhagen, and D'Albert played these early sonatas. Let your presto be a moderato ; but let your adagio approach andante."

It must not be imagined that these orations were uninterrupted. It is only fair to give Kligerman's point of view, and this I reconstruct from his vigorous splutterings and expostulations. Had we given him time for a considered speech it would have gone something like this :

"That what you say is very well. But you suppose I shall make great success with methods which are so reactionary ? What will people call me ?—they will call me tame, with no life and no fire and no passion. You say ' von Bülow.' Good. But I am told he played like a volcano extinct. I—I am twenty-two. I am Siegfried, not Wotan. I do not believe that the critics want this, or that, or the other. I believe the critics want a sincerity, an enthusiasm, and I do not think they want the beaten track, a performance like every one else. To me, my tempi in Beethoven are right. He was young when he wrote these sonatas : you think then one shall play them like an old man ? No, no. Beethoven was virtuoso also : shall one then not play quick passages like virtuoso ? In ' classic ' Beethoven I do not believe : I believe only in Beethoven romantic, poetic. Is he not a prince, a prophet, a pioneer ? . . . Is he not. . . ." By this time our good Alexis had become so excited that his face had become dead-white, his eyes shone like arc-lamps, and he thumped my mantelpiece until I was afraid he would injure his wrist. Then the decanter came to our aid, and thus ended the "struggle for an artist's soul." In novels and on the screen this means whether some starving artist should degrade his soul by allowing some rich woman to seduce his body. But Leo and I are not concerned with any such twaddle. The point is : Can we detach this young man's mind from his fingers ?

Sept. 17 *Thursday.* To the Coliseum for the revival of *The Belle of New York.* The instantaneous success of the *Belle* in England was due not to its tunes, but to the English passion for confounding opposites. Pale curates conquered by the flesh—see that absurdity, the play called *Romance*—Rosaries and Monastery Gardens. Did I not, on Sunday last, see the Aldershot audience enthralled by a nightgowned mite of eight singing Schubert's "Ave Maria," followed by imitations of Carmen Miranda and Sophie Tucker, winding up with something of which the refrain was "When I lift my little knee and show my garter"? About the *Belle* Montague wrote: "From a sympathetic presentation of a young hero drunk and lying on his stomach on the saddle of a bicycle and paddling in the air with his legs, the whole thing seemed to pass into an ecstatic fantasia on sex questions as these might be understood in fowl-runs or by cats in our backyards." Alas, that at the Coliseum they omitted the bicycle incident—the one funny bit of business in the entire piece! Did the tunes play no part in the triumph? Again, no. Reverse the plot and show the young woman putting the tambourine to its proper use instead of kicking it, and the play would not have run a week. Grand opera is good, but the music-hall has always held Gracie Fields's mock at it to be better. Salvation may not be a bad thing in its way, but cocking a snook at the Salvation Army is more fun. At least that was the 'message' of the *Belle*. Yet how good Kerker's score is, and how well it has worn! Twelve numbers with so much inherent life that they are still whistled by your butcher's boy; they are the preservative that has kept this preposterous nonsense alive. Evelyn Laye is excellent in the first scene, where she wittily matches the Belle's shyness with a wisp of ersatz singing. Later on the old bogey of intonation raises its head, and I bethink me that, like Hazlitt and all the best dramatic critics with the single exception of G. B. S., I must suppose myself to be without ear. But why should this popular artist worry, since she received an ovation at which Evie Greene would have goggled, and Schneider swooned?

Sept. 18 *Friday.* "I told you so" is impermissible only when a catastrophe is calamitous, not, I hold—using "catastrophe" in its dramatic sense—when it is triumphant. Readers of *Ego* 5 may remember how I came to be interested in Pamela Brown. "But she's amazing!" said everybody after the first act of *Claudia* last night, and again at the fall of the curtain. But I wasn't amazed, being in the position of the chemist who, having poured sulphuric acid on to zinc, isn't surprised to see hydrogen released. I had already seen the flame of Pamela's talent. In the autumn of 1940, at the Oxford Playhouse, I noted a performance of extreme distinction by a young and unknown actress. Her attack, intelligence, and quality generally convinced me that she could play Hedda Gabler. Now the saving grace of a repertory company is that it will listen; your commercial manager has ears only for finance. I proposed the play, Eric Dance gallantly acceded, and six weeks later the new Hedda was launched and received great praise from the principal London critics. But did any London manager inquire further? I heard of none. I tried to get the piece transferred to town for a matinée. The company was eager. Dance offered to sacrifice the evening's receipts, and I pointed out that, any modern set serving, there would be no expenses except the front of the house and a man to pull the curtain up and down. The managers refused to listen. They went on with the old game of wringing their hands and deploring the lack of new talent. The newcomer has that *petite frimousse éveillée* which was Sarcey's way of describing Réjane's departure from conventional good looks. She has great gift of facial expression, and when she feels emotion can show it, and the kind of emotion. When she must express grief she does not, as more trumpeted discoveries have done, bury her head in a cupboard. Her acting possesses both pace and variety. It is good enough to stand up to a heroine who is a tiresome combination of the innocent in Besant and Rice's *Golden Butterfly*, Ibsen's Nora, and Bret Harte's M'liss, to which is added a strong infusion of mother-complex. *Now*, perhaps, some manager will give us a play that can stand up to Pamela. Why not a matinée of *Hedda*? I should not dream of suggesting a run for this masterpiece unless one could entice the public with a cast including Deanna Durbin as General Gabler's daughter, Harpo Marx as Tesman, Bing Crosby as Lövborg, and W. C. Fields as Judge Brack!

Sept. 20 *Sunday.* Took Kligerman to the Cambridge Theatre to hear Kentner. He made quite a long speech in the taxi, something like this: "I am not so little artist as Mr Pavia thinks. I pay great attention to all he says, and you can see by way I play at your house I improve. Mr Pavia is worried because when I play at concert I follow own imagination, I forget things he has told me. I am not monkey. I like not to imitate. When I play it shall be myself, and not rendering after some one other. What Mr Pavia tells me I am grateful, I observe, and I think. Later I go home and try this, try that. . . . At last such new ideas shall become part of me. That is the way I should gather that an artist shall make himself." After the concert I collected Harold Holt, Boyd Neel, the oboist Alec Whittaker, and Osbert Sitwell, and took them all to the Savage, where I made them listen to K., who played better than I have ever heard him. He certainly has the gift of rising to an occasion. What with this and the endorsement by all the Sunday papers of Pamela Brown's success, I go to bed exhausted by triumph and slightly drunk.

Sept. 22 *Tuesday.* Letter from L/Bdr. John Clairmont Bowdery. "Curly" joined up when war broke out, and even in peace-time was a bundle of nerves. A strange mixture of inferiority complex and arrogance. Writes good stories; I have arranged for one to appear in Leonard Russell's *Saturday Book*, or whatever it's called. (I seem to be developing a patronage complex.)

> In three weeks' time I shall be on leave again, thank God! For one awful moment last week I thought I should never see my friends again, on this earth. Three Focke-Wulfs thought they'd play. They machine-gunned the site from about 50 feet, and I couldn't distinguish between the whistle of their bullets and the swish of *that* angel's wing! But one of those miracles happened—no one received the slightest hurt. The next night walking back to camp alone thro' the night I saw two nuns, who disappeared as I stepped aside to let them pass. The two incidents have rather shattered my nerve, temporarily. Suggestion to the M.O. that a little brandy was called for resulted in my being forbidden smoking and drinking. I am, consequently, in a worse state of nerves than ever!

Sept. 26 *Saturday.* A busy week spent principally in minding other people's business. Did a little work on my own account, such as explaining to *Tatler* readers that the composer of *Messiah* was not the gaunt, sardonic creature Wilfrid Lawson makes him in the new film, *The Great Mr Handel*, but a stout, red-faced, choleric German, full of the roast pork of old Saxony, and with enough sense of his own importance to insist on an Abbey funeral and leave in his will the sum of £600 to pay for it. Also tell them about the *Largo* and how Handel, far from intending it as a gift to organists, conceived it as an air for the male soprano Casarelli, having to do with a tree, and how that "amiable vegetable" was more comforting than a woman's arms. Also dealt with Noel's film about a destroyer. Very good.

Did short broadcast to America about the kind of plays and films this country wants in war-time:

> In the lounge at a seaside hotel a week or two ago a young woman asked me what was on at the theatre. I said *Macbeth.* She said, "Anything else?" I mentioned the name of a popular farce. "That ought to be good," said the young woman. I said rather rudely, "Yes, and so should *Macbeth.*" She said, "I wouldn't know about Shakespeare." There is nothing your Britisher enjoys more than physical hard work under the name of recreation. He will bat and bowl his head off and enjoy it. But he cannot bear to do anything with his head except bat and bowl. He just doesn't believe that using his brains can be amusing.

But the greater part of the time has been absorbed by Alexis. On Thursday I took him and the Kentners to lunch at Canuto's, after which we went to their studio and Alexis played really well. Kentner very sympathetic. Said the boy was a pianistic marvel but musically not ready. On Friday took Harold Holt to lunch at the Café Royal and afterwards dragged him up to the Villa Volpone, where Alexis played, I think, a little below his best form. Holt said he was satisfied on the technical side, but advised intensive study and provincial concerts with orchestra before crashing the Albert Hall.

Sept. 29 *Tuesday.* My excellent doctor, Norman Newman, who has taken a house behind Sadler's Wells Theatre, gave a housewarming last night, which I utilised to warm up Kligerman. K. played for three-quarters of an hour, every one was enchanted, and Norman jumped at my suggestion that we should make the boy accept a small cheque. (Three guineas.)

The Villa Volpone was much excited this morning owing to the secretary of the Philharmonic Orchestra, Thomas Russell, ringing up to say that he would give K. an audition. When ? To-morrow. Whereupon we rushed round to K., who thrust the score of the Grieg Concerto into Leo's arms, saying, " Now you shall be orchestra." After which we repaired to a charming little room in the Wigmore Studios containing two excellent Bösendorfer baby grands. K. in good form, and that incalculable Leo supplying everything from flute to kettledrum at least as well as the Philharmonic Orchestra ! All the more remarkable because I don't think he had seen a copy of the Concerto for twenty-five years, and then only the solo part. Parry Jones turned over for him, and the afternoon was full of romantic excitement with the portraits of Wagner and Brahms glowering at one another, though in the latter I detected a glimmer of a smile for the young *aspirant*. Parry is an admirable talker and convulsed us with some of his musical yarns, and Leo amused us with a story about Hans von Bülow, who once travelled to Birmingham to rehearse the Emperor Concerto with a well-known orchestra. Bülow, always like a Prussian general, said " Begin ! " Whereupon the orchestra gave out the first chord of E flat. " Now the tutti," commanded the pianist. " But, Herr von Bülow," remonstrated the conductor, " you haven't played your solo before the tutti yet." " Bah," said von Bülow, " I do not come to hear how *I* play ; I come to hear how *you* play ! "

Sept. 30 *Wednesday.* This afternoon was very embarrassing. The studio at the Steinway Galleries turned out to be excessively tiny, with harsh, uncomfortable lighting. Present were Solomon, who always looks as if he were dividing the child, a Dr Mosco Carner and a Herr Franz Reizenstein, as alike as Jewish Tweedledum and Tweedledee, and Thomas Russell, a nice little man. They all had to stand ; except, of course, J. A., who always takes the only chair in the room. I suppose there may be some point in seeing what a newcomer can do under the most unfavourable circumstances. K. did his best, but I should not have been surprised if he had walked out. However, he kept his temper, though I saw the muscles in his Muscovite neck thicken and swell. The result was probably the angriest performance of the Grieg Concerto ever given. There is a grandeur of self-valuation—not altogether conceit—about this young man which pleases me. Coming away from the Albert Hall the other day we climb on to a bus, and he says, " From these famous pianists I learn nothing. Pavia is not great pianist, but from him I learn. From A., from B., from C. most of all . . . no. They are what you call small fry."

Oct. 3 *Saturday.* My preoccupation with K. is getting me into trouble with my friends and taking up too much of my Diary. Because K. was recording with Decca (five guineas) I had to cut yesterday's date with Jock to see *Sweeney Todd.* Note from Jock this morning to say that he considers himself slighted, but looks forward to a time when I shall be " unbepianisted and devirtuosified." To which I have replied :

Villa Volpone
October 3, 1942

DEAR JOCK,

Sixteen years ago, on the strength of a few lines scribbled in a notebook, I gave a talented boy of twenty-one his first chance. On the strength of a few bars overheard in the foyer of a suburban theatre I am moving heaven and earth, Myra Hess, and Thomas Russell, to give his chance to a talented boy of twenty-two of whom Ernest Irving said, after hearing him play the Bach-Tausig Toccata and Fugue in D minor, " Whether you call it young Busoni or young Kligerman, it's grand playing and shows your friend to be more than a mere virtuoso." It was not by my wish that I became unsecretaried : you should be the last person to want me to be unmusicianed.

JAMIE

This morning I receive a letter from my bank manager asking " what has happened to destroy the peace and harmony of the financial situation ? " Charmingly put, but I know what he means. Also a curt note from the Hampstead Borough Treasurer. Whereupon I do some arithmetic and find that if I can raise £50 in cash to pacify the bank, get Stanley Rubinstein to pay the rates, and live for the next few weeks on what is left in the Savings Bank, plus the sale of half my library and pictures —everything is going to be all right, as they say in the films. So off to Wine Office Court and Cork Street, first dispatching this letter to Stanley, who pretends that my finances are worrying him:

10 *Fairfax Road, N.W.*6
Oct. 3, 1942

DEAR STANLEY,

Your "debilitated frame and shaken health" are pure fiction. And how clumsy of you not to stage your little play better! I make sympathetic inquiries from Benno about you, and the report I receive is that you are obstreperously well.

But how is't with your James, when every knock appals him? Merely that the far from wither'd bailiff, with Tarquin's ravishing strides, moves towards the Villa Volpone. A most substantial ghost. £29 14*s.* 3*d.* for rates as per enclosed. They can, I suppose, seize my furniture, which suggests that we ought never to have paid off the bill of sale! Or isn't a bill of sale good against rates? Now comes the real point. I understand they must leave me my bed but can take my writing-table. What I want to know is: Can I have it the other way round? While I have no objection to sleeping on the floor, working on it is different. My writing is sufficiently *terre à terre* already.

Ever your
JAMES

Oct. 4 *Sunday.* "He does not discept and distinguish like Walkley and Master Hugues's Two; nor can he be watched reasoning steadily from point to point like William Archer." The critic of the *Times Lit. Supp.* on the author of *First Nights*. What about to-day's article in the *S.T.*?

THE CRITIC SUMS UP

Members of the Jury, the charge against the prisoner at the Bar, Eric Maschwitz, is murder, in that on the 29th day of September, 1942, at the Cambridge Theatre, in a piece entitled *Waltz Without End*, he destroyed the reputation of Frédéric Chopin. The Prosecution says that to alter a composer's rhythms, keys, and tempi is to murder that composer. That to debase to blatant, mischievous, and comic purpose part or parts of the B flat minor Scherzo and the finale of the B minor Sonata, to divert from the piano to the voice some part or parts of the third Etude, the E flat Nocturne, and the Waltz in D flat, and to make such voices sing words that are the acme of tawdry nonsense, is to destroy the reputation of an exquisite composer. The Defence argues, and I must ask you to consider this very seriously, that Chopin's reputation cannot be harmed by these vagaries, however extravagant and nauseating, since musical people will keep away, and what the unmusical think is of no importance and can be disregarded. You will ignore the evidence of the witness A, who said he was ashamed to belong to a country which not only tolerated but welcomed artistic vulgarity of this order. Buffooneries in this kind are not intended for him.

But the Defence goes further. It maintains that the prisoner, so far from destroying the reputation of a great composer, has actually given him a fame which he did not enjoy before. (I see from my notes that 'enjoy' was the word the learned counsel used.) That tens of thousands of ignorant and uncultured persons, who had never heard of a Scherzo in B flat minor or any other key, will now go about the town singing "Fools Follow a Rainbow" to a tune of greater elegance than they normally use. That this musical comedy, for which the prisoner admits responsibility, will presently be filmed, and that hundreds of thousands of persons even more ignorant and less cultured will be stimulated by the waltzing and vocalising of, say, Miss Jeanette Macdonald and Mr Nelson Eddy, to the point of buying a gramophone record of a tune which must heighten their musical perceptions. And that all this creates fame in minds in which that fame did not previously exist. It is for you to weigh the validity of this argument.

I come now to that part of his speech in which Counsel for the Prosecution suggested that musical plays of this nature tempt the public away, and hold them back, from such admirable revivals as that of *Hedda Gabler* at the Mercury Theatre. You will give that argument its due weight and no more. You may think that Ibsen's play is a masterpiece of dramatic art, and as such presents no attraction to the musical-comedy public. You may hold that the force, distinction, intelligence, and sheer acting capacity of Miss Sonia Dresdel, and the fact that she does not burst into song, are a further discouragement to that public.

The prisoner is not charged with failing to encourage the arts of music and drama. You may conclude from the evidence that the only charge which he is called upon to answer is that of furthering the business of public entertainment, of meeting the lawful requirements of a large section of the community in a straightforward and demonstrably successful way. You may think that in presenting an imbroglio of maximum inanity in which history and sentiment contend which can be the falser, in eliminating wit in favour of gross and stale humours, in completely disregarding everything we know about the principal character to the extent of presenting him as chubby and bucolic, the prisoner has done what he set out to do, and with commendable skill. The Prosecution admits that the principal performers, Mr Ivor Sheridan and Miss Jane Carr, acquit themselves in the manner approved by custom and the kind of audience they are seeking to please, that the dresses are agreeable, and the dancing less lumpy than some more pretentious cavortings.

In conclusion, the Defence contends—and the Prosecution has put forward no counter-argument which is at all convincing—that the music of Chopin, however garbled and mutilated, is more beneficial to uneducated taste than the atrocities of jazz and swing presented in their horrid integrity. Counsel for the Defence has gone so far as to claim that Chopin himself would have preferred the destruction of his melodies—if, *before this audience*, the mutilations amount to destruction—to that degradation of the public ear through jazz and swing which, the Defence claims, is the only alternative.

Putting that aside as not being the real question, can you say, taking the evidence as a whole, that you are satisfied beyond reasonable doubt that the reputation of Frédéric Chopin no longer exists, and that it was the hand of the prisoner and no other hand that destroyed it ? If you are not so satisfied, whatever your feelings or prejudices may be, then it is your duty to find the prisoner not guilty. If you *are* so satisfied, equally it is your duty to find him guilty. Members of the Jury, will you now consider your verdict ?

Oct. 6 *Tuesday.* Telegram from Jock saying " Rebuke justified," and a 'phone message from Stanley saying he has paid the rates. Dined at Barton Street with Mrs Belloc-Lowndes. A sumptuous meal served by a Sitwellian butler. Felt like Disraeli at Balmoral. Mrs B.-L. is a first-rate talker, and I listened beautifully. Gave me her *Edmond and Jules de Goncourt*, an unashamed gutting of the *Journals*, which I read till three in the morning. Perhaps some account of my reading arrangements may be of interest. I find that by lying on my bed the reverse way and balancing a candle on the bedpost I can just see to read. The candle falls off at least three times a night, but always *away* from the bedclothes. When I'm tired of reading I get up, re-make the bed, and go to sleep with my head the proper way. All of which is rather a business. Why don't I have a reading-lamp ? No paraffin available, and because the electric light works only in four of my eleven rooms, and my bedroom isn't one of them. I called in an electrician over a year ago ; he said the whole house wants re-wiring and advised me to continue as I am doing unless I want to face a bill for sixty pounds, or some other unenvisageable sum.

Fatras. About Mnemonics. Bethinking me that I have to write to a man named White and mustn't forget a story about elephants, I naturally hit on " White Elephant " as the mnemonic. But how do I make sure of remembering " White Elephant " ? Spike Hughes says, " That's easy, James. White Elephants never forget." Spike is a charming person. Disapproves of Beethoven's Sonatas because he " doesn't like the sound that comes out of the piano." Whereas he dotes on Duke Ellington and the sound that comes out of his band. Presumably also on Donald Duck and " the sound that comes out of its bill."

Oct. 7 *Wednesday.* I wonder if I have found the missing motive in the case of William Herbert Wallace, the Liverpool insurance agent found guilty of murdering his wife and sentenced to death. Wallace's Diary contains this entry :

> *March* 20, 1929. Listened-in to *The Master Builder* by Ibsen. This is a fine thing and shows clearly how a man may build up a fine career, and as the world has it, be a great success, and yet in his own mind feel that he has been an utter failure, and how ghastly a mistake he has made to sacrifice love and the deeper comforts of life in order to achieve success. Curious that Julia did not appreciate this play. I feel sure she did not grasp the inner significance and real meaning of the play.

Wallace's counsel stressed the absence of motive. But I can quite well imagine a row about the exact meaning of Hilda Wangel's " I heard harps in the air," followed by a Biff and a Bang. The medical evidence showed that the wretched woman had received six biffs and five bangs, eleven in all, on the cranium and delivered from behind, apparently by the time-honoured blunt instrument. Who was the murderer ? Could it have been what Damon Runyon would call Julia's ever-loving husband ? Perhaps " ever-loving " gives us a clue. Winifred Duke, in her excellent novel *Skin for Skin*, founded on this case, suggests that the husband, whom she calls Bruce, murdered his wife for the reason that he just couldn't stand living with her any longer.

And a very reasonable reason too. After all, an Old Dutch on the cover of a song and an Old Dutch at home are two very different propositions. We shall never know how many Darbys have put away their Joans. Or what things other than blessings have been poured on the frosty pow of John Anderson, my jo, John. Life at the old-age pension stage is a brittle thing, and an overworked doctor will not be tempted to look beyond natural causes, provided, of course, that there has been no amateurish work with a hatchet. And the Wallace case was a highly professional affair. It was planned with extreme care and extraordinary imagination. Either the murderer was Wallace or it wasn't. If it wasn't, then here at last is the perfect murder. If it was, then here is a murder so nearly perfect that the Court of Criminal Appeal, after examining the evidence, decided to quash Wallace's conviction. He died in 1933. There was great competition among the more excitable newspapers for the statement it was presumed Wallace would make on his release. The *Empire News* won. At least, it was in that paper's motor-car that he drove away from the Court of Criminal Appeal. And at once fell asleep. The special reporter kept a sharp ear for any words that might fall. " She was bending down," he heard the sleeping man murmur. And then Wallace woke up.

Oct. 8 *Thursday.* The first copies of *Ego* 5 to hand. Quite good paper, I have now got used to the smaller margin, and I think that in view of all the difficulties Harrap's have done extraordinarily well. After my colossal efforts I now know that it is impossible to produce a book without a misprint. In spite of Jock's eagle eye, George Mathew's steady gaze, and Leo's vengeful glare, to say nothing of my own owlish brooding—there, staring us all in the face, is a song-title which not even a dance-band leader could get wrong. The trouble is that one's eye flits too quickly over whatever is too familiar. When the first copies of *Ego* were bound and waiting to go out for review I discovered an allusion to " Johnson's *Boswell* " which meant that the page had to be cut out and a new one inserted. Bill Barrett tells me that I ought to adopt the classical method of reading every line and word backwards, so that familiarity cannot breed contempt. By the way, if ever these Diaries should be reprinted I direct the editor to make a correction on page 123 of *Ego* 2. To keep his feet warm before the empty grate my brother Edward used to wear *two* pairs of socks. Also *Ego* 5, page 173, where Macbeth's going hence should, of course, be Duncan's.

Oct. 9
Friday.
Criticism as it used to be. The occasion is the production on November 9, 1758, of Ravencroft's *London Cuckolds.* Author unknown.

This monstrous production of nonsense and obscenity, is the spawn of one Ravencroft, a Writer whose wit was as contemptible as his morals were vicious. He does not seem to have had one sentiment either of a man of genius, or a Gentleman; at least if we may judge by the characters he had daubed, which are a pack of reprobates of the lowest kind. Nor are the things which look like incidents in this Play the produce of his own invention; but squeezings from an extravagant novel by Scarron, and two or three ill-chosen fables of La Fontaine; from which ingredients he has contrived to mix up a sort of hog-wash, sweetened with a few luscious expressions, and a large portion of the grossest lewdness, to the palates of swine, or, what is the same thing, of men like them, but which must be odious to, and nauseated by all people of delicate taste, or common modesty. Let me add, the upper-gallery was crowded with applauding spectators, and once for all, that the *London Cuckolds* is a spectacle fit only to be represented before common w——s and blackguards.

Oct. 10
Saturday.
Kligerman was awarded a great ovation at the Savage Club Luncheon to-day. He is the first artist in the history of the club to be asked to make a second appearance at a later part of the entertainment.

Oct. 12
Monday.
Lured Walter Legge to lunch at the Savage and brought the talk round to Kligerman's performance on Saturday, which at once started a buzz. Then back to the H.M.V. Studios in Abbey Road, where who should be waiting but Alexis! The best Steinway being trotted out, K. performed so grandly that Walter, *tout emerveillé,* rushed us into a taxi down to Drury Lane, where he obtained a permit for K. The idea is a tour with E.N.S.A., which would not be too good for him at his present stage. Shall try to do better for him. In the meantime he has left the "Q" Theatre.

Oct. 13 Letter from Norman Collins:
Tuesday.

Evenlode
Nicholas Way
Northwood
October 12, 1942

DEAR JAMES,

Let's begin another amusing correspondence!

Your review of my novel *Anna* has been read, re-read and deeply regretted—for your sake. About the merits of the book you may be right. Or wrong. But you of all people must not let yourself be right—you may be, and certainly were about those of my novels which you liked—for the wrong reasons.

You contend that novelists ought to write about things which they know at first-hand. Really, James, I am surprised at you! Without a blush for mixing the company, I ask whether Sigrid Undset was drawing on recollections of her early youth when she wrote *Kristin Lavransdatter*. Did good Sir Walter go galumphing across the plains of Asia Minor before he wrote *The Talisman*? How much of *The Fortunes of Richard Mahoney* derived from Henry Handel Richardson's experiences gold-digging in Australia? Did Dickens go through the French Revolution? Was Shakespeare ever in Rome or Illyria? Did not James Agate (to fly high for a moment) write a book on Rachel without being exactly a contemporary?

And for the second time, really James! To suggest that there can be a "reasonable" length for a novel! "Reasonable" length for whom? For those who like short novels? Or medium-length ones? Or long ones? On this point let me tell you a little parable. There was once a University Extension Course on "The English Novel" for women teachers. At the end of the lecture an imposing harridan said acidly, "The lecturer has told us about short novels, and about long novels. Would he now tell us what is the *correct* length for a novel?" (I know the truth of that story, because I was the lecturer.)

In short, James, you have blundered. You have stepped down. You are dishonoured. As I see it, there is nothing for it but hemp or hemlock for you now. I do not see how even the privilege of reprinting this letter, free of charge, and with my cordial good wishes, in *Ego* X, could possibly ease your conscience sufficiently for you to face the indignity of going on living.

Yours,
NORMAN COLLINS

My reply :

10 *Fairfax Road, N.W.*6
Tuesday October 13, 1942

DEAR NORMAN,

Delightful !

But why not let well alone ? Why walk into the lion's den twice ? Daniel didn't. Since playing with you is no good I must now get to work on you.

About first- and second-hand novelists. The best shot at confounding me would have been *Salammbô.* I agree that Flaubert never saw dead and dying elephants piled one on top of another, or heard one called Fury of Baal, caught by his leg chains, scream from noon till night with an arrow in his eye. But he makes me see and hear them, and smell the blood and taste the sweat of the soldiers' naked bodies. The book reeks of Carthage, whereas *Anna* reeks of Camberwell. But then it is very difficult to write like Flaubert. My *Rachel* reeks of Paris in the 'forties and 'fifties. But then again it is very difficult to write like Agate ! In other words, you are just about a good enough writer to set down the things you know. To write about things you don't know wants genius, and you haven't got it, my dear boy. At least, not that kind.

In the matter of length. There is a correct length for every novel. This is attained when the verbal envelope fits the emotional or intellectual content exactly. From which it follows that *War and Peace* and *The Young Visiters* are both the right length. Your book is like the Cromwell Road : it doesn't know when to stop.

Will you now please sit down and write a novel about the middle-aged publisher who becomes a Home Guard ? You might begin with a party at Northwood, in the grounds of Norman Collins, Esq. But you must stop at the moment when your Home Guard goes into action against an air-borne German tank, since, your name being Norman and not Gustave, you don't know about such things. Correct length for this book 87,362 words.

End of amusing correspondence.

JAMES

Oct. 14 *Wednesday.* Marie Tempest is dead.

The essential truth about Mary can be put into a sentence. She had a small, exquisite talent and was generally recognised as an actress of the first rank. Yet I do not remember that she ever played in Goldsmith, Sheridan, Pinero, Wilde, Galsworthy, Shaw. New movements passed her by : or rather she passed them by. And she was wise. I remember an occasion when, on the wireless, she played Mrs Alving in *Ghosts*, and over the air came the accents of *The Marriage of Kitty*. Inside its limitations Marie Tempest's art was superb. Over all her acting was a *patina*, the result of years of study to make perfection yet more perfect. Her technique was flawless, and her comedy had everything that comedy should have, except the gift of tears. Mary hadn't a shred of pathos, and her rare attempts in that direction could have made only a crocodile weep. She had unsurpassable elegance, exquisite poise, and a sense of proportion which enabled her to give her effects their exact value and no more. Oddly enough, she overdid one gesture which she took from Jeanne Granier—that of putting finger to forehead. She had a great sense of humour. I remember the first night of a piece called *Her Shop* in which she had to say, " It's very nice, of course, to be young and beautiful. But there are other qualities, thank God ! " I think I never heard a line better delivered. Her voice was indescribable and inimitable ; her ' squawk ' will not be heard again. Beneath the patrician layers there was a note which suggested that, like Rachel, like Réjane, and our own Mrs Jordan, she knew her plebeian world.

Off the stage Maria, as many people called her, was a continual delight. My most endearing memory of her is finding her in pyjamas on the morning after the fire in Avenue Road, preparing to demolish the piano with the coal-hammer. On my objecting that the result wouldn't look in the least like fire damage, she turned the hammer round and ran the spike along three shelves of rather shabby calf bindings. Again I protested. " The hose-pipe, dear, the hose-pipe ! " she said. Her letters show that she looked upon the provinces as an unspeakable No-man's Land, and regarded first-rate acting as something to be seen only in the Capital. In this she had the support of the French, who long ago invented that useful tradeswoman, the *tragédienne de province*. Mary would have cut out her tongue sooner than go down to history as a *comédienne de province*. She hated touring. " Quelle vie de DOG ! " she wote.

Her *volonté* became legendary ; she was the very genius of the indomitable. In great measure a tartar, she gave that side of her character full rein. Her best rôle was that of Marie Tempest. In this she was superb.

Oct. 16 *Friday.* Letter from Jock :

33 King Street
Covent Garden, W.C.2
15th October, 1942

DEAR JAMIE,

(1) My old Peggotty at home—who brought me up " by hand "—has just written one of her rare letters to me, and it has the sentence : " I hope you are not becoming too high and mighty in the company you seem to be keeping these days. Who for instance is this Lady Bracknell whose remarks you are always repeating in your articles ? "

(2) Snatch of a recent conversation between me and a certain young person :

ME. I'm devoted to James, but just at the moment he's a terrible bore about some young pianist.

Y. P. My dear, he was a terrible bore about *you* fifteen years ago ! (*Close of conversation.*)

(3) I did enjoy the brief drinky-winky with you and Leo.

Love,
JOCK

Oct. 19 *Monday.* A letter :

2 *Carlyle Square*
*S.W.*3
18*th October* 1942

DEAR JAMES AGATE,

Our common friend Osbert Sitwell tells me that you have a passion for Sarah Bernhardt—indeed, a most natural passion. Wd. you like, as a present, a picture painted by her for the Red X sale at Christie's during the last war, and re-sold at the Red X sale at Christie's 2 years ago and bought by me ? I have also a letter written by her explaining that she wanted to help the Red X. This goes with the picture and therefore to you, if you like the idea. The picture cd. do with a clean as I have not touched it, and the varnish is dirty—the subject is 2 Macaws—however you spell that form of parrot—and it is not very well painted. But it has a quality of silliness wh. is delightful. And who else owns a Sarah Bernhardt ?

I plan to take a week's leave from the Air Ministry on Sunday, and suggest that you shd. come and lunch here when I return, and inspect the picture.

Yours sincerely,
DAVID HORNER

Oct. 20
Tuesday.

Another misprint in *Ego* 5. This is that Mistinguett has an *e* too many in the text, but is spelt all right in the Index. These things are impossible to avoid; they happen because the mind runs ahead of the eye. An evening paper went through all its editions recently with the heading "Coal from Oil," and nobody detected anything wrong. On the same day the *News Chronicle* leader-writer complained that the Government was still putting the horse before the cart.

Oct. 21
Wednesday.

Disappointed with Lillian Hellman's *The Little Foxes*, the film of which appears to have gammoned everybody. Fay Compton makes Regina an undisguised bad lot, Hedda Gabler piled on Vittoria Corombona with Goneril and Regan thrown in, and none of the redeeming features of any of them. People try to tell me that the film presented a study in deterioration; which must be all my eye and Bette Davis. In the play Regina is "mean" from the beginning; her declaration that she can conceive no state between nigger and millionaire makes this plain. She has neither desires of the flesh nor outreachings of the spirit. About her wickedness there is nothing poetical, intellectual, metaphysical. She is no heroine of Greek drama in thrall to some pitiless goddess. She is not concerned with a husband's advancement or a lover's career. She does not want to have a finger in the world's pie. Her aim is simply to have a great deal of money, to live in Chicago, and spend the money giving dinner-parties to the right people. Her mind is utterly vulgar, and Fay is superb. But I quite see what people mean when they insist that Bette Davis was better; they mean that the screen play gave the screen actress opportunities denied the stage player. I can imagine Bette going all out for charm in a canter through those Virginian woods on the back of Hedda Gabler's saddle-horse, and the bemused film public marvelling at the turpitude presently revealed. Fay is in different case, having no choice but to tragedy-queen it in black velvet. It is quite possible that she would not be so good on the screen as Bette, who is a superb screen actress. On the other hand I do not believe that Bette would give as good a stage performance as Fay, who is a superb stage actress.

Oct. 23 *Friday.* A busy day. Looked at some books, dictated my *Daily Express* and *Sunday Times* articles, did a broadcast on *expertise* in dramatic criticism, and went out to lunch. Kligerman called in the afternoon. Also a photographer who took flashlight photographs all over the house, by arrangement, he said, though I had forgotten. Kenneth Hopkins arrived in the middle of all this, and I abandoned work for the day to listen to this pleasant young soldier of twenty-eight explain in a Cockney accent why he is the greatest living poet. Showed me seven lines about a sundial, and then told me that in his world I am looked upon as superficial and conceited. Implored me to give up the Diary at the first sign of my being written out, of which, he was good enough to add, he saw no trace at the moment. I liked the young man very much and so did Leo, and we made him promise to come again.

Fatras. From a book about Jane Austen :

> There is nothing about Jane Austen of what Proust calls the Dostoevsky side of Madame de Staël. . . . We could never picture her being tied to a mast to realise a snowstorm, like Turner.
>
> DAVID RHYDDERCH, *Jane Austen*

Oct. 24 *Saturday.* If there is anything those two citizens, Jock and James, despise it is a gabby highbrow doll, and such a doll as X is apt to have at his parties. Have written to X declining to dine with two female highbrows, pleading that Jock is too young and I am too old to be bothered. Women, especially intellectual women, have no social tact; whenever they meet a dramatic critic they fall on him hammer and tongs and want to know what he thinks about the new plays. Which means that he has to listen while they tell him what they think. Women have no notion of letting a man be. They go on clicking their brains at him like knitting-needles, until he is exhausted. At the Club the other day the company at my table included Bud Flanagan, Benno Moiseiwitsch, Douglas Furber, Spike Hughes, and Joe Batten, who had brought along Herbert Sutcliffe and Abe Waddington. Not one word was spoken about cricket. Added a postscript to my letter to X, giving a list of the women we *will* dine with.

Oct. 27 Jock writes :
Tuesday.

33 *King Street*
Covent Garden
*W.C.*2
26*th October*, 1942

But, dear Jamie, you have no right to identify me with your views on ladies to sup with (copy of your letter to X just received) ! I wouldn't be very willing to sup with any of your Permissibles or Impermissibles (excepting Mary Hutchinson, who sometimes asks me, and Queen Mary, who doesn't !). Clemence Dane—I suspect it is through some ass's practical joke—has long been convinced that I am a telephoning blackmailer. Caroline Lejeune once overheard me calling her a Wallachian peasant in disguise (she always ties her hair up in a hanky) and has never so much as glared at me since. Caryl Brahms has never begun to forgive me for dubbing her—to some common friend—as " a remorseless mixture of intensity and vivacity." Dilys Powell is a darling *but* a film critic (and I want to forget films at supper-time). Gladys Calthrop—though I met her once at a birthday party of yours—is oblivious, and looks at me unrecognisingly at first nights through her serenely handsome eyelashes. And Rebecca West once said she wouldn't be seen dead with me. (At least she said *that* of all your satellites in *Ego*, and I naturally took it to include me. Very soon afterwards I was caught in a severe air raid in Baker Street near her flat. While waiting for a train at Marylebone I sent her a letter-card saying, " Dear Miss West—You were very nearly seen dead with me to-night —Jock." I don't think R. W. ever got this missive, because the pillar-box outside Marylebone Station had vanished next morning when I returned from the country.) I don't know any of your other ladies, and have no desire to meet or not to meet them. Give *me* actresses to sup with. I see you don't mention a single actress. They are the jolliest. They usually eat a good deal, which saves a lot of talk, whereas literary ladies just pick and wrangle. Besides, all the actresses I know act quite badly off-stage. They nearly always flatter you in an obvious way (which is always pleasant). Or else they indulge in blunt reprisals (which makes them look absurd to everybody). And later on (over the coffee, I mean) they tell you their secret ambitions and their private antipathies (which are respectively impressive and delicious). I find them, in short, sincere and natural, as ladies go.

Always your
JOCK

Oct. 29 *Thursday.* Apropos of Hesketh Pearson's Life of Shaw, am telling *Express* readers that just as Minerva sprang from the head of Jove, so Shaw's plays spring from the author's brain, innocent of heart, stomach, bowels. That, like Schubert, Shaw has never known when to stop and, unlike Schubert, has not had the luck to leave even one of his plays unfinished. That with these reservations Shaw is our greatest playwright since Shakespeare. And I end by saying that taking on trust the account of Shaw as social reformer, polemist, and politician—about which I know nothing—I pronounce this to be an admirable book, doing full justice to its subject's integrity, diversity, sanity, wit, invective, style, vitality, industry, larkishness, and colossal sense of human responsibility.

Oct. 31 *Saturday.* Have sold Jonathan Cape *Brief Chronicles: A Survey of the Plays of Shakespeare and the Elizabethans in Actual Performance.* £150 advance. Of this at least eighty-five pounds goes to income tax. Add fifteen pounds for typing and I shall be lucky if I make fifty pounds out of it.

Nov. 3 *Tuesday.* The last three days taken up in reading *Sodome et Gomorrhe.* This is the only book of Proust's into which I have not dipped at one time or another, and when I found a beautiful copy (Knopf) at the Chenhalls's I determined to make a frontal attack. I know now that I shall never be a Proustian, though perfectly remembering how Walkley declared the first two books had given him "more pleasure than anything in modern French." I recognise the genius of Proust and marvel at his craftsmanship; a blind man reading him in Braille would be dazzled. Yet he does not hold me as Balzac holds me. The snobbery? Rather like those dinner-parties at Eaton Gate, when Monty Shearman would suddenly recover his social sense and say to Maurice Ingram, "Yes, yes, Maurice, but tell me about your Ambassador's wife afterwards. James isn't interested," and turn to me and ask if I had seen any exciting cricket at Lord's recently. (More and more I miss Monty's never-failing sympathy and counsel.) The hypocrisy about Albertine? I just cannot be bothered to read "him" for "her" six times a page. When I knew Albert he was, I suppose, about fifty, and had acquired a certain saturnine distinction. He told me, a year or so after Proust's death, that he had some four hundred letters from him "which, when it rains, will keep me." But it never rained. "Monsieur Albert est mort," I was told the next time I went to Paris, "d'une pneumonie féroce."

Nov. 4 *Wednesday.* A coincidence. At Clarke-Hall's, the Wine Office Court bookseller, I discovered a copy of Van Vechten's *Nigger Heaven.* Reading this to-night I came across the sentence "René Maran, the author of *Batouala,* he had actually been acquainted with." The name sounded familiar, and I remembered that in the Charing Cross Road on my way home I had picked up another book. I look at it again and find it is *Batouala, Véritable Roman Nègre,* by René Maran.

Nov. 5 *Thursday.* Ernest Short's *Theatrical Cavalcade* revives the old Irving-Shaw controversy. I have never understood why Shaw was angry that Irving refused to put on any of his plays. Confront an actor of Irving's calibre with one of Ibsen's parochial quandaries or Mr Shaw's sociological debates, and obviously he will say to himself, "This is all very fine, but there's nothing for *me* to act." Meaning that an actor of lesser virtuosity will do the job as efficiently. After all, it doesn't take a Liszt or a Rubinstein to play Beethoven's Opus 14 No. 2 or Mendelssohn's Rondo Capriccioso, charming works though they both are. Say you enjoy spending an evening discussing the sanitary affairs of some poky little hole in Norway or worrying about the pronunciation of a Cockney flower-girl, all well and good: it needs no Ghost come from the grave—and there was always something of the apparition about Irving—to tell the playgoer about these things. In his account of *The Lyons Mail* Short recalls Dubosq's callousness in humming a bar of the Marseillaise. Has he forgotten that after Dubosq had rifled the body of the murdered post-boy, Irving, still humming, would first wipe his hands wet with blood on the horse's flank, and then pat the animal's neck? Ellen might have made a shot at Ibsen's Nora. But what scope would Helmer have afforded for her great partner wrapped in himself and nobody else?

And suppose H. I. had diminished each corporal agent to the feat of being Helmer ? I hold that one would have left the theatre with possibly more respect for Ibsen, but certainly less for Irving. Short reminds us that " Always, a special limelight ray followed the Chief's face with a small ' pin ' light of steel blue." Splendid ! I never think of Irving without this lighting, and I cannot possibly see it being used in any play of Ibsen's. Shaw abused Irving ; he should have gone down on his bended knees and thanked him.

Nov. 8 *Sunday.* The title of my *Tatler* article next week is going to be " Announcing the Dilysians." To-day my beloved but ferociously highbrow Dilys Powell, who henceforth gives her name to the abstruse coterie, writes :

> But to instance a scrap of literature embedded in a film is beside the point ; if the film has its own validity as an art it must affect us by its own methods, which are basically, though not exclusively, visual. . . . The pictorial effect in *Green Pastures* of the hands touching Moses's shoulder in farewell is more moving than speech.

What a bungler, then, was Shakespeare ! What a time-waster to bother with :

> It is the cause, it is the cause, my soul,

and all that rigmarole about quenching flaming ministers. Unless I am being wildly unfair, we shall presently be reading, " The pictorial effect in *Green-eyed Monster* of Othello's dusky fingers snuffing the candle is more moving than any speech."

With an appositeness that is quite miraculous the programme of the Bing Crosby absurdity, *Road to Morocco*, which I saw this afternoon, contained this note :

> Every once in a while movie-makers remember their medium's voiceless beginning and revive for a scene or two the art of pantomime. Often these scenes are among the best in the picture, which must prove something. Maybe what it proves is that films always were and always will be based on visual appeal.

I am not sure that this film does not make the best of both worlds, that of the Dilysians, and mine. There comes a moment when a camel puts its head through the wall of a tent and, with its chin resting on Bing's shoulder, says, " This is the screwiest picture I was ever in." Perhaps some day this intelligent animal will be given a chance to dilysiate in the highbrow films; he will find them far screwier than this one.

Fatras. Our highbrows :

> He once told Aldous Huxley of his intention to go to the West Indies to live among the negroes to collect material for a novel about Mayfair.
>
> G. U. Ellis, *Twilight on Parnassus*

Nov. 9 *Monday.* A glorious day, in every sense of the word. Alexander's great victory and the invasion by the Americans of French North Africa have put the people of this country into better fettle than they have known since 1925, when, at Melbourne on the third day of the second Test Match, Hobbs and Sutcliffe put on 283 runs for England's first wicket and sent the Stock Exchange up two points. I am so far Conservative that I believe almost nothing I see in the popular Press, and very little I hear on the wireless. Unless a thing is corroborated in *The Times* it remains, for me, rumour. To-day's good news has received the august sanction, reinforced by the " Old and True " selection. This is Chesterton's

> " The high tide ! " King Alfred cried.
> " The high tide and the turn."

Nov. 10 *Tuesday.* About Edna May Oliver, the film actress who has just died in Hollywood, I read that :

> Her biggest successes were as the Nurse in the £400,000 *Romeo and Juliet* and as Betsey Trotwood in *David Copperfield.*

Apologists for the popular Press might argue that to its readers the bare mention of a Shakespeare play means nothing, but that the addition of the figures indicates that this one was a film and an expensive one. Such an argument would be plausible but not valid—the young man who writes the paragraph has no sense of its vulgarity, and his editor applauds it. As the cheaper papers see it, the choice is between no mention of Shakespeare and a vulgar one. Which is the better ? The popular Press has been able to make its up mind about this. I haven't.

Nov. 11 *Wednesday.* *Best Bib and Tucker* at the Palladium. Tommy Trinder very funny; he has his being in that Atlantis "out of which our coxcombical moral sense is for a little transitory ease excluded." The Cairoli brothers superb, and Nat Jackley slithers about the stage like Walt Disney's illustrations to Stravinsky's *Sacre du Printemps.*

Nov. 12 *Thursday.* *Ego* 5 officially published to-day. It had been announced for November 5, which accounts for some of the notices being a trifle premature. The one most obviously flattering is by Elizabeth Bowen in the *Tatler:* "When, from day to day, the top of the furnace is opened for restoking, one finds oneself almost intimidated by the expectant interior roar."

I put *Punch* next. "H. K." (Hugh Kingsmill ?) writes:

> Every one, it is said, has one good book inside him, and, if this be so, it would be unkind to suggest that Mr James Agate is the exception that proves the rule. All one can in fairness say is that his good book is not among the thirty-six he has so far produced.

To justify this statement "H. K." must have read all thirty-six books. To continue in feverish search after thirty-five disappointments—here's tribute indeed !

As always happens when an article is cut, most of Osbert Sitwell's wit has evaporated from his notice in the *Sunday Times,* of which he had sent me a copy. I should have liked the sentence: "When Mr Agate is summoned to the office of his solicitors to discuss new methods—on the top of those already in force—of cutting down his expenditure, my soul is purged with terror and with pity." But it was not to be, and even without it the review is a beauty. I like the notion that I join Dr Johnson as one of the tantrumists of letters.

Most notable, perhaps, is the *New Statesman* review by Raymond Mortimer, which is magnanimity's self. About this George Richards writes to me this morning:

> You could have knocked me down with a flock mattress when I picked up a *New Statesman* with a pair of tongs to-day and read of your Famous Victory. The conquest only included acres of barren sand-dunes, it is true, but what a Rout! Mortimer was never one of your True Blue, *i.e.*, Pink Yapping

Bloomsbury Yahoos, but merely runs with the wrong pack, a survivor from a comparatively civilised epoch when skill in one's craft (if that happened to be a writer's) was not necessarily held against one. He's not, in other words, classifiable as Monotremata : " the lowest order of mammals, consisting of the duckbill and the echidnas, belonging respectively to the subclass Ornithorhynoidæ and Tachyglossidæ, restricted to the Bloomsbury region. They lay large-yoked, thin-shelled eggs, the young being enclosed in a shallow pouch during lactation. The genital, urinary, and intestinal organs open into a common chamber or cloaca. The brain has no corpus callosum, the testicles are permanently abdominal, the coracoid articulates with the sternum, and epipubic bones, clavicles, and an interclavicle are present. True teeth occur only in the embryonic stages."

Nov. 13 *Friday.* Thomas Griffiths Wainewright has turned up again. The late A. J. A. Symons used to begin his letters to me "My dear Egomet Bonmot," and there is a passage in John Lindsey's *Suburban Gentleman* which seems to justify this.

> Mr Wainewright had his horse, Contributor, harnessed to his new gig and drove into London to see and be seen. Contributor was a good horse. Wainewright had bought him at great expense, greater than he could afford. But the name pleased him. With a horse named thus he would drive into literature. . . .

About this Hazlitt wrote :

> The hackney coachman who drives him [Wainewright], or his horse Contributor, whom he has introduced as a select personage to the vulgar reader, knows as much of the matter [Vulgarity and Affectation] as he does.

Remembering another journalist of horsey inclination, I turned up the Goncourts and found :

> *June* 19, 1861. In Grossetête's restaurant we caught a glimpse of Ponson du Terrail, with his dogcart waiting on the boulevard ; it is the only carriage owned by a Parisian man of letters. Alas, the poor fellow pays dearly for the privilege, by the sweat of his brow, and by the sacrifice of all his literary pride. He is known to have said to the editor of a paper in which he was publishing a long serial novel, " Give me notice a few days ahead if your public is getting bored, and I will finish up in one chapter."

Am contemplating sending a similar note to George Harrap !

The justification of Lindsey's book is, I suppose, that it puts into popular form Jonathan Curling's much better work, the masterly and exhaustive study entitled *Janus Weathercock*, published some four years ago.

Dined with my old friend Trevor Blakemore at the Sesame Club. Other guests were Lance Sieveking and Louis Gautier, grand-nephew of Théophile, but much prouder, I gathered, of being President of the conjurors' club known as the Magic Circle. Talked to L. G. about something which has intrigued, and sometimes worried, me for thirty years and more. It began one evening when I was sitting in the kitchen in the little Derbyshire farmhouse where I had rooms. I lit a cigarette, and throwing the match into the fire, was surprised to find it stand on end on the bar of the grate. I was so much impressed that I collected some neighbours to bear witness. We removed it gingerly and tried to put it back again by hand, but without success. A few days later I was practising the Christmas trick of throwing cards, one at a time, into a hat. The first card I threw landed on the threadbare carpet, and remained erect. At Doughty Street I threw a half-smoked cigarette out of the window and it stood up on the area railings. For thirty years these balancing tricks have persisted. Knives remain precariously poised, see-sawing on the edges of marble-topped and even glass tables, in the presence of other people. I remember going to my bookcase—an open one—to look for a quotation, when the volume I wanted fell out upon the floor. No, it did not open at the right page. But I have so often opened a book at random and found the quotation I was looking for on the page at which I opened it that I am no longer surprised. It would be tedious to multiply instances. I am consciously totally incapable of any kind of legerdemain, and these things never happen when I am thinking about them. They seem to me to be in some way allied to the subconscious reproduction of other people's handwriting which sometimes happens when I am thinking about those people, some of whom are still alive; consciously I cannot imitate anybody's handwriting. Louis Gautier could give no kind of explanation, and I have an entirely open mind on the subject, merely rejecting the theory that these things happen to everybody and that my observation of them is exceptional. About the happenings there is no disputing; Jock has witnessed many of them.

Fatras. Looking in Wilde's *Intentions* for something about Wainewright, I read : " I said to you some time ago that it was far more difficult to talk about a thing than to do it." That, of course, was the bosh of the period. It is, and always was, much easier to write beautifully about, say, a sewing machine than to make one. Old man Hugo couldn't have mown two inches of a field of hay without amputating both feet. Whereas he could write

> Quel dieu, quel moissonneur de l'éternel été
> Avait, en s'en allant, négligemment jeté
> Cette faucille d'or dans le champ des étoiles

without mulcting his verse of a syllable.

Nov. 14 *Saturday.* Being reviewed by Willson Disher is rather like being reviewed by Alice's White Knight. Nevertheless I detach from the woolly entanglement that I shall not win fame by " emptying wastepaper baskets into publishers' laps instead of salvage bins."

The reviewer of the *Times Lit. Supp.* cannot decide whether *Ego* 5 is causerie, scrap-book, or diary. Astonishingly, for a *Times* reviewer, he holds that " what the audience he [the diarist] eventually reaches hopes to get from him is a view of people and things unclouded by fear of the law of libel or even respect for the rules of common courtesy." In other words, I should have done better to hold up my Diary during my lifetime and fill it with accounts of how X, the well-known actor, never goes on the stage until he is drunk ; with what persons and what kind Y, the famous pianist, sleeps ; and how Z, the great painter, cheats at cards. I would not desire immortality at this price ; I could have it to-morrow with a volume of *chroniques scandaleuses* beginning with myself ! What my Diary tries to do is to give some kind of permanence to such fleeting interests as come my way. I have published in my lifetime, because, as Doctor Johnson so nearly said, we shall not treat with publishers in the grave.

Nov. 15 *Sunday.* Violet Vanbrugh, who died last week, had stature, presence, gait, and a deep, resonant voice, but she brought more than these qualities to her Lady Macbeth, one of the best I ever saw. To any sensitive playgoer it was at once obvious that the actress had been stirred out of her normal orbit and projected into a world other than that of her Muriel Glaydes and Lady Aletheas. The late Allan Monkhouse divined the actress's intentions when he wrote: "The exaltation of the part requires that Lady Macbeth should move above and beyond the human levels; there must be no lapse from the diction of high passion; the great, dim exemplars like Siddons and Ristori must have one more worthy follower." But, alas, this Lady Macbeth was handicapped by her spouse, who made the Thane of Cawdor a city magnate with accesses of hysteria. Which prompted A. N. M. to ask as we left the theatre whether I thought murder could be "as serious as all that came to?"

But Violet was not always on her high horse, and perhaps more's the pity. Yet of her performances in the comedies of Sutro and others it was possible to write that she "contrived with astonishing skill to put a human edge on to creatures of frivolity." No one would have proclaimed her a great actress, but she was a very good one. Her name did not appear in the casts of Ibsen and Shaw; there was a world elsewhere which she illumined by her own special talents. She brought to the theatre a dignity which nothing could impair, and when the fashion and the favour ebbed—as they will after fifty years—she continued in her loyal devotion to the stage and what she judged to be its best interests. During her later years she was frequently to be seen at first nights. No need on these occasions to instruct the young playgoer on which side of the footlights distinction of the old school was to be found.

Nov. 16 *Monday.* Portia opines that "Nothing is good, I see, without respect." Antonio's mouthpiece might have said equally that nothing is bad without respect. There are moods in which I could consider *Panama Hattie*, inflicted on me immediately after breakfast this morning, the worst picture I have ever seen. And then I reflect that not even a film can be deemed bad without respect. Montague once left the theatre in the middle of a wretched performance of *Romeo and Juliet* because, said he, "the carts in the street were so much jollier." What's the alternative to seeing even the worst possible picture? Well, for millions of people there is spending the evening at home quarrelling with the family and trying to hear the news above the baby's crying. Or there is sitting in a frowsty public bar, drinking more flat warm beer than the pocket-money can run to. If I lived in, say, Widnes or Walsall I can well believe that I might take *Panama Hattie* for a masterpiece. But I live in London, and rather than listen to lyrics like

> I thought I was a lady until last night,
> I thought I was a lady till I got tight,
> Boy, did I get stinking at the club Savoy!

I would prefer to spend this film's eighty minutes standing in the black-out signalling to non-existent taxis.

My preference for *A Yank at Eton*, on view after lunch, is that there is no damned verisimilitude about it. Do those Olympians who belong to "Pop" process down the High Street chorusing the Eton Boat-song? No. Does a brand-new pupil, even an American, begin his scholastic career by pommelling a member of the Sixth Form? No. Is the stickjaw episode credible? No. Is this film a greater libel upon Eton than that other was upon Oxford? Yes. And shouldn't even an Eton housemaster realise that when Mickey Rooney wears his Yes-I-did-it-so-what look he is merely sheltering Freddie Bartholomew? Yes. Doesn't Edmund Gwenn ever go to the pictures? It would seem not. It all comes back to something I am never tired of saying—that when you are in the presence of genius, or let me say great natural talent, it doesn't matter very much what that talent is exercised on. No doubt it would have been better if Ben Davies had eschewed Songs of Araby and John McCormack had adjured Hearing You Calling Him, and if both had devoted themselves to the song-cycles of Schubert and Schumann. But better for whom? The gain to lovers of *Lieder* would have meant the loss of these artists to their warm-hearted if less musical public. It is the same with Mickey Rooney. There are people who deplore the zoom and rush of this great little artist's genius, which they call vulgarity. I am content that Mickey's genius should be vulgar; I no more want this actor not to be vulgar—in the sense in which the release of boundless energy is always vulgar—than I want Trabb's boy not to be vulgar. This film should have been called *Trabb's Boy at Eton*.

Nov. 17 *Tuesday.* Alexis is drawing crowds to the Swiss Cottage Odeon, where, twice daily throughout the week, he is giving a twenty minutes' recital. (14 guineas.) Being asked by the management for a popular programme, he begins in a pink light with Grünfeld's charming Fantasie on waltz themes by Johann Strauss, following this in a mauve light with the *Liebestraum*, and ending in a sunset glow with that awful Second Rhapsody. He looks very well in evening dress, and has plenty of showmanship. The pretended *affaissement* in which he sinks back in his chair at the end is beautifully calculated.

Nov. 18 *Wednesday.* Rang up Gwen Chenhalls and proposed myself for dinner. Found her alone and very gay. Excellent food and drink, and the run of her husband's cigars, Alfred being away for the night auditing Metro-Goldwyn-Mayer's pocket-money, or something. Many women have wit ; Gwen has humour. Gave me a delicious and entirely fanciful account of going to the Albert Hall to hear Kentner and his talented wife in Béla Bartók's Concerto for two pianos, percussion, and orchestra. Gwen had had a preliminary look at the score, and found that the piano parts consisted " entirely of chords of at least six notes in each hand, including two and sometimes three for the thumb with mountains of double flats and sharps, played fortissimo in 29-64 time. Both players were obviously at the top of their form, but what with the echo and the fog, and of course the percussion, I didn't hear a note from either piano ! " Gwen added—and I am sure it was her inventive genius at work—that both artists had come all the way from Invergordon, having spent the previous thirty-six hours standing in the train. She kept me laughing from eight till past midnight.

Nov. 19 *Thursday.* *Let's Face It* at the Hippodrome. From my point of view this is a dreadful show. But then I don't find Bobby Howes funny. We are always being told that the secret of your great comedian is his power to suggest thoughts too deep for tears. Bud Flanagan, says this school, would not be so funny if he were not at times extraordinarily like Old Man Wordsworth. I accept this on condition that I am allowed to laugh first and cry afterwards. I just cannot do it the other way round. Howes, puckering up his face to laugh, makes me pucker up mine to cry. All the same, I have a great admiration for Bobby, who is a beautiful actor. Many clowns have wanted to appear in Shakespeare, generally as Richard III. I see him as the perfect Fool in *Lear*.

Nov. 20 *Friday* At the National Gallery to-day (five guineas) Kligerman played the following programme :

Toccata and Fugue in D minor .	. Bach-Tausig
Ballade in F minor, Op. 52	. . Chopin
Etude in C major, Op. 10, No. 1	
Etude in A minor, Op. 10, No. 2	
Polonaise in A flat, Op. 53	

Myra Hess came up afterwards and complimented Alexis on his " superb tone." Jock, who was hearing him for the first time, said that he had not heard the Fugue given that organ quality since he was a boy and heard Moritz Rosenthal play it in Glasgow. And that nobody could have played the A minor study better. Ralph Hill concurred. Leo reserved his fire till we got to the Savage Club, where I gave a little party to Alexis, Leo, Ralph, and Jock. Leo, who was in his mood of not liking anything, said, " I don't think Alexis played particularly well, but at any rate he is getting rid of his worst faults, so that we may quote Churchill and say that it is the end of his beginning. The Fugue was over-pedalised and sounded muddy. The Ballade was ineffective and the end a mere scramble. The Etudes were good, with too much bass at the end of the second one. And the Polonaise had no breadth and no dignity. But we will make a pianist of him yet." And, turning to Alexis, he added, " What on earth made you play that terrible wrong note in the Fugue ? I nearly screamed." " You did scream," retorted Alexis. " I heard you ! "

Jock showed me a delightful review of *Ego* 5 in the *Manchester Guardian*. After comparing me with Nero and Pepys, the review concludes :

> It is a poor heart that cannot find diversion from the gloom of the time in the æsthetic amours and vendettas which he continues to pursue with all the swagger of Cyrano, something of the irony of Swift, and that sure feeling for certain sorts of perfection that is his prime claim upon an audience.

At last a reviewer who sees what I'm after! Get home to find in the *Daily Telegraph*: "There is a lot about dull people." What the inexact fellow means is: "He writes uninterestingly about lively and exciting people." But he doesn't say this and so I pink him, very much as I did his predecessor two years ago:

> The *Telegraph*
> (Don't make me laugh)
> Holds that Baring, Beecham, Beerbohm, Belloc, Bridie, Cocteau, Coward, Henson, Hicks, Lutyens, Margot, Maugham, Priestley, Shaw, Wells, my beloved Rebecca, and some six hundred illustrious and witty dead whose names I cull,
> Are dull.

Nov. 21 *Saturday.* Believing in striking while the iron is hot, I again put up Kligerman at the Savage. Among the guests were Lord Vansittart, Aneurin Bevan, and Jack Hobbs, and as the rest of the crowd was not particularly musical I made him turn on that awful Second Rhapsody, into which he manages to infuse a certain nobility.

Nov. 22 *Sunday.* An odd note has begun to creep into my reviews: "Whatever the arguments for and against the lasting quality of *Ego* . . ." "Has an eye on posterity. . . ." "The diarist hoping for immortality . . ." "Has for some years been laying traps for posterity. . . ." Concern as widespread as this for the permanence of *Ego* begins to look like fear of its happening. In to-day's *Observer* Alan Pryce-Jones has this:

> It is not wise, I believe, for a diarist to ignore his own time. Nobody will quarrel with Mr Agate's belief that the fact of Beethoven is of greater permanent interest than the fact of a bomb in a back-street; all the same an extrovert, to survive in literature, must marry the two. Mr Agate, moreover, not merely dislikes his own times, he seems not to be interested in them. It is as though a keen mind, vividly and quickly stored, were applying to all its faculties—of the heart Mr Agate never speaks—an intellectual apparatus acquired at one effort, embellished with one range of taste and example, and tuned to one tensity. The style never slackens or surprises; the evidences of reading and sensibility, though generally sufficient, are never renewed.

Not interested in my times? I read every scrap of news about the war, not because I care who rules Norway or Greece but because I will not tolerate German self-sufficiency. If I don't read about post-war reconstruction, it is because I don't believe in it. Though you may drive a road straight through from Maida Vale to Mile End I realise that there will always be crooked Jews and fat, ill-mannered Jewesses at both ends of it. Ditto Christians. Holding that human nature has not changed in the last billion years, and isn't going to change now, I regard the world as divided into rare spirits and vulgar ones, artists and non-artists, of whom only the first in each kind interests me. I am told that I should renew my stores of reading and sensibility. At what fount, pray? Modern novels? In the last twelve years I have read no novel which I would not gladly have dropped half-way through in favour of the dullest volume in the *Comédie Humaine*. Painting? Is anybody improving on Renoir? My occasional visits to the galleries do not tell me so. Music? Must I persevere with that hideous Bloch quartet? "Of the heart Mr Agate never speaks." I think Pryce-Jones has got something here. I refuse to write my *Liber Amoris*, the one book of Hazlitt I deplore. He was unhappy with his drab and should have shut up about it. Whether I have been happy or "perplex'd in the extreme" is my affair and not the public's.

Nov. 24 *Tuesday.* If I were involved in a murder charge à la Herbert Wallace would any jury believe this? Invited to dine with Lady Juliet Duff at 3 Belgrave Place, I left my house at 7.30. Went by tube to Oxford Circus, say 7.45. Took a taxi and was put down at 7.55—"Here you are, sir"—at what turned out to be the wrong end of Eaton Square. Another taxi landed me at a vast mansion which turned out to be unoccupied, in, I think, Pont Street. After which two policemen and four civilians misdirected me. Dearth of taxis. Finally I got a third, whose driver was on his way to supper. I explained my plight, and, being a kindly soul, he offered to help me. He set me down in a mews which I had explored some three-quarters of an hour earlier. I was about to give up when a pleasant voice said "Can I help you?" It turned out to belong to Simon Carnes, the revue-writer, sent out as a search-party. It was 8.55. I had wandered about for exactly one hour.

When I got home I found this letter:

1 Barton Street
Westminster, S.W.1

DEAR MR AGATE,

I am longing to talk to you of *Ego 5*, of which I have read every word with the most intense interest. I think what struck me most was your brother Edward's letter in his 'teens. I feel sorry I never met so remarkable a being. My heart was warmed by your fine tribute to C. B. C. I have only met him and his Evelyn once, out at lunch. I sat next him, and I fear he thought me dull, but it was a great pleasure to meet some one who had given me such delight, especially when he brought over the Guitrys, and when he produced that odd version of *La Belle Hélène*.

The quotation I most enjoyed was that describing Junot's passion for Napoleon. It is most touching, and I have not seen any allusion to it in any book, although I have read an immense number of works connected with the First Empire. Eight of my great-uncles were officers of Napoleon.

Of the theatrical stuff, I was by far the most interested in all you said concerning the famous Othellos. By the way, I note that you knew St John Hankin. My husband was fond of him, and I was fond of the lady he married. We were among the very few people invited to their wedding, and when he came to his strange and, indeed, piteous, end, my husband went down to the Welsh watering-place where Hankin drowned himself, and naturally did all he could for the widow.

I am looking forward with eager curiosity to the collection of Barrie's letters. He was a most amusing, indeed a delightful letter-writer, and in some ways the most singular being I have ever known. I knew him before he was famous, and I used to see him when he was courting Mary Ansell. So for nearer fifty than forty years I used to see him at intervals. More often in Lady Northcliffe's house than anywhere else, but also now and again in a country house.

Well, I must not go running on, as old-fashioned people say.

Yours sincerely,
MARIE BELLOC-LOWNDES

Nov. 25 Wednesday. Lunched with G. B. ("Peter") Stern, at the Potomac in Jermyn Street, a smart restaurant unknown to me. Felt rather guilty about turning up as I had in my pocket a murderous review of the last instalment of her Rakonitz Saga, which runs to over a quarter of a million words. "One has grown to expect a Stern chase to be a long one, and I calculate that anybody getting steam up now and abjuring theatres, cinemas, concerts, dog-racing, parties, listening to the wireless, newspapers, and all other reading, may with luck sight land somewhere about Boxing Day." I try to keep my reviewing and my friendships in water-tight compartments. Women don't understand this, and I expect I have had my last meal with Peter.

Nov. 26 *Thursday.* *Ego's* excuse for having an eye on the future is that its compiler has an ear for the present. Compare a letter of J. M. Barrie written during the last war:

> Hardy was staying with me lately, and he and Wells and Shaw and Arnold Bennett and I sat one night watching the strange spectacle. It is an exposed spot, tho', and after raids I always find shrapnel on the roof. Callers who don't find me in might have better luck if they tried the cellar.

Did Hardy and Wells and Shaw and Bennett not say one single word between them worth recording? Was Barrie himself mum? Give *Ego* such a roof-full and see what would come of it! Barrie's *Letters*, edited by Viola Meynell, tell us nothing we didn't know about the wee giant. On one page we are given a superb passage from his speech on the unveiling of the Hardy Monument:

> "There were years certainly when I thought him the most unhappy man I had ever known; but if he had escaped his weird we could not have had our Hardy. And, after all, can one be altogether unhappy, even when ridden by the Furies, if he is producing masterpieces? May we not suspect that he has moments of exultation which are denied to other mortals? I daresay the shades of the departed great gathered in that room at Max Gate to watch their brother write the last page of *The Dynasts*. Happily after that he was to pass into a long evening of serenity. The President of the Immortals had ended his sport with Hardy."

How on earth can the man who wrote this have been capable of the mawkishness of:

> The primroses give me enormous pleasure. They stand on this table in four happy little bowls, and smiling at me every time I look up. The courage of flowers in these days to go on just as usual!

To think that I used to give J. M. B. credit for faking the nauseating stuff. I was wrong. Mawkishness was as much a part of his make-up as tawdriness was of Liszt's. He wrote a play about a Little Boy David and had him played by a Little Girl. He was a genius with a passion for baby-ribbons.

Nov. 27
Friday.
Cookman, of *The Times*, says of the new farce at the Ambassadors Theatre that its humour is "such as the exhilaration of a char-à-banc trip from Southend to Clacton might have engendered." As one who has made this trip many times, I resent this on behalf of both terminuses. Incidentally:

> Where your sharrybangs are buses
> Termini are terminuses.

In neither resort, nor at any stopping-place between, have I found anything comparable to the witlessness of this farce, in which situation and dialogue contend which can be the staler.

A letter to Charles Morgan:

10 *Fairfax Road, N.W.6*
November 27, 1942

DEAR CHARLES,

Do you remember Kipling's Colonel Dabney in *Stalky and Co.* and his "Don't attempt to deny it"? Don't attempt to deny that you are "Menander" in the *Times Lit. Supp.* Ye are! Your article on George Moore is sheer loveliness from beginning to end, and every word of it bears your unmistakable finger-prints. There was some argument at the Savage Club about the identity of Menander, whereupon I read aloud your peroration about Moore being saved by the singleness of his faith. Somebody said, "But Morgan's in the Navy." I said, "I don't care if he's in the Sea of Azov!" Mrs Belloc-Lowndes, with whom I dined to-night, confirmed my best suspicions. What a delightful woman! Ten times more like Queen Victoria than Anna Neagle will ever know how to be. I love the way her skirt dips to the ground.

Your faithful admirer, always and *quand même*,

JAMES AGATE

At one end of the scale I regard Charles as—well, a bit inhuman. At the other end I realise that my blatancies must give him pain. But I feel that there is a lot of middle where we meet on common ground.

Nov. 28 *Saturday.* As I perambulate London I see pictures which demand this and that painter. In certain lights on summer evenings Fairfax Road is the perfect Utrillo. To-day in the purlieus of Camden Town I saw something which called for a poet. This was an aged rocking-horse, so begrimed that it had lost its spots. Hardly a hair left on its mane, and where the tail should have been merely what George Carney used to call "a naperture." Even the littlest kiddies, passing on their way from school the miserable junk-shop outside which it stood, heeded it not. The deadest deaths are the best, says Montaigne, and the indifference of the children should have told the rocking-horse that his day was done. But did it? As I got into the taxi again I turned round and caught, or thought I caught, a late spark in that glazed eye and the remains of defiance in those dusty nostrils. Or am I drooling in the worst Barrie manner?

Dec. 1 *Tuesday.* Watching an old, worn pony pulling a heavy load up the steep, slippery slope of Lower Regent Street, I reflect how much closer I am to the poor beast than to Betty Grable.

Dec. 2 *Wednesday.* A poor day. Morning broken up by telephone callers and making arrangements for Kligerman to play for the L.P.O. at Golder's Green a week on Sunday (10 guineas). Trade show of a film: then back to work. Remember a first night at Kew. Slog out there. Absurd drama about an artist who commits a murder and paints a portrait so brilliant that there is talk of making him a peer. Desist from watching, and decline into an argument with Jack de Leon, who wants to know why, in my last *Ego*, I haven't dealt with Life, Death, Space, Time, Eternity, Sex, Philosophy, and Religion. "An autobiography should contain something of what a man thinks about all these, or it should have some other title. In so far as your book is almost wholly objective it is neither autobiography nor diary." In the meantime the car which is to take me to my supper-party in Park Lane at nine fails to turn up, which means that I do not arrive till ten. Ask for my hostess, a charming actress, and am told by the porter that nobody of the name lives there, that the flat is occupied by a

Mrs Wotherspoon-Whifflebottom. Wander round in the rain and black-out till eleven, and arrive home exhausted at twelve. Ring up my hostess, whose 'phone number I have now recovered, and find I was right about the address, but that she lives there with a ridiculously named husband I didn't know she possessed.

Dec. 3 Thursday. Lunched in Carlyle Square with David Horner in a house which Osbert Sitwell has lent him. The meal turned out to be a banquet, for which we repaired to a bicycle-shed at the bottom of the garden furnished with things which might have been from the brush of Sebastiano del Piombo or a bit of junk out of the King's Road. D. H. is a witty and delightful talker. All the same, the Bernhardt picture he gave me was covered with dirt to such an extent that there was nothing visible. Have sent it to the restorer's. I am told that there is too much about Sarah in my books. If only people realised how much I leave out, and the effort this costs me!

Dec. 4 Friday. On the lines of Eckermann's *Conversations with Goethe*, I am thinking of starting a series of *Conversations with Kligerman*. Here is the first:

KLIG. You know I play Tschaikowsky Concerto with Philharmonic?

J. A. You mean the Philharmonic are playing the Concerto, and have got you to fill in the piano part at ten guineas.

KLIG. If you like. Perhaps you tell me that you know where is Leicester?

J. A. I do.

KLIG. Then perhaps you tell me nearer the time I play Concerto?

J. A. I will.

KLIG. Your friends Moiseiwitsch, Hambourg, Kentner, and such others as Solomon, Curzon, Pouishnoff—when they play Concerto it is Polish, it is German, it is Hungarian, Turkish, or maybe it is only Jewish. But never is it Russian. I shall play it Russian.

J. A. Good for you, Alexis. Suppose you sit down now and play it Russian?

KLIG. What, without orchestra?

J. A. You don't need an orchestra to be Russian.

Klig. pulls a long face, J. A. helps himself to a large whiskey and a cigar, and the performance begins. As the last chord dies away :

KLIG. What you think of that ?

J. A. I think my friends Moiseiwitsch, Hambourg, Kentner, and such others as Solomon, Curzon, and Pouishnoff play it better.

KLIG. But was it not Russian ?

J. A. It was not.

KLIG. (*furious*). You 'ave never been in Russia !

Dec. 5 *Saturday.* Sat next to Mark Hambourg at the Savage Club Annual Luncheon to-day. The First Lord of the Admiralty (A. V. Alexander) made an admirable speech (ten minutes), the Russian Ambassador (M. Maisky), first-class (five minutes), the Home Secretary (Herbert Morrison) had prepared a full-dress oration which managed to say nothing. (A mistake to treat us as though we were Queen Victoria.) I gathered from H. M. that while the worst is probably over, the worst may well be to come. Parry Jones sang some Handel beautifully, Mark played four Chopin preludes, including the nostalgic one in F (I think this is my favourite) which he does better than anybody living, and then launched an assault on Bach's D minor Organ Toccata and Fugue which was like a demolition squad attacking St Paul's. When my turn came to entertain I gave them four minutes of my best, or rather other people's best. Wound up with a too-little known fable which I culled from Carl Crow's book, *My Friends the Chinese.*

A tiger caught a monkey and was about to eat him when the monkey pointed out that he was too small to provide more than a mouthful, and offered to guide the tiger to a satisfactory feast if his captor would spare his life. The tiger agreed, and the monkey led him to a hillside where a donkey was browsing —an animal which the tiger had never seen before. The donkey took one look at the tiger, gazed reproachfully at the monkey and said, " Little brother, you have always brought me two tigers for supper. Why to-day do you bring me only one ? " Then he let out his loudest bray, and the tiger fled for his life.

This went very well, and M. Maisky laughed a lot.

Fatras. Two ways of putting the same thing.

"Malta is as bright a diamond as shines in the King's crown."

THE RIGHT HON. WINSTON CHURCHILL,
in the House of Commons

"Malta is just a lot of guys."

Letter in the "Manchester Guardian"

Dec. 6 *Sunday*. Our Ernest in the *S.T.*:

Smith's great Symphony in Q flat minor, let us say, is, at any concert, as to 98 per cent. Smith and only 2 per cent. the conductor: the symphony would have remained just as fine a work if the conductor at that particular concert had never been born, whereas our measurement sticks are too tiny to enable us to estimate what the conductor would be without the symphony.

But a Derby winner would be as fine a horse if his jockey had never been born. And Ormonde's jockey would have been as fine a horseman if Ormonde had never been foaled. That Wagner could have done without Ernest doesn't justify me in asking where Ernest would be without Wagner. Either my old friend has got himself muddled, or he puts too low an estimate on the intelligence of the ordinary music-loving public. As a member of that public I no more compare Weingartner with Beethoven, or Ernest with Weingartner, than I do Kean with Shakespeare, or Hazlitt with Kean. As I see it there are A, the creator of the work, B, the interpreter, and C, the critic of the work and the interpretation. The fact that A is a genius does not prevent B and C from being in the genius category also. Ernest is a very great critic who sometimes writes demonstrable nonsense.

Dec. 7 *Monday*. I really don't care very much whether there is life on Mars or why Hannibal turned back at Cannæ. There's nothing logical about the things which puzzle one person and not another. Or even oneself. For example, I care nothing at all whether Wagner's father was or was not a Jew, while desiring immensely to know the answer to the Shakespeare-Bacon riddle. Rossini's idleness intrigues not me: no, nor Congreve's silence neither. But I am practically on fire, as Damon Runyon would say, to know why Rimbaud abjured poetry. I am not in the least anxious to continue *Edwin Drood*, whereas I hanker after more of *Weir of Hermiston*. I want to know the identity, not of the Man in the Iron Mask but of the Third Murderer in *Macbeth*. I would not cross the road to know whether Mary Queen of Scots connived at the killing of Darnley, but would go all the way to Liverpool to learn who killed Mrs Wallace. To the permanent fascination of the *Marie Celeste* mystery another has been added during the last few days—meaning that I have been dipping into Cyril Foley's *Autumn Foliage*. The mystery is that of Alletson, the Notts cricketer, who in the Notts v. Sussex match at Hove in 1911, during the thirty minutes of cricket which Foley was privileged to see, scored 139 runs. He finished up by making 115 out of 120 in seven overs, hitting Killick for 22 in one over, and 34 (4, 6, 6, 4, 4, 4, 6) in another, there being two no-balls, and scoring 34 off two overs from Leach, or 90 in four overs. The mystery is not how Alletson came to do this but why he never tried to repeat it. Foley writes:

> After these fireworks his appearance at Lord's against Middlesex was eagerly anticipated. An enormous crowd assembled to see him. He certainly made a fair score, including a gigantic drive over the clock, but was otherwise disappointing. From then onwards he retired into his shell and absolutely refused to hit. Later in the season I went to see him at the Oval and happened to sit in the Notts dressing-room next to A. O. Jones, the Notts skipper. "Jonah" was in despair. He said to me, "The man can't be normal. I've told him that I will play him in every match right through the season, even if he makes recurrent cyphers, as long as he will hit, but he just won't do it. You'll see for yourself presently." And I did. In came Alletson with a huge crowd on tiptoe with excitement, and made the most scratchy 11 runs possible. Never once did he attempt to hit the ball. As he was not a bowler he had to be dropped from the side.

What is the psychology of the cricketer who, knowing that he can hit and knowing also that he will be dropped from the side if he doesn't, refuses to make the attempt? Why should that two-handed engine which was Alletson stand ready to smite once, and smite no more?

Dec. 8 *Tuesday.* A delightful letter from Liverpool saying, " My gratitude for *Ego* takes the form of what may be loosely called a poem. Whatever you think of it, it very likely has a ' rarity ' value, since it is the first time—I will venture to guess—that you have been praised in verse by a Catholic priest." The poem :

HOMMAGE A JAMES AGATE

The critic of the *Sunday Times*
Discourses of departed mimes,
Turning his bright AGATIAN limes
　On Garrick, Irving, Kean :
He likes to put the modern race
Of actors in their proper place,
And though he writes with charm and grace,
　His *plume* can be *maligne.*

Enstalled and comfortless, forlorn,
He views the modern stage with scorn,
And if you say " a star is born "
　Remarks (in French) " Boloney ! "
He sighs for Malibran (*la feue*),
He writes some *Nouveaux Contes Scabreux*
Pour tromper son ennui un peu . . .
　Then goes to buy a pony.

Ah ! *certes*, a brilliant pen he wields ;
What riches rare his mem'ry yields
From lowly and exotic fields—
　Amanda Ros to Stein.
Pale highbrows shrink, pretensions die,
Before that keen, judicial eye :
Producers quail when he is nigh—
　But ask him out to dine.

ENVOI

Before that " great resolver, Death,"
Deprives both you and me of breath
(Like " golden lads," as Shakespeare saith
　—And who could say it better ?)
Permit, me, Sir, to call you friend,
And say, " Though suits and writs impend,
And you can ne'er make end meet end,
　Here's one, at least, your debtor."

CHARLES W. RIGBY

Dec. 9 *Wednesday.* Ran into Moray McLaren at the Café Royal and found him in great conversational form. " The Poles are like the Irish. They have a contempt for time, a contempt for death and the material things of life. Yet they are, in the long run, far more realistic than their Saxon neighbours and overlords. Do you realise that Poland is the only over-run country which has not produced a single Quisling? The Slovaks are the Welsh, full of spurious charm and bogus religiosity. The Czechs are Lowland Scots, patient, industrious, worthy, and dull. The Serbs are the Highland Scots—the best. After the war I should say to Germany: 'You have made the best toys in the world. With the assistance of the Austrians you have made the best music in the world. You have the second best scenery in Europe. Your philosophy, if not translated into action, is harmless, amusing, and, for young men, intoxicating. Therefore you shall be allowed to go on making toys and music and attracting foreign tourists. You shall philosophise to your hearts' content. You shall be rich and well-fed and happy. But never again shall you be allowed to make so much as a single popgun. And we shall come over every three months to see that you don't.'"

Dec. 10 *Thursday.* On Sunday at the Hambourgs' I sat opposite Mrs Marks (Marks and Spencer). To-day at Quaglino's I sat next to Lady Moss (Moss Empires) wearing a mink coat she had insured for £1700, and at least £10,000 worth of pearls and diamonds. I think my liking for rich people is something more than vulgar snobbery. It is the natural reaction from the penury which has surrounded me ever since I came to London; with the exception of Monty Shearman, none of my intimate friends has had a penny to bless himself with. I don't mind this, since wit, charm, and fun are all other names for being hard-up. But I dislike the sense of humiliation whenever I must slip the cab fare into a departing friend's hand under the pretence of tapping the barometer. I get no pleasure out of ordinarily well-to-do people; they must be twice as rich as Crœsus, and able to slip *me* ten thousand cab fares and not notice it. On my other side was a large, handsome creature who said, "With your exciting life, dear Mr Agate, you ought to keep a diary." Sir William Murison, the host, told us of a young barrister who would have gone far in the law but for his inability to curb his wit. A solicitor proposed to brief him on behalf of a wealthy City magnate whose yacht had run down a fishing smack—"We did all we could; we luffed." The young barrister said, "'Tis better to have luffed and lost than never to have luffed at all." Murison's son completed the party. There was a lot of good talk, of which I did my share. Anyhow, I was so exhausted afterwards that when I got home I slept for three hours. Perhaps the three bottles of Volnay 1929, of which I did more than my share, had something to do with it.

Dec. 11 *Friday.* Lunched at the Ivy with my old friend the New York dramatic critic, John Mason Brown, now in the American Navy. Introduced me to the new adjective "hilarious," meaning first-class or extraordinary. About *In Which We Serve*: "It took me almost as long to get used to Noel Coward as a naval captain as to myself as a naval lieutenant." About the hilarious liqueur brandy: "I expect they distil it from the Crown jewels."

Dec. 12 *Saturday.* Seeing how I manhandle Kenneth Hopkins in *Ego 5,* his review of that book in *Time and Tide* is magnanimous as well as exquisitely written. I reproduce part of it here not because it flatters me but because it shows what these young poets can do when, reversing Mr Wegg's habit, they drop into prose:

> For some of us this is like news from nowhere. Not for us the stage door and the ringside seat and calling the great by their first names. But it is a world into which by Mr Agate's help we can escape out of our dull preoccupations and away from importunate reality. . . . In this book the sense and nonsense, the "didactic and grotesque," the author and his friends, blend most happily: "He was a master of his trade it curiously that builded."
>
> Mr Agate has much in common with Praed's Vicar:
>
> His talk was like a stream, which runs
> With rapid change from rocks to roses,
> It slipped from politics to puns,
> It passed from Mohamet to Moses;
> Beginning with the laws that keep
> The planets in their radiant courses
> And ending with some precept deep
> For dressing eels or shoeing horses.
>
> Into this book he puts them all and there emerges a portrait by inference; if we do not get Mr Agate (and I think we do) at least we get Mr Agate's Mr Agate, who is a fine fellow. He is

busily concerned in "scattering compliments, tendering visits, gathering and venting news, following feasts and plays . . ."; he cheers himself up with ends of verse and sayings of philosophers, like another Hudibras; he hears ghosts, quotes Goethe, and can't pay his income tax. He likes accuracy and doesn't like being left alone. He likes Mr Leo Pavia, as anybody would, and doesn't like the younger poets, which is understandable. He records his sayings and doings with unflagging enthusiasm, and from the result he may justly say (if he has read Cowper), "Forth steps the Man, an emblem of myself."

Dec. 13 *Sunday.* Andrade did me a witty turn yesterday at the Savage Club. An elderly and obvious bore, a visitor, coming up and saying, "Mr Agate, I generally agree with the things you write in the *Sunday Times*, but to-day . . .," Andrade cut him short: "Excuse me, Professor, this is not Mr James Agate, the critic. This is his cousin, Mr William Agate, a stocking manufacturer from Dorking." Whereupon the old gentleman withdrew after profuse apologies. The philosophy of boredom has been insufficiently explored. In my case it is quite simple, and can be put into one sentence: I don't want to talk to anybody unless I get something in return. I am not like Leo, who will talk to the fronts of empty houses if he can't get people to talk to; in fact, he has been seen in the street doing it. Put Leo in a bar among complete strangers and in ten minutes he is entirely happy. But that is because he is eternally young, and talking to impress is one of the qualities of youth. Whereas I am old and curmudgeonly: I want to be paid for my talking. Most of all I hate conversation about the theatre. When anybody says to me, "What did you think of Gielgud's Macbeth?" my mind goes back to those four days of hard and painful thinking compressed into a column. Am I now to go through the further labour of condensing that column to a sentence which shall express what I think exactly? And this for the benefit of some silly fellow who only wants to misquote it to somebody else.

Dec. 14 *Monday.* Gerald Moore says that if he had his time to come over again he would ask the gods for one gift—that of being unable to play a single note on any instrument. With this asset he feels that he could have climbed to great heights in the world of recording, broadcasting, conducting, and musical criticism. He told me how the other day one of the Big Noises at H.M.V. insisted on a passage being played differently. "Show me!" said Gerald, getting up from the piano-stool, whereupon Big Noise perforce collapsed. Very enthusiastic about Kligerman's performance last night at Golder's Green, where Gerald had been playing for Tatiana Makushina. Jean Pougnet also played, but it seems that Alexis brought down what there was of a house, the empty seats being due to the fact that the Chief Rabbi had prescribed a week of lamentation for the victims in Poland. Gerald remarked: "Yes, I know. Beating their breast with one hand and eating pickled herring with the other." He had previously described the three great Jewish Festivals as the Day of Atonement, the New Year, and the concerts at the Golder's Green Orpheum.

Dec. 15 *Tuesday.* Sarah's painting has come back from the cleaners, and I like it as much as I shall ever like a picture of two macaws.

One of the most tragic things in the world is to have talent but not enough. Better to be born without talent and to know it, than to have a sprinkling and not realise that it is only a sprinkling. This is why when the *Tatler* rang me up this morning and asked if it would be all right if they put under a portrait of Kligerman and me, "Encouraging talent is one of Mr Agate's hobbies," I replied No, it wouldn't. Encouraging talent and discouraging lack of it are two of Mr Agate's hobbies. Take the late Willie Ranken for example, a charming man who very nearly had talent. Ernest Thesiger, his brother-in-law, kindly sent me to-day some of Willie's drawings which he thought I might like to have, the subjects being Coquelin as Cyrano, Réjane as Sapho, Duse and Sarah as themselves, all dating from the early nineteen hundreds. The Coquelin drawing is quite undistinguished; Réjane, losing all her *chic*, has borrowed Jane Hading's looks; Duse has a faint air of Evelyn Laye; Sarah's nose is given the uncompromising Jewish curve instead of the straight line with the little ridge in the middle which she was careful to reproduce in her bust of herself. Yet there is something in each drawing which shows that Ranken saw what we saw, though his pencil could not reproduce it. I should not be more grateful to Ernest if the drawings were masterpieces, or less grateful if they were rubbish. But assessing the merits of a work of art is different. To recognise the will behind the deed is the first duty of a critic ; to mistake the will for the deed is the first betrayal.

La Thorndike made her *rentrée* to-night in her brother's preposterous play, *The House of Jeffreys.* " Not where he eats but where he is eaten," said Hamlet. Georgina reversed the process ; after spending thirty years arranging not to be devoured by cannibals she took to adopting their diet—to wit, devouring a sister missionary. How had she evaded the spit ? By falling on her portable harmonium and blasting the poor savages with ecstasy. How did she come to find herself at the heart of African darkness ? A descendant of the infamous Judge Jeffreys, she had thought to get rid of the taint in her blood by the old dodge of converting the heathen ; unfortunately, the heathen had the opposite idea and converted Georgina. Whereupon, having made Africa too hot, she came back to England to resume business as a publisher (!) and, annoyed at the flippant treatment of equatorial mysteries by one Roberta, a gossipy globe-trotter, gobbled her up ! After which she slew the body of her coffee-coloured accomplice to save his milk-white soul, and went mad. An odd sort of evening, in which Mrs Jellyby seemed to have taken Herman Melville's Queequeg into partnership. And yet a trifle of ten minutes with the blue pencil could have made this arrant nonsense into quite a good thriller ; all that was necessary was to delete the references to cannibalism and make Georgina the victim of some horrible but non-gormandising form of mania. With this alteration there might have been some shadowy reason for looking upon the thing as a psychological study ; as the play stood, to watch our old friend throw the mantle of Hecuba, Medea, Phædra, Queen Katharine, Lady Macbeth, and St Joan over a witch-doctored " rump-fed ronyon " seemed as incredible as to gaze upon Madge Kendal sitting down to a meal of ' long pig.' In fact, I shouldn't have believed any of it but for Robert Adams, an " Anthropophaginian " after Mistress Quickly's heart, and Russell, who, as Georgina's right-hand man in the publishing business, stood about in trepidation very much as we may imagine Thackeray in Smith and Elder's sanctum balancing himself first on one foot and then on the other in imminent expectation of Currer Bell making a meal of him. The skill and tact of Sybil's performance are to be gathered from the fact that we did not laugh at Georgina once, not even when she came back from the wine-cellar clutching a bottle of Amontillado with which to wash down Roberta.

When I got home I found this nostalgic postcard from Jock, written from Southend :

> DEAR JAMIE,
>
> Here for Sunday. A cold semi-gale whirls round our old Palace Hotel ; and from our chosen table in the restaurant I gaze out at a sulky December sun, a sky of pearl, and an oyster-coloured sea. That ingratiating Irishman Irvine, now manager here, seems by his affectionate inquiries to think that all is dross that is not James Agate, and conciliates mere Me with an excellent lunch, almost Agatianly after hours. The little ships don't sail nearly so grand as they used to, my immoderate Pier doesn't seem to want to be visited, and there is not a soul in sight—except one peculiarly Tchehovian seagull.
>
> Love,
> JOCK

Dec. 16 *Wednesday.* Forster, in his *Life of Charles Dickens*, quotes from an unpublished letter of Bulwer Lytton : " It follows that art and correctness are far from identical, and that the one is sometimes proved by the disdain of the other. For the ideal, whether humorous or serious, does not consist in the imitation but in the exaltation of nature." I can think of no better criticism of *The Petrified Forest*, revived at the Globe to-night, Sherwood's killer sunk in melancholy, his hero babbling half-baked stuff about world unrest being Nature's revenge on Man for thwarting her careful arrangements for disease, pestilence, and famine, his little waitress who in the middle of the Arizona desert reads Villon and paints like Vuillard—all these impress me as being profoundly untrue to life. On second thoughts, perhaps the hero is reasonably true ; he reminds one of those pacifists *à outrance* who see in the present conflict not the resolve of civilisation to preserve its standard, but the general will to war ; the Dutch flying at the throat of Poland, and Norway passionately desiring to tear Italy limb from limb. About which one can only say with Sir Toby, " Tillyvally, lady ! "

Dec. 17 *Thursday.* According to Sir Evan Williams, who has been talking to the Coal Utilisation Research Association, the world is getting near the end of its petrol resources. Not, I am afraid, in my time. If the aeroplane could be abolished I would consent to do away with taxis, even if it meant staying put at Swiss Cottage for the rest of my days hearing nothing but Bergnerese. As I get older I care less and less about the future, and more and more about the past. I am certain that the world of to-day is a much more vulgar world than it was fifty years ago, and that all that half a century of so-called education has achieved is to multiply the ways in which the common mind can express its commonness. When I was a boy women were divided into ladies, and modest young women who had no desire to be anything else. To-day there are very few ladies, and the streets are filled with baggages whose minds are still at the stage of Dickens's Marchioness—all of them perfect examples of Montague's "vulgarity that is seldom far from the human animal when it has only decorated its animal life and not built an ampler life on it." George Slocombe, the writer, assured Basil Cameron and me at the Café Royal last night that under the forthcoming U.S.S.B. (the United States of Soviet Britain) the three of us will be graded as first-rate because intellectual workers. But workers in what sort of world ? I have no use for the communal soup-kitchen. Let me have the old world with its elegance and squalor, luxury and starvation, noblemen's parks and fœtid slums, bawdy-houses and debtors' prisons, gala nights at the opera and the chance of getting your throat cut as you come out. If the J. B. Priestleys have their dreary way the post-war Bank Holiday will be spent sitting in a municipal park listening to municipal music performed by a municipal band, followed by a visit to a municipal theatre to see a municipal drama performed by municipal actors, after which we shall be allowed an hour to drink municipal tea out of a municipal samovar and then home in time for the municipally-minded wireless. Not for me ! Yet I am terribly exercised about it all. I recognise a scale of values in which I and my kind are less than the dust beneath the dustman's little finger-nail. I am prepared to vote for and support a Brave New World for the Dustman and his kind. But I take leave to have no interest in it or him. Is this asking for whatever the New Order uses for tumbrils? "*On y va, canaille!*"

Fatras. From the *St Pancras Chronicle, People's Advertiser, and London Independent*, circulating in Camden Town, Kentish Town, King's Cross, Somers Town, Euston, Regent's Park, Tufnell Park, Gospel Oak, Highgate, Holly Lodge and Brookfield Estates, Chalk Farm, Tottenham Court Road, Gray's Inn Road, etc.:

> Police observation was kept on the premises for four days, and during that period five women took seventeen men there. The warrant was executed that morning, when twelve unmarried couples were found at the address, eleven of the men being American soldiers.

Any but a nation of hypocrites would publicly thank the landlady for providing accommodation so obviously needed.

Dec. 18 *Friday.* *Barry Lupino has given me Charlie Chaplin's cane!* And with it a formal guarantee in the form of a letter:

> 1 *Granville House*
> *Granville Place*
> *London, W.*1
>
> DEAR JIMMIE,
>
> Herewith Charlie's cane as promised. It was given to Stanley by Chaplin when Stan was last in America. It is the original cane used by Charlie in his first film. Here is something which may interest you: Mrs O'Shea, Stanley's mother-in-law, who died a few years ago aged 86, used to look after Charlie when he was a young boy, and in fact made him his first pair of long pants without pockets, to enable Charlie to control his hands and not slummock. Charlie slit the sides and sewed two socks on. Thus defeating the Old Girl.
>
> Yours always,
> BARRY

Taking care between whom I sat, I lunched at the Club, keeping both eyes on the cane, which I laid on the table in front of me, afterwards taking it to a picture-framer to have a case made for it. Then to the Paris Cinema in Lower Regent Street, where I broadcast with Gerald

Moore about chamber music. Rather nonsense as far as I was concerned, and I really don't know why I do this sort of thing as at best my musical opinions are amateurish, the rehearsing and expressing of them takes up the most of an afternoon and evening, and what I get after deducting tax and expenses is less than the price of a bottle of champagne.

Having left Leo to finish an article on a silly film, I am staggered to find under my name in this week's *Tatler*:

> I always think the happiest solution to this business of two men in love with one woman, or two women with one man, is that of Goethe, who ends his *Stella* by making the hero go off with both his wives, saying in effect: "Now, girls, you can just share me, cut and come again. No jealousy or any of that silly caper, or I'll sack you both and take another coupla broads, see?"

Dec. 19 *Saturday.* What does Raymond Mortimer mean by "Balzac's vulgarity of thought, feeling, and style"? I agree that the man who took all society for his theme lacked the uncanny precision of Proust's niggling differentiations between more authentic duchesses. But where in that miniaturist is to be found any approach to Balzac's sublimity? Could Proust have penned such a line as "La gloire est le soleil des morts"? However, to say of Balzac's style that it is a "foaming, sparkling, hasty, scummy and opaque boulder-encumbered whirlpool-forming torrent" is something. In to-day's *Express* I give *Channel Packet* all possible praise this side adulation. In the same article I fall foul of Clifford Bax's *Evenings in Albany* because of the sentence: "Dickens had, it seems, a gift of immortality which must always puzzle the judicious." Seeing red, I quote from *Bleak House* Chadband apostrophising Poor Jo, and the tremendous, "Dead, your Majesty. Dead, my lords and gentlemen. Dead, Right Reverends and Wrong Reverends of every order . . ." I turn to my Ruskin and I find: "Nobody cares much at heart about Titian; only there is a strange undercurrent of everlasting murmur about his name, which means the deep consent of all great men that he is greater than they." What was murmur in Titian's case is, in the matter of Dickens, a roar after Boythorn's own heart! Clifford should see an aurist.

Dec. 20 *Sunday.* Christmas collation at Francis Sullivan's from one o'clock till black-out. Larry, a magnificent host, stood most of the time a Colossus in his own drawing-room, letting the party swirl about him; it was fun to sit on the stairs and watch the guests dart under his arms and between his legs like the Chevalier Tannhäuser's " *valets de bain* or little fish " in the Beardsley story. Half the stage seemed to be there, and the talk was as good as one would expect. I sat in a knot with Mary Merrall and Martita Hunt, and listened to Eric Portman telling wholly malicious and wildly probable stories of the leading ladies he has played with, including one famous for her " sex-repeal." When the conversation got back to Irving—it always does—Franklyn Dyall told us the following. It seemed that during the American visit one of his company left him to start in business on his own. Then Irving: " I went to see the—er—the young man in *The Forest Lovers* [heavily accenting the last word]. Somebody called Prosper le Gai [again the heavy accent]. Hmmm. Romantic *figure*. Beautiful *armour*. Hmmm. Looked as though he'd piddled himself. Beg your pardon, Ellen." I am aware that this story is meaningless for anybody who does not realise that Irving looked like every English prelate since Lanfranc.

Sent the following Reply to a Young Jew in the East Surrey Regiment wanting to learn the Art of Acting before appearing on the Operatic Stage in opposition to his Parents, who desire that he should manufacture Brassières:

10 *Fairfax Road*, N.W.6
December 20*th*, 1942

DEAR SIR,

1. Let's get the war over first.
2. You are quite right to follow your own bent, if it's strong enough.
3. Have you got a really good *voice*, or do you just let your friends tell you so ?
4. If the first, nothing can keep you back. If the second, go in for brassières or women's knickers, and keep your voice for your own solace.
5. I don't think it fair to use a repertory company to learn acting, and then desert the stage. You are taking up room which belongs to a non-vocal and persistent actor.

6. These things settle themselves. Get your parents to allow you enough to starve on in London for two years, under your word of honour that if you have not shown signs of making good—and I will act as umpire if you and they approve—you will go into the lingerie business.

7. What do you look like? Jewish? All right. Too Jewish? Not so good.

8. Are you a musician? Or just a singer?

9. Are you prepared to go through hell?

10. If you have real talent, I will help. If not, I will turn you down without any compunction whatever.

11. If you are a real singer with a real voice and real musical taste, can go without food and drink for long periods, and are prepared to leave sex alone, nothing and nobody, including your parents who are advising you for the best as they see it, can stop you.

12. Show your parents this letter.

JAMES AGATE

P.S. You have given me an idea for a story. This is about the frustration of a young man born of stage parents and compelled by them to pull the damnable faces of the actor while knowing himself to be the supreme genius of the *soutien-gorge*.

Dec. 22 *Tuesday.* Took part in a Transatlantic debate. The American team consisted of Dorothy Parker, Ilka Chase, Arthur Schwartz, the composer of light music, and a revue comedian name of Bolger. On our side were Susan Ertz, Pamela Frankau, Osbert Lancaster, and myself. Mrs Parker asking me why men insist on giving women vanity-bags as presents instead of war bonds, I told her about a film I saw yesterday concerning a woman who, inheriting a million dollars, said to her husband, "I've decided what to do with the money. From to-day on, I'm never going to let you see me in the same frock twice!"

Dec. 24 *Thursday.* So great is Fay Compton's sense of style that even the tights of a Principal Boy cannot mitigate her complete artistry. A great artist in another line is Charlie Naughton. Montague once likened Walkley to "one of those cross-bench or mugwump angels who were neither on the side of Jehovah nor on that of Satan in the day of battle." Naughton, though he may not know it, arrived at much the same conclusion in to-night's pantomime at the Stoll when he defined the mugwump as " a curious bird which sits astride a fence with its mug on one side and its wump on the other." Odd that while Charlie reminded me throughout of Coquelin's befogged bourgeois, Teddy Knox was like any Célimène from the Comédie Française enjoying the Indian summer of retirement and a grateful State's pension.

Christmas Day. The daily papers are furious at not being able to get their teeth into the news about Darlan, which they have had to leave to the wireless and the Sunday papers. Went to a party at Louis Sterling's and was heckled by the well-known woman pianist of whom a conductor once said : " She's not bad really ; she always knows when to come in." In the evening to Gwen Chenhalls's, where, the other guest being the conductor George Weldon, I did some rooting for Kligerman. Talked till 2 A.M., relying on Gwen to get a taxi for me. Which that angel did.

Boxing Day. Rehearsed Kligerman in the Tschaikowsky and read him that bit of Damon Runyon's story *Blood Pressure*, in which Rusty Charley knocks down the wop ice-dealer's horse, and told him to take that punch as model for his opening chords in the concerto. Spent the rest of the day reading Sala's Autobiography. Staggered to find on page 587 : " Nothing remarkable happened to me in 1874." And this was the year of Irving's Hamlet !

Dec. 27
Sunday. Heard this story : " An Evangelical Bishop, visiting Dublin, went to Phœnix Park and started feeding the ducks on an ornamental pond. Two charwomen passed by, and one was heard to remark, ' Sure, isn't it a foine sight this blessed morn to see his Lordship over there with the halo of sanctity round his head, and him with all his larnin' and piety like an innocent choild playing with the drakes and the ducks ? ' Whereupon her friend said, ' Gwan now, Norah, it's not the Catholic Bishop at all, at all.' ' The Saints bless us and save us,' says Norah, ' it'll be a Protestant wan, will it ? Look at the bloody ould fool now. It's in his second choildhood he must be ! ' "

Dec. 31 *Thursday.* The year's work:

Sunday Times	47,000	words
Daily Express	45,000	,,
Tatler	55,000	,,
John o' London's Weekly	26,000	,,
Ego 5	47,000	,,
Ego 6	35,000	,,
Odd articles	10,000	,,
	265,000	words

In the four years before the war I wrote an average of just over 500,000 words a year; in the four years beginning with and including 1939 I have averaged some 315,000 words. And, of course, worked harder than ever. Earnings pretty much the same as last year, or some £2000 less than in the pre-war period.

1943

Jan. 1 *Friday.* Unfestive letter from Stanley Rubinstein pointing out that at the present rate with increasing tax and diminishing income I shall not be straight with the Revenue till 1959.

Jan. 2 *Saturday.* Donald Wolfit in a feminine version of Robertson's old play about David Garrick. Does the authoress really expect us to believe that vapid little Ada Ingot was changed by marriage into a clever woman who dined with the Bishop of London and, widowed, twice refused Lord Monboddo, a Scottish peer and the author of a book to prove that men are merely monkeys *sans* tails ? And what a good play there is here, done with any competence ! The period being that of the interminable quarrels with Kitty Clive, why not lay a scene at Drury Lane on the first night of that ranting piece *Barbarossa,* when, Tate Wilkinson tells us, Garrick entered the green-room arrayed in all his Eastern finery, expecting the flatteries of his company, and Kitty coarsely said, " Make room for the Royal lamplighter," a rude speech which quite overset him, as well it might ? Round the room the author would place, taking a few pardonable liberties with dates, Mrs Cibber, Mrs Pritchard—babbling about her *gownd*—Mrs Woffington, Mrs Clive, Macklin, Barry, Quin, and my great-great-something-or-other, Shuter. And who are these crowding the doorway ? The painter Reynolds, Topham Beauclerk the man-about-town, Burke pondering on what he would say in the case of a revolution in France, Gibbon weighed down equally with Heliogabalus and hydrocele, and little Goldy arm-in-arm with Mr Thrale, the fat brewer looking as well gorged as ever and obviously wondering where his next election is coming from. These are ready to flood the room and wait only for that tidal wave which is the great Samuel Johnson. Settle *him* in the best chair, with Boswell in attendance, and the scene is set for that to which " the Pivy," as Garrick called his Kitty, alludes in that letter which she addressed to him on his retirement, and which at Oxford two years ago I got by heart: "I have always said this to everybody [praise of Garrick's genius as a spur to the talent of whoever acted with him] even when your horses and mine were in their highest prancing."

Jan. 3 *Sunday.* In his exquisitely written *Observer* article Ivor Brown describes *A Midsummer Night's Dream* as being "full of earth and timber; magic glimmerings do indeed light the sky, but that same sky is also dotted with 'russet-pated choughs' and bordered by 'far-off mountains turnèd into clouds,' a perfect image of our misty landscape." Lovely! After which comes the statement that "the forest is anywhere in England, not somewhere in Mendelssohnia." M'yes. And last, "The fairies are not alien other-worldly creatures, but ourselves in our livelier, more fantastical moments." At which I call a halt. Ivor gives as basis for his Theory of Shakespeare's Fairies, Titania's

> Playing on pipes of corn, and versing love.

Could anything be more naughty? He knows as well as I do that this is the Fairy Queen's description of Oberon when he stole

> *away* from fairy land,
> And in the shape of Corin sat all day.

(Italics mine, not Shakespeare's.) Surely there is one respect in which the little people must conform to human logic: they are not to be defined in terms of that which they are not. In citing Titania, Ivor, with maximum infelicity, has called a witness for the other side.

He is tremendously impressed by the fact that the Fairy Queen, after providing "the finest description ever made of that familiar imposition, the English summer," launches out into some stuff about the female ivy enringing the barky fingers of the elm. Can my friend really think that because Titania botanises on occasion she is no immortal but a mortal like the rest of us? Judged on these lines the First Murderer in *Macbeth*, with his

"The west yet glimmers with some streaks of day," is no murderer but a poet; and the First Carrier in *Henry IV, Part I*, with his "Charles' wain is over the new chimney," is no carrier but an Astronomer Royal *manqué*. Now if these murderers and carriers remain murderers and carriers despite the poetising and star-gazing forced on them by their author, then I contend that Titania remains fairy in spite of the fact that, when Shakespeare's gardening fit is on, she talks pure Mr Middleton. If the immortals in this play are mortals slightly above themselves—which is Ivor's case in a nutshell—then there might be some excuse for the late Cecil Sharp's arrangements of old folk tunes, sounding like four-square, rather stuffy Christmas carols, which were used in the Old Vic production in 1929. But if they are, in Oberon's words, "spirits of another sort," then I challenge the most frenzied Tudorite to point to a single passage in the English music of the period which breathes the insubstantial air, or begins to turn the key in that door which a German Jew of the early nineteenth century threw wide open. Were, indeed, the fairies of this play unethereal "emanations of the English country," then one might well suppose them spiritual first cousins of Hardy's eldest Dewy. "Your brassman is a rafting dog—well and good; your reed-man is a dab at stirring ye—well and good; your drum-man is a rare bowel-shaker—good again. But I don't care who hears me say it, nothing will spak to your heart wi' the sweetness o' the man of strings." I take it that Ivor wants us to believe that the wood in this play is Yalbury Wood, and the proper music to it the Mellstock villagers discoursing Tudorly. But, of course, without clarinets. "Clar'net's was death," said Old William. "Death they was!" echoed Mr Penny. I suspect our Tudorites of finding death in Mendelssohn's horns blowing of Elfland, oh, so little faintly and so triumphantly! In the meantime, is it not significant that, whereas Berlioz, Tschaikowsky, and Ambroise Thomas handled in some sort *Hamlet*; Locke, Verdi, and Milhaud *Macbeth*; Rossini, Verdi, and Coleridge-Taylor *Othello*; and Nicolai, Verdi, Elgar, and Vaughan Williams the plays enshrining Falstaff, no composer, great or little, has dared to lay a finger on that play which, in 1826, Mendelssohn with four chords made his own for ever?

Jan. 4 *Monday.* A broken day. I am just in the thick of preparing Thursday's Book Talk for the wireless when the telephone-bell rings. Will I put up twenty-five pounds bail for an old waiter who has got himself into trouble? Hardly have I weakly consented than the telephone rings again—will I discharge a five-pound fine for an old friend who appears to have been drunk and capable enough to assault a policeman? The suggestion is that if I don't I shall find him hanging outside my flat. I come back to find Charlie Rogers, my ex-houseboy now in the Air Force, Bombardier Bowdery with a pocketful of new stories, Kligerman poring over the score of the Tschaikowsky Concerto, and, of course, Leo—all clamouring for lunch. We repair to the local, and gorge ourselves on cold meat-pies and pickles. I then return and have just started taking up the broken threads when a little old lady, looking exactly like Dickens's Miss Flite and claiming that she has an appointment, wants to know what right the B.B.C. has to stop her marrying Noel Coward, and what am I prepared to do about it? She then hands me a list of other people she proposes to marry; these include the Home Secretary, Leslie Henson, and Commander Campbell, if she can find him. I calm her down, except that she is calmer than I am. And about five o'clock, having locked my door and disconnected the telephone, I resume my article. Dine with Simon Carnes at the Café Royal. This is a young man of considerable looks and charm but inconsiderable income. Is now instructor in naval fire-watching or army Morse-signalling or something. Gets four pounds ten a week, out of which he proceeds to entertain me more than handsomely. In return I produce Michael Shepley and also Veronica Rose, a pretty woman, and quite a good actress. We talk till the doorkeeper comes along and chivvies us out.

Jan. 8 *Friday.* Dined with Basil Cameron at the Dorchester. The food exquisite, with a beautiful bottle of Mouton-Rothschild and some good brandy. Basil was at his best, talking a great deal about Joachim, whose pupil he was, and how Joachim had been the high priest of the violin—in contradistinction to the modern virtuoso-entertainer with the fiddle. Said some people think me a better music critic than Newman.

I said, "You mean I'm not so tired of listening to music. Ernest tells me he only wants to read it."

Jan. 9 *Saturday.* Letter of congratulation to Osbert Sitwell on his coming into an unexpected legacy of £10,000.

10 *Fairfax Road, N.W.*6
January 11*th*, 1943

MY DEAR OSBERT,

Here's Richness indeed! To be envious, says the invaluable Noah Webster, is "to be pained by the good fortune of another." In that sense I am not envious. But the pretence that the news of your legacy has not stirred an unfamiliar and, I think, not very laudable emotion in my breast, would be as thin as this paper! Anyhow, my best congratulations.

Do you remember Bulwer Lytton's *What Will He Do With It?* You will not, I imagine, buy an honour: but what *will* you do? Will you add a wing to Renishaw, start an intellectual theatre at Sheffield, endow a home for the Cantrell-Cookseys (what a masterpiece—I shall read it again before I go to bed to-night), keep a boxer, finance an orchestra on condition that it plays nothing later than Purcell—see William Glock *passim*—head a fund on behalf of ballet-dancers suffering from rheumatoid arthritis? I am fertile, even fecund, in suggestions.

I, too, can boast a windfall—the sum of five shillings and one penny—last year's profit on *Ego*. The first volume—the others have never yet earned their advance royalties. And now that *Ego 5* was sold out before publication I cannot get paper to reprint.

But I wander from the real point of this letter. Which is that if some vulgar, envious person should hint that you were already sufficiently bestowed, you should counter with Mrs Erlynne's remark in Wilde's play: "Margin is everything!"

In conclusion, may I hope that I now know where my next glass of champagne is coming from?

Ever your
JAMES

Jan. 10 *Sunday.* On the point that I ignore the world outside my immediate interests. Has anybody else noticed that the essence of the Beveridge Report is contained in two of Ruskin's Lectures—one delivered to the Working Men's Institute at Camberwell, the other at the Town Hall, Bradford? Both in the eighteen-sixties. See *The Crown of Wild Olive*, pars. 42 and 79. I am aware that Ruskin says nothing about insurance. But the underlying notion—" that whatever work is done shall be fully paid for, and the man who does it, paid for it, not somebody else "—is the same in both cases. As for par. 79, I hold that the scarifying picture of the capitalist notion of what constitutes a happy and contented society is as true to-day as it was then. That I do not diarise about the Beveridge Report does not mean that I have not heard of it, or hold it to be unimportant.

L'esprit de l'escalier. From Catherine Whitcomb's *I'll Mourn You Later.* " 'Mother, when, or rather—*if* you ever get old and queer, may I just give you a tasty little dish of cyanide for your tea, or something ? It'd be a kindness to you, I'm sure.' 'Yes, dear,' answers Elizabeth absently, ' do.' " Why didn't I think of this for my notice of *Arsenic and Old Lace* ?

Jan. 11 *Monday.* Moiseiwitsch tells me this story, characteristic of the way artists, brains-trustees, and others are treated. Engaged to give, and I mean give, a recital for the Russian Red Cross, he arrives at some miserable hole about the size of, say, Luton. The recital is at three o'clock, and his train gets there round about 1.45. Nobody to meet him, no taxi, a mile-and-a-half walk, with bag, to the cinema where the recital is to take place. Cinema closed, also pubs. No lunch and nowhere to go out of the bitter wind. Presently one or two people start forming a queue, which he joins for warmth. " Somebody tells me," says Benno, " that the next two trains to London are the 4.50 and the 7.25." I ask which he caught. " Never," says Benno, " were so many wrong notes played to so few people in so short a time ! "

Rehearsal with Kligerman at the Wigmore Studios, Leo reading the orchestral part of the Tschaikowsky at sight on another piano and doing it *con brio*, filling in the brass with whoops and shouts which cause me to say, " Well roared, lion ! " K. makes good his promise of " playing it Russian." He takes the last movement more slowly than anybody I have heard, thus giving it a breadth and dignity one hasn't known that it possessed. These occasions give me a peculiar thrill. I feel that for once in a way I am doing, or helping somebody else to do, something creative instead of this perpetual criticising.

Fatras. Part of a letter from Mrs Norman O'Neill :

In the days of Bach, Beethoven, and Mozart, and even much later, in the Romantic period (Schumann, Chopin), the allegros and prestos were not meant to be played at great pace. We have now in the middle of the twentieth century reached such a pitch of virtuosity that players are apt to over-emphasise rapidity of execution—through this, the classical and romantic music loses much of its characteristic, and very often sounds mechanical. My authority in expressing this opinion is based on my connection with Clara Schumann with whom I had the privilege to study. Already then (end of the nineteenth century) she was deploring the fast *tempi* adopted by the great pianists of the Liszt school—she specially laid stress on Schumann's works as always being played too fast, and how Schumann himself could not bear it. Another great pianist with whom I studied was Wilhelmina Claus-Szarwadi (an exquisite interpreter of Chopin). Through her one got a distant connection with Bach ! As a child prodigy she studied Bach with old Griepenkerl, who had been a pupil of Philipp Emanuel Bach ! So these two real traditions were not too remote !

Jan. 12 Four letters.
Tuesday.

1. From C. B. Fry :

T. S. " *Mercury* "
Hamble, Hants
January 11, 1943

Dear Agate,

If I may . . . ? A girl called Joan Begbie, daughter of Harold (who " did God " for the *Daily Mail*), told me she had heard you talking about me and cricket on the air—something to do with Clifford Bax's *Evenings in Albany*. You were there, and I remember our symposium on the finer points of the much misinterpreted field-game so murdered by most writers and talkers. But the point is I've been trying to extract from the Brains Trust and other less likely sources a definition of *Rhythm*. The term is used of Music, Poetry, Prose, Dancing, a horse galloping, the façade of a cathedral, pictures and what-not.

Now what do the users have in mind when they use the term ? Even if you ask a musician or a dancer they say " Oh, well, it means . . . rhythm." I asked Josephine

Bradley, the best ballroom dancer in the world (who taught me for four years), and she said, " Well, *you've* got it. *I* gave it you, but I can't put it into words." Then there is the negro song, " All God's Chillun got Rhythm." Of course, if it is an ultimate emotional experience it *can't* be defined . . . but it can be " indicated " by metaphor or analogy.

My *own* notion is this: " Ruthmos," the Greek noun, originally meant " flowing." " An *actual* flowing of a river " —*i.e.*, it was originally used of things which were fluid and did really flow. But there are things and experiences which *seem* to flow though they are not fluid but totally different actually, *e.g.*, music, a dancer's movements, etc. So rhythm was used in a transferred sense, *i.e.*, applied metaphorically (by selection of *one* character) to any experience or *cause* of an experience which was smooth and fluent. But there is a muddle at this stage between (*a*) the emotional effect in *me* and (*b*) the character or features in the music which cause this feeling in me. It is clear that in poetry or music the rhythm effect depends on repetition and expectancy of a pattern, vague in prose, more definite in the Psalms, definite in strict metre and rhyme. So in some way one may say that rhythm as an effect felt is due to repetition of a spatial or temporal or sound pattern in such a way, with variation, as to excite and satisfy expectancy of a pleasurable kind.

Yours truly,
C. B. Fry

2. From Kenneth Hopkins, containing a Thought from Robert Southey :

> Spider ! thou needst not run in fear about
> To shun my curious eyes ;
> I won't humanely crush thy bowels out
> Lest thou shouldst eat the flies ;
> Nor will I roast thee with a damned delight
> Thy strange instinctive fortitude to see,
> For there is One who might
> One day roast me.

3. From a doctor in Cornwall :

Dear Mr Agate,

In the absence of the celebrated Dr Johnson, I can imagine no one more qualified than yourself to express an opinion on a matter of some conversational interest.

Every two months I have to visit a lady of rather unusual age, one hundred and four years in fact. She is in the best of health, eats enormously, sleeps like a babe, suffers no strange symptoms, and is probably not aware that I am a doctor. She does not read, does not listen to the wireless (this wisdom may have contributed to her longevity), has no hobbies, and sees no one but her niece who looks after her. She lives in a remote place along the coast.

There is between us a difference of some seventy-two years, and while this imposes some limitations upon our conversation, it should leave a small but definite field to develop. Can you suggest any line of conversation that Dr A. can pursue? All my usual claptrap about the weather and the news as provided for us by the daily papers seems strangely inappropriate when attempted upon a stolid old lady who was born in the days when Dr Johnson could be well remembered by many men.

4. From an old friend, an ardent Runyonite, with whom I had a tiff:

I am afraid I lost my temper *More Than Somewhat* last night when I came near to boffing you on the noggin. *Furthermore* I realise that you and I are not such guys as citizens care to have sored up at one another. So what about exchanging a big hello at one of Good Time Mr Charley's tables? In other words, let's *Take It Easy*.

Jan. 14 *Thursday.* Brains Trust by the Staff of the *Express*. Caxton Hall crowded, including standing room. Hore-Belisha in the chair, as suave, plausible, and amusing as ever. But I still think that, like Wilde's General Moncrieff, our former Minister for War is essentially a man of peace. Questions mostly political, and a lot of impassioned nonsense by everybody, including the audience. When I made the obvious point about not bombing Rome because the Nazis didn't bomb Athens, whose buildings I said were the equivalent of Shakespeare's plays or Beethoven's symphonies, somebody shouted, "Wot abaht the 'uman architecture of the Whitechapel Road?" But I got an unexpected round of applause when I said: "Until we are all completely educated, better education means worse taste. Formerly society was divided into two classes—the educated who had taste and the uneducated who had none. Society is still divided: the educated who have retained their taste and the half-educated who have acquired a lot of taste, most of it bad."

Kligerman made his début with orchestra to-night at Leicester. In the Tschaikowsky with the Philharmonic. Stayed up late thinking he might 'phone or come round to say how it had gone off. But he didn't.

Jan. 15 *Friday.* Took the chair at the meeting called by Leslie Henson at the Saville Theatre on behalf of the Opening of Theatres on Sundays. Had Lewis Casson on my right and Will Hay on my left. It was all most amusing and muddle-headed, and I felt like the calm spot in the centre of a vortex in a whirlpool of red herrings. Nobody put forward the essential thing to be debated—that if the general weal demands Sunday opening the profession should acquiesce and arrange its conscience and its business affairs accordingly. In my view actors and actresses who cannot do this should abandon the profession in favour of those who can, and see if they have any better luck as printers, nurses, and everybody else who has to work on Sunday night. I kept this to myself, however, and gave no inkling of which way my sympathies lay.

Some time after midnight a well-known actress rang up. She and her husband were coming round to the Villa Volpone. I tried all sorts of things—including my Sarah record—to keep them off the vexed question. But it was no use, and what, after all, can an elderly critic do when a beautiful woman throws herself at his feet like Mrs Kendal at the feet of Mr Kendal in *The Ironmaster* ? They had ordered a taxi for two o'clock, and at half-past I suggested that the driver might like a drink. They acquiesced, after which the lady resumed her impassioned appeal to be allowed to spend Sunday evening darning her husband's socks with her husband looking on. Bed around four.

No word from Alexis.

Jan. 16 *Saturday.* "Is your journey really necessary ?" Perhaps not. But I couldn't resist the implication in Blanche Robey's letter that I might like to see the old man in pantomime again. The 11.15 to Bristol was practically empty. Lunched at the Grand, and then drove round to see the sights—horrid, depressing sights. Complete desolation over small, sharply defined areas. Many churches gone, but the most beautiful of them unharmed. I get the impression that Bristol is much more touched by the war than London ; this is probably true of all the big provincial cities. Nobody about except the troops.

The first pantomime in which I saw George was *Robinson Crusoe.* " Old, old, Master Shallow," said Falstaff, when asked whether a certain *bona roba* still held her own. And Shallow said : " Nay, she's old ; she cannot choose but be old ; certain she's old ; and had Robin Nightwork, by old Nightwork, before I came to Clement's Inn." That which befell Robin's mother must equally befall Robinson's ; she cannot choose but be old. It is a matter of forty-five years since I first saw this great player assume bonnet and dolman. I saw him just above the horizon, decorating and cheering the elevated sphere he just began to move in, glittering like the morning star, full of life, and splendour and joy. And never, as Burke didn't say, were these optics dazzled by a more delightful vision. If not in this pantomime then in an earlier one, an elephant used to call for the star at his lodgings and squat on the kerb till a sufficient crowd had collected, when a frock-coated figure, collarless, with brow circumspectly cinct, and carrying an odd little cane, would mount on to the animal's back and ride down to the theatre indifferent to the mob, wrapped in his own thoughts, and as if this were his usual mode of conveyance. Was some of the old exuberance missing to-night ? Possibly. But will anybody insist that Beethoven in his Third Manner retained everything of the frolicsome First or tempestuous Second ? To Robey, too, must be allowed his third period. After the storm comes the calm, and it is to be conceded that those over-the-wall squabbles with Mrs Moggridge belong, and may now be relegated, to the order of happy, far-off things and battles long ago.

Jan. 17 *Sunday.* Was entertained at lunch with some members of the company. George seemed a little tired, I did my best to keep the talk going, and he whispered, " I'll bet the folks around are saying, ' There's Robey making 'em laugh ! ' " And I thought I detected something very like wistfulness. His modesty is unimpaired, witness his confession that he once refused to be one of Cinderella's Ugly Sisters on the ground that the other was to be Fred Emney. " Fred *was* a woman ; I should have been merely a red-nosed comedian in petticoats."

Jan. 18 *Monday.* Alexis came round, and I gathered that although the Leicester audience had leaped to its feet and cheered wildly, he was a little dashed at the orchestra remaining seated. Then he said with pathos : " In train they occupy two coaches, I see they carry instruments, I get in with them. I sit in corner of compartment, I wait for discussion. How do I play, am I better than X, am I not so good virtuoso as Y ? But no. Not a word do they speak with me. Only do they talk of the price of beer and about football teams." I comforted him by saying that the Philharmonic had played for every great pianist from Carreño to Clifford Curzon, and were probably sick of the Concerto anyhow. Whereupon Alexis retorted, " These players are Philistines, they make no approach to art." I replied that they probably preferred making the approach to St Pancras. Terribly busy with my Robey article, I got rid of him as soon as I could, I am afraid a trifle unceremoniously.

Jan. 19 *Tuesday.* Enormously flattered to read the fourth leader in to-day's *Times* beginning :

> It is pleasant to think that the name of Mr James Agate will go down to posterity indissolubly joined with that of Mr Joseph Smiggers. When occupying the chair at a somewhat tempestuous meeting of the theatrical profession he smoothed the wrinkles on many sable brows by ruling that certain expressions were to be understood in a Pickwickian sense. Everybody knows who Mr Agate is ; he needs no further fame, but his companion has scarcely enjoyed his due, and many people might have to scratch their heads before recalling him. Yet Joseph Smiggers, Esq., P.V.P., M.P.C.—let us accord him his full title—took the chair at the meeting when the immortal phrase was first used.

And for the rest of the day I went about the house murmuring the article's last sentence : " We are all, comparatively speaking, brimming over with *l'esprit de l'escalier*, but only genius can seize the irrecapturable moment."

Jan. 20 *Wednesday.* Here is a really brilliant pun reported by Spike Hughes, himself a first-class wit. (" The Metro-Goldwyn-Meyerbeer Choir " was his invention.) The discussion had turned upon a newspaper article entitled

"Nervousness in the Vatican." A wine bibber, normally reputed to be slow-witted, chipped in: "But they've got the wrong heading. Surely it ought to be: 'Shattered Nerve du Pape'!"

Percy Cudlipp, editor of the *Herald*, a most amusing fellow, pretended at lunch to-day that he had heard the late Mr Justice Rigby Swift, whom nothing could deprive of his parentheses, deliver sentence of death in the following manner: "The sentence of the Court upon you (*kindly close the doors, Usher, for the noises of the street are a considerable distraction and the prisoner may not hear the sentence*)—is that you be hanged by the (*I must also request that the windows be fastened; there is a severe draught in the Court*)—neck until you are (*persons in the public gallery will be ejected unless they realise that this is not a theatre*)—dead."

Jan. 21 *Thursday.* The difference between Capitalism and Communism. Under Capitalism the customer is always right; under Communism the customer is always wrong.

Jan. 23 *Saturday.* Having noticed in a sale catalogue two "large" photographs of Sarah Bernhardt, I left a bid of £5 for the pair. Learned that I had got them for £1 18*s.* 0*d.* They arrived in a taxi-cab into which they would just fit, each of them measuring four feet by three! One is an exquisite portrait of Sarah as herself in 1886. The other, Sarah as Pelléas, is a coloured horror, which was exhibited in Willie Clarkson's window for years. I shall hang this prominently, though it is a poor work of art. Thrown in was a water-colour of Willie as Alfredo in Verdi's opera!

Leonard Russell 'phones me this morning for an article for *Printer's Pie* to be entitled "Are We a Nation of Grousers?" Knocked off the stuff in something under two hours. Perhaps it would be more correct to say that Job, Carlyle, Kipling, Mrs Hemans, Dickens, Gilbert, Browning, Philander Chase Johnson, Benjamin Franklin King, and the authors of *The Anatomy of Melancholy* and *Mrs Wiggs of the Cabbage Patch* knocked it off for me. One hasn't got the knack of quotation for nothing. Twenty years ago I heard some wit say "Originality is the thief of time," and I have never forgotten it. I think it was

Pavia at our first meeting in the saloon bar at the Duke of York's, next to the Victoria Palace. However much we may quarrel, that first encounter and Jock's first call on me are the two events which have made the greatest mark on my life.

Jan. 24 *Sunday.* To the Mercury for a performance of *La Parisienne.* This is the piece to see which, some time in the late 'nineties, or early nineteen hundreds, I motored from Manchester to London, taking two days over the journey. Réjane was in the title-rôle then ; Sonia Dresdel very fine now. The scene in which Clotilde sits on the couch listening for a full five minutes to that ass Simpson in succeeding waves of pique, umbrage, boredom, and exasperation, was a masterpiece of facial mobility. Why this actress, incidentally a superb Hedda Gabler, is not given her chance in the West End is a mystery ; with the exception of Edith Evans I know of no comedy actress who can hold a candle to her. Or rather, it is not a mystery at all. She can *act*, and what the West End wants is an odalisque with the full complement of clothes.

When I got home I found that Leo had left on my desk the following :

EPILOGUE AT "IBSENSHOLM"

(*The scene is a Christmas party ten years after the end of the plays. A number of people are sitting round a small fire, shivering.*)

HELMER. How cold it is !

KROGSTAD. How the rain pelts !

MRS KROGSTAD (*formerly* MRS LINDEN). How the wind howls !

HELMER. Ten years since Nora left me.

ELLA RENTHEIM. Ten years since Erhart left me.

MRS BORKMAN. Ten years since Erhart left *us*.

KROGSTAD. Ten years since Rank died.

MRS KROGSTAD. Ten years, Nils, since we married.

HELMER. How the wind howls !

MRS BORKMAN. Ten years since Borkman died.

ELLA RENTHEIM. How cold it is !

MRS BORKMAN. How old we are !

KROGSTAD. How the wind howls !

TESMAN. Ten years since Hedda shot herself.

MRS TESMAN (*formerly* MRS ELVSTED). Ten years since Eilert shot himself.

OLD EKDAL. Ten years since Hedvig shot herself.
MRS ALVING. Ten years since Oswald went mad.
IRENE. Ten years since I went mad.
MRS SOLNESS. Ten years since Halvard fell off the steeple.
MRS HELSING (*housekeeper at Rosmersholm*). Ten years since my mistress fell in the millpond.
DR WANGEL. Ten years since Ellida ran away to sea.
MRS ALLMERS. Ten years since little Eyolf fell in the sea.
THE INSPECTOR AT THE BATHS. How cold the water is!
DR STOCKMANN. How dirty the water is!
MRS BORKMAN. Play us something, Mrs Krogstad.

(MRS K. *goes to the piano and plays* "*The Death of Ase.*")

Jan. 25 *Monday.* Looking forward to-night to Wolfit's Lear. Ellen Terry in her *Memoirs* writes: "Henry was just marvellous, but indistinct from nervousness. Terriss spoke out, but who cared! Haviland was very good, and my Ted splendid in the little bit he had to do as Oswald. I was rather good to-night. Cordelia *is* a wee part, but a fine one all the same. *King Lear* was one of our rare failures." It is an old story how, after the curtain had fallen, Irving came forward and thanked the audience in words every one of which carried to the back wall of the gallery. Whereupon a voice from the gods rang out: "Why didn't you speak like that before?" This morning I receive a letter from Acton saying that the voice was the writer's.

Later. Disappointed with a very good performance. Probably because between the very good and the supreme actor there is a great gulf fixed. An admirable performance by Richard Goolden, except that he makes the Fool more than half Lear's age, whereas he should be a stripling. At least, Macready thought so. See the Diaries:

> *January 4th*, 1838.—Went to the theatre, where I went on a first rehearsal of *King Lear*. My opinion of the introduction of the Fool is that, like many terrible contrasts in poetry and painting, in acting representation it will fail of effect; it will either weary or annoy or distract the spectator. I have no hope of it, and think that at the last we shall be obliged to dispense with it. Settled the scenery, which will be very striking.
>
> *January 5th.*—Speaking to Willmott and Bartley about the part of the Fool in *Lear*, and mentioning my apprehensions

> that, with Meadows, we should be obliged to omit the part, I described the sort of hectic, fragile, beautiful-faced boy that he should be, and stated my belief that it never could be acted.

But I have seen it acted! This was in 1927 at the O.U.D.S. production of the play. Komisarjevsky did a wonderful setting, the Lear wasn't up to much, Cordelia ditto, Dorothy Green and Martita Hunt played Goneril and Regan like two hooded birds of evil, and there was the best Fool I ever saw, played by a boy whose name I noted at the time. It was Tandy, and he is, I believe, a brother of Jessica Tandy.

Jan. 26 *Tuesday.* In a letter from George Richards:

> It struck me the other day that Irishmen and Catholicism (Roman, of course, not Anglican) are like hand and glove. No one who is not pure Irish should be allowed to be a Catholic—and every Irishman should be compelled to be one. Any Irishman who does not reek of Catholicism is only half Irish. Italians, Spanish, Germans, French, and even Mexicans only play at being Catholics; no one who has not set foot in Ireland, not even the Pope, can have an inkling of what membership of the apostolic church really is.

Moiseiwitsch said to me, " By the way, Jimmie, I've got some good news for you about your protégé, Kligerman. I asked about him from Jean Pougnet [the leader of the Philharmonic], who said, ' It was obvious the Concerto [Tschaikowsky in B flat minor] was beyond him. But he never lost his head and played quite well for a beginner.' " Alexis will be furious. " Such insult! I a beginner!! "

Jan. 27 *Wednesday.* Letter from Ashley Dukes:

> *26th January* 1943
>
> Dear James,
>
> Here are some of the few notes I have been able to collect about Henry Becque (1837–99) without consulting any full-length biography: I don't even know if one exists.
>
> At a stretch one might call him the Parisian counterpart both of Stendhal and Synge, and it would be easy to talk of the Empires and Republics and the Commune and what they

made of him ; but there seems to be little indication that they troubled him at all.

Nobody seems to have liked him much. He was respected, if only because his refusal to compromise with anything or anybody became, as somebody said, " une coquetterie." No desire to please, complete indifference to the public. He would have been astonished to hear that the first-night audience for *La Parisienne* stood up and clapped their hands on the line " Prenez garde, voilà mon mari." He was not present, he had quarrelled with the manager or some member of the cast.

Les Corbeaux was the play that nearly made him the first dramatist (in the sense of the foremost) of Antoine's group when the Théâtre Libre was founded. But it was personal as *La Parisienne* is personal, and the mood of the time was social and Ibsen's *Ghosts* became the standard-bearer. *Les Corbeaux* is still given at the Français ; I saw it only a few years ago.

All the Mandarins affected to despise Becque for writing *La Parisienne* at all. They used even its success as a reproach to Becque. Some critics said it was his revenge upon a woman. When he died they found a scrap of paper among his manuscripts with the lines :

> Je n'ai rien qui me la rappelle,
> Pas de portrait, pas de cheveux ;
> Je n'ai pas une lettre d'elle ;
> Nous nous détestions tous les deux.

Afterwards a group of his followers thought they had found his grave (which had no headstone) in Père Lachaise, and they began to visit it regularly and leave their flowers ; until they found other flowers laid beside them, and one day encountered a widow whose late husband's grave it really was—another Henry Becque who had been a clerk in a gasworks. And somebody murmured, " Comme Antoine." (He also was in a gasworks at first.)

A street in Paris—I think it is just behind the Palais Royal —was named after him, and his statue was erected ; but a few days later a lorry backed into it and knocked it down so that it had to be put up again without ceremony.

Les Polichinelles, Becque's unfinished comedy, was published some years after his death.

La Parisienne is the only play of the modern school, or the only play with any pretensions to be a work of art, that has been continuously performed by the Français for fifty years. By comparison, *Les Corbeaux* is treated as an occasional or museum piece.

Now that I have got them on paper, these notes look very

slight. But you asked me to send them and the subject has a good deal of interest. Lydia Yavorska (Princess Bariatinsky) performed the only previous version of *La Parisienne*, which was made for her by W. L. Courtney. I did my best to trace it before beginning the present version used at the Mercury. No version has been published. I have an idea that the comedy would suit the Lunts, and perhaps they will do it one of these days.

Yours as ever,
ASHLEY DUKES

Jan. 28 *Thursday.* A man came up to me at lunch to-day and introduced himself as Anthony Heckstall-Smith, the author of the play called *Juggernaut.* Is now an officer in the Navy. Told me about taking his men to an E.N.S.A. concert at Mersa Matruh, where he heard Alice Delysia sing her old songs in tent, sandstorm, and backless Hartnell frock.

At the Cambridge to-night they guyed, but did not perform, Dion Boucicault's *The Streets of London.* Ten minutes of guying at a very late hour, in a very small room, at the top of Bloomsbury's steepest stairs, might be amusing. Three hours of it ? No. Unable to *rigoler*, I go over the way to *Rigoletto*, and my eyes nearly pop out of my noggin to see that the Carl Rosa Opera Company is taking the old nonsense seriously, and doing it beautifully. But I will lay plenty of 6 to 5 that Bloomsbury gives me a big hello when I set Verdi's music to Damon Runyon's story *Sense of Humour*, with Frankie Ferocious, Joe the Joker, and his ever-loving wife Rosa in place of Sparafucile, Rigoletto, and his ever-loving daughter Gilda. After all, it's much the same tale.

Afterwards with Frank Singleton to supper at his new house, where I meet Lieutenant Richard Charles Schuckburgh, a great-grandson of Charles Dickens. A nice boy. To get a taxi after midnight I use a dodge which Ronnie Squire first put me up to. You ring a well-known sporting club, say you're Cochran's valet 'phoning for a friend of his master's who is willing to pay double fare. This never fails. Home about one and spend the next two hours re-writing my *Lear* notice. Rather pleased with : " Those who see a moral purpose behind the phenomenon of the artist must be discouraged when they realise that the faults of the great actor are more impressive than the virtues of the player who has no more than talent." And: "What is peculiarly tantalising about this business of the artist is that talent, produced to infinity in the Euclidean sense, never attains to genius any more than perpetual burnishing of silver turns that metal into gold. However, there is one glory of the sun and another glory of the moon, etc., etc."

Jan. 29 *Friday.* Wake up this morning realising that there is still a lot to be done to my *Lear* article. Which means that I must simultaneously tinker with this and write my *Express* stuff. Kligerman calls for the first time in ten days, the reason being that on the last occasion I had to shoo him off owing to excess of work. He comes round to-day to play us the Beethoven No. 3 which he has just got by heart. Whereupon the shooing process has to be gone through all over again; *two* articles and Alexis being beyond even my powers.

Jan. 30 *Saturday.* Spend the morning working on proof of *Lear* article. Must guard against the feeling that, judging by the time I take to write my stuff, my grip is weakening. The point is to give the readers in two half-columns as much intellectual—forgive the word—content as in the old two full columns. Every word counts now, one must write "because" and not "for the reason that." It is the condensing and compressing which take the time. On the whole I hope to be pretty good to-morrow.

In the evening to the Tatler picture-house for the superb *Lenin in October*. This was preceded by a film of Shostakovich conducting an orchestra of badly dressed, hairy, and be-warted Communists in a medley of waltz tunes more commonplace than anything that ever came out of Czarist Russia. Is it possible that the Black Sea has its Blackpool?

Jan. 31 *Sunday.* An unknown friend has sent me a copy of *The Times* for June 12, 1882, in which he has marked the passages having to do with the theatre. I have no doubt that the idea was to lure me to an article comparing the theatre of to-day with that of sixty years ago. Well, let's look at the theatre of 1882. Sarah Bernhardt in *Le Sphinx* ; Rossi in *King Lear* ; Irving, Ellen Terry, and Mrs Stirling in *Romeo and Juliet* ; Bancroft, Arthur Cecil, A. W. Pinero (!), Modjeska, and Mrs Bancroft in *Odette* ; Mr and Mrs Kendal, T. W. Robertson, and John Hare in *The Squire* ; Tree in *The Colonel* ; Mrs Bernard-Beere in *Far from the Madding Crowd* ; Toole as Robert Macaire ; Wilson Barrett in *The Romany Rye* ; G. W. Anson, Henry Kemble, Forbes-Robertson, John Clayton, Lottie Venne, and Marion Terry in *The Parvenu*. Among forthcoming events Ristori as Lady Macbeth, and Edwin Booth as Richelieu. At the Italian Opera Sembrich, Patti, Pauline Lucca, and Albani. At the German Opera *Tannhäuser* with Richter. Will the like come any more? Never, never, never, never, never, as Lear says.

I note an account of the Chester Musical Festival :

> To musicians two instrumental selections were of the highest interest, a quartet by Schubert in D minor, and Beethoven's in C minor, Op. 18, No. 4, played by four principals of Mr Hallé's band, Herr Straus, first, and Herr Jacoby, second violin, Herr Bernhardt, viola, and M. Vieuxtemps, 'cello.

This puts the clock back to my earliest days. Herr Jacoby was my brothers' music-master. I remember him well—a saturnine, witty, cultured Jew, and a sound musician of the old school. But for lack of self-confidence he would have led the Hallé Orchestra after Willy Hess left. I remember him telling us that for years he never read anything except the farces of Labiche, from the six volumes of which he was never separated even when he travelled. Is the world less good to live in than it was sixty years ago ? Sixty times Yes would be my answer. The columns of *The Times* were half an inch wider, and the type, though smaller, was not only more elegant and more readable, but allowed a greater number of words.

A young man to whom I have just shown the foregoing was only faintly interested, if at all. " You see, it's before my time." Very much the same thing was put forward the other night at the Café Royal by a young intellectual who knew all about the Baron de Charlus but had never heard of the Baron de Nucingen, was *au fait* with Daphne's Rebecca but did not know William Makepeace's.

Feb. 1 *Monday.* The *Star* has a photograph of Flying Officer Wickham, of Rusper, near Horsham, who took part in the first daylight raid on Berlin. I am to admit here that while my thoughts ought, by all that is patriotic and proper, to have been centred in the gallant airman, what they actually dwelt on for the next half-hour was his birthplace. Rusper is a village of no size at all, but it was there that I went to buy my pony, Rusper Maryan, exactly thirty years ago. I have told in an earlier volume how she won London for me at the first time of asking. My family, as Mrs Micawber would say, comes from Horsham, and I remember asking the groom who drove me to the Ward-Hargraves' whether among the gentry in the neighbourhood there were any of my name. He replied, " Lord, sir, there's a power of Agates, but none of 'em gentry."

Feb. 2 *Tuesday.* A correspondence :

Red Court
Pudsey
29th January 1943

DEAR MR AGATE,

When you read the name at the bottom of this letter I don't think that it will convey much to you.

I think, however, that you may remember just before the war, while you were staying in Worcester, a certain young gentleman about twelve years of age approached you with an autograph album and asked you if you were a county cricketer. Upon hearing that you were not a cricketer but " only " a writer he was disappointed, but upon being asked he decided that he would like your autograph.

You may also remember that this same young gentleman, although he came from Bradford, had never heard of J. B. Priestley. This brings me, who you will have realised was that " certain young gentleman," to the point of my letter.

It had often puzzled me since our meeting why you were so surprised that I had no knowledge of Mr Priestley. I am no longer puzzled. Last night I went to see his new play, *They Came to a City*, at the Prince's Theatre in Bradford. I was so intrigued by this play that I decided to write immediately to tell my friend Mr Agate (I have always looked upon you as my friend since our meeting) that if he has not already seen this play he must seize the first opportunity that he gets to see it.

This is the first of Mr Priestley's plays that I have ever seen, but I am determined that in the future I shall never miss the opportunity to see another. Hoping that now, after having gained some slight knowledge of Mr Priestley's work and his views, my education is more complete, and that you consider me as a more worthy citizen, I am

Yours sincerely,
NORMAN G. WILSON

10 Fairfax Road
London, N.W.6
4th February, 1943

DEAR NORMAN,

But of course I remember you. And here's something for you to puzzle over. At twelve years of age I would very much rather have been a county cricketer than a writer of books. Now that I am sixty—and even a little more—I still think it may be better to be a county cricketer than to be an author.

I am very glad to hear you like Mr Priestley's play, and I shall certainly take your advice and go to see it when it comes to London. In return will you let me tell you a few things which will turn you into a good playgoer, which is the next best thing to being a good playwright or a good actor?

1. Ask your father and mother to take in a good Sunday paper for you, and let it be known as YOUR PAPER. I should like to think it was the *Sunday Times*, because I write for it, but the *Observer* is just as good. Read the column about the theatre, first of all: and whenever you get the chance, go to see the plays recommended in that column of YOUR PAPER.

2. I have thought of something even better. Spend your pocket-money on whichever of these two papers you choose, and get your parents to take in the *Manchester Guardian* for you. You may get it a day late, but that doesn't matter. The news about the London theatres is written by Alan Dent ("A. D."), who has been a friend of mine for over fifteen years and is one of the most brilliant critics of the younger school.

3. I expect there is a repertory theatre in Bradford. If so, get your parents to let you join it. You see I am old-fashioned. In my day a boy of sixteen had to ask his parents' permission to do this and that.

4. Until you are twenty play as much cricket as the war will let you.

5. I don't think what I am going to write about now will be any good to you until you are twenty, but you might think about it from time to time. Remember: What is written about the theatre or any other subject by a vulgar or trivial mind—however much you agree with it—will always remain

vulgar and trivial. Just as the outcome of a fine and earnest mind will always be worthy of respect, however much you may disagree with it.

6. Read as much as you can of the works of Charles Dickens.

7. As you know, a good general never asks his subordinates to do anything he is not prepared to do himself. When I was a youngster I promised my parents I would neither smoke nor touch alcohol until I was twenty-one. On my twenty-first birthday I was in London, and I remember going into the Salisbury Hotel in Fleet Street at eleven in the morning and ordering my first whiskey-and-soda and smoking my first cigar. With the result that I was exceedingly ill for the rest of the day! To ask you to follow my example is probably asking too much of a boy of your generation, so I shall amend it slightly and say: Don't smoke or drink till you are eighteen. Nineteen would be even better. If you have already started, STOP: or you will have no eye for fast bowling.

Here I cease, as by this time you must think me an unconscionable bore. Or a prig. Or a spoil-sport. Or even a kill-joy. But, actually, I am none of these things.

Yours sincerely,
J. SANDFORD MERTON SAMUEL SMILES AGATE

Feb. 3 *Wednesday.* To the Regal Cinema to see the Russian film *One Day of War*. Enormously impressed by the dignity of this documentary embodying the courage, devotion, steadfastness, cheerfulness, and self-sacrifice of an entire people. The women come out of it splendidly, particularly the girl who had brought back to safety one hundred and sixty-one men lying wounded in the open, and in every case had retrieved his rifle. A great poem. And then, of course, being English, we must follow up this superb picture with a Government snippet showing an encounter between a business damsel and an A.T.S. transport driver seated at the driving-wheel of her truck. Gurgles the business lass, "Darling, I had no idea the A.T.S. uniform could look so marvellous. I envy you, my sweet!" Whereupon the patriotic driver seizes her cue and retorts, "In that case, angel, why not try wearing one yourself?" From which it would seem to be officially recognised that clothes and not duty are the Englishwoman's cue for action. The "musical" was some appalling rubbish entitled *Orchestra Wives*. In no other country would that snippet and this inanity have been bracketed with the Russian film.

Feb. 4 A letter :
Thursday.

9 *Weymouth Street*
Portland Place
London, W.1
31*st January*, 1943

DEAR MR AGATE,

Your analysis of talent and genius in to-day's *Sunday Times* has called to my mind a conversation with my great friend Marguerite Moréno. Talking of Sarah Bernhardt (whom she detested) we did not seem to get any farther than anecdote. I had seen Sarah act when I was so young that acting meant nothing to me, so that of a *Dame aux Camélias* endured at the age of fourteen no memory remained but that of a tattoo with knives and forks on plates in the supper scene and of Sarah's unusually long lace cuffs which I either imagined or had been told were worn to hide the scragginess of her wrists. Later, I sometimes met her and once or twice saw her play, but it was in her decline, culminating in that rather gruesome display at the Opéra when she recited *La Nuit de Mai* in a *voix d'outre-tombe.* I wanted to know something about Sarah's genius, and Moréno wasn't delivering the goods. Then honest admiration got the better of her hate (Moréno is a good hater) and she said more or less this :

" Le génie de Sarah—c'était qu'une ou deux fois dans la soirée l'assistance était pénétrée et transformée—cela ne durait pas longtemps mais pendant ces quelques minutes on était en proie à un ravissement que je ne peux comparer qu'au plaisir de l'amour. Le reste de son jeu n'était trop souvent que de la conversation entre des actes de volupté. . . ."

The tingling thrill that is unmistakable (the Arabs have a word for it, and if you will forgive me an anthropological frankness, it is explained by the commentators as a " curdling of the scrotum ") seems more elusive as time goes on. The last time I experienced it was when I sat through a night of dances at Angkor.

Forgive me troubling you with a lot of subjective and self-centred stuff, but I thought that you might be amused by Moréno's comment, and she is a very intelligent woman.

Yours very sincerely,
ALAN HOUGHTON BRODRICK

There are several references to Moréno in Arnold Bennett's diary for 1903, at which time she was the wife of Marcel Schwob, who made the version of *Hamlet* for Sarah. After Schwob died Moréno married a second-rate actor called Daragon, and I think

I remember her in French films playing old women. She was a member, I believe, of the company from the Comédie Française which came to Windsor for the 1887 Jubilee, which would make her a very old lady indeed.

Feb. 5 *Friday.* To Kligerman's in response to an invitation to hear two pieces he has added to his repertoire, a Rachmaninoff Prelude (G minor) and the Op. 42 Valse by Chopin. He is going to play both at a concert in Harrogate which I have arranged for him next Sunday (five guineas plus expenses). Arrive to find an excellent tea and Leo fussing and fuliginating all over the place. Then Alexis, after the usual fifty excuses—" I do not like this piano, I am tired of practising, the room is too cold, the room is too hot, it is too early, it is too late," and so forth—plays the Prelude. Quite good. Then the Valse. Not so good. The first theme, which should be coaxed out of the piano, sounds like a butcher's boy whistling. When these are over Leo says : " Tell me, Alexis, which was the prelude and which was the waltz ? " Then I ask for the much advertised Beethoven No. 3. K. plays the first solo in the first movement. Dreadful, like a not over-intelligent schoolboy. And my beloved second subject—without any expression or charm, just as though he recites the grocer's bill. No breadth, no sentiment. He stops at the second *tutti*, and I look at L., whose eyes are raised to the ceiling in horror. " Alexis," I say, getting in my oar first, " this is the worst thing I have heard you do. It's no good your saying you feel it that way. You don't feel it any way. It is without form, and void, like the earth before the Creation ; if you play like that with an orchestra the leader will throw his bow at you." Then L. shows him how this second theme should be played. But K. has the unshakable conviction that he is playing like an angel. . . . What am I to do ? I can think of nothing except to forbid his ever playing the Concerto in public until he plays it properly. I cannot and will not risk the damage to my musical reputation —such as it is—if ever I let him make such an exhibition of himself. I am not going back on what I have said. I still maintain that he has a grand technique ; I still insist that his virtuosity is astounding. But his fingers control his brain instead of the other way round. I have done my amateur, and

Leo has done his professional, best. In other words, we are much worried. I had supper last night with Julian Herbage, the musical director of the B.B.C., and it took a lot of moral courage to introduce the subject of K. However, I did introduce it and arranged for a meeting. But I shall confine K. to Liszt, who doesn't need any brain.

Feb. 7 *Sunday.* At the Café Royal an ex-dramatic critic who has gone all Russian came up to me and said, " About that rubbish you've been writing in the *Express*. Critical standards are all rot. You'd have been a better dramatic critic if you'd never read Montague or seen Bernhardt. And a better book critic if you'd never read Sainte-Beuve or Dickens."

" Tell me," I said with all the mildness I could muster, " should I be a better film critic if I'd never seen Emil Jannings or Charlie Chaplin ? "

" Yes," he said. " Don't you realise that you're over forty ? "

" Over sixty."

" Forty will do. No man has a right to be a critic after forty. It's a young world we're living in to-day, and we've abolished the old standards."

" Tell me something about the new standards," I said.

" There's only one," he replied, " and that's actuality. Go into the streets, the shops, and the pubs, and if the actors you see on the stage are like the people you meet there, that's good acting. And if the characters in novels are like them, that's good novel-writing."

" I did think of doing a little dog-racing on Saturday," I murmured.

But he didn't hear me.

" Don't you realise," he shouted, " that Max Miller is of more value to the present generation than Michael Angelo, and that Vera Lynn is more alive than Leonardo da Vinci ? "

" I quite agree," I said, using a poor joke to keep my temper, " that the Marx Brothers are funnier than Karl Marx."

But the young man wasn't listening. He went on, " Must you be ninety before you realise that a live donkey is worth more than a dead lion ? "

" But surely," I protested, " you've got it the wrong way

round. What you've been trying to tell me is that your live lions are better than my dead donkeys ! "

Alas, he was already out of earshot.

I think I put up a pretty good defence, but I must confess that I am a little worried about my attitude to modern art. When I got home I looked again at *Modern Reading*, opening it at a poem by Mayakovsky :

> And you who spend the nights
> carousing
> and mornings reading in warm lavatories
> about newly decorated heroes—
> I'd rather spend my time
> serving pine-apple juice to whores in brothels
> than sit with you
> trouserless bastards.

Try as I will, I cannot regard this as poetry. In my *Sunday Times* this morning I find Desmond MacCarthy telling me that T. S. Eliot has never written with " a more musically modulated, careful simplicity " than in his new religious poem *Little Gidding*. And here, too, is Ernest Newman announcing that he is prepared to be told that people find Britten's Sinfonia da Requiem " ugly," " shapeless," and " confused." Ernest's explanation for this is that once in every three hundred years music undergoes " a fundamental upheaval in vocabulary, in idiom, and in imaginative background." Music began by being " basically contrapuntal," after which it became " basically harmonic." It is now moving on, says Ernest, " under an inexorable law to a phase for which we have as yet no adequate distinguishing name." And I remember how, in that pantomime of *Jack and the Beanstalk* long ago, George Robey used to say, " First it was gold, then it was beans. *What is it now ?* " It may, of course, be that the Hamlet of the future will be right to take his standard of English from the four-ale bar ; that critic would certainly be a fool who failed to recognise the energy in the Russian poet. It may be that there is some kind of non-Tennysonian music in

> If you came this way,
> Taking any route, starting from anywhere,
> At any time or at any season,
> It would always be the same : you would have to put off
> Sense and notion. You are not here to verify,
> Instruct yourself or inform curiosity
> Or carry report.

(I have, of course, carefully picked Eliot's flattest lines.) It may be that this afternoon's wireless excerpts from Alban Berg—I could not have tuned in more opportunely—excruciating to my ears, are enchanting to those which Ernest manages to project into the future. As a critic I am perilously poised and cannot afford to come down on the wrong side. That *all* the arts should agree in moving in the direction of what seems to me to be ugliness is a danger-signal no critic can afford to ignore. I cannot believe that all artists have suddenly gone out of their minds. Or that they are merely forcing themselves to feel in this new way, all originality on the old lines having been used up. This would make them charlatans in spite of themselves, and I do not believe that all modern artists are charlatans. I am old enough to remember the time when the plays of Ibsen were considered immoral, the operas of Wagner and Richard Strauss cacophonous, and the paintings of Gauguin and Rousseau libels on the human form. Wherefore I will not come down on that side of the fence. Now I have re-written my favourite quotation from Balzac : " Il est si facile de nier ce que l'on ne comprend pas," so that it reads : " Il est si facile de *louer* ce que l'on ne comprend pas." I must suppose that Ernest would know if somebody played a wrong note in the middle of *Wozzeck*, that Eric Newton would never mistake an unmeant goitre for the genuine Modigliani article, and that Desmond is unspoofable. And since I do not possess this gift of intuition I shall not come down on that side of the fence either. What is left ? Obviously I must remain poised above the maelstrom, coupling grace with dignity, and feeling like Mrs Crummles when she stood upon her head on the butt-end of a spear surrounded with blazing fireworks. But I have a shrewd suspicion that even in that situation the lady knew the acting of the company's Mr Lenville from that of Mr Kean. Some day when I have more time I shall return to this question of modern art. A critic should declare where he stands.

Feb. 8 *Monday.* *The Moon and Sixpence*, the film made out of Willie Maugham's novel, flabbergasted the Odeon audience to-night. I remember when I was a boy being enormously impressed with George Moore's " What matters the slaughter of ten thousand virgins if they provide Delacroix [I think it was] with a fine canvas ? " It was about this time that Wilde was writing " No artist has ethical sympathies." And : " Vice and virtue are to the artist materials for an art." I remember how, reading this, vicious little schoolboys took to enlarging the scope of their diversions under the delusion that they were turning themselves into artists. Later I remember how Montague tried to demolish the pernicious, amusing nonsense in a single sentence. " Wilde, when slowly dying of a retributive disease, with all his splendid gifts already dead before his body, was still chattering about the amplitude of the career of moral uncontrol." Unfortunately for Montague's argument, the disease from which Wilde died was retributive only in the time-sense ; twenty years later the medical profession made that discovery which would have saved him, body and mind. The original of this film's Strickland died, not of a disease which he had contracted in Tahiti, but of one that he caught in Marseilles and presumably spread among the islanders. If this is so, it would take a more convincing argument than Wilde's and a greater brush than Gauguin's to make a pretty picture out of that kettle of fish.

The second theme—the attitude of artists to marriage—brought up something no cinema audience can know anything about. Long before Maugham wrote his novel there was a play called *Hedda Gabler* which dealt with the subject of woman's indifference to all the artist lives for—his art. In that play Ibsen showed how Hedda was willing to go through fire for Eilert Lövborg, provided it was she who inspired his book ; and how equally ready she was, when the book turned out to have been inspired by another woman, to put the manuscript *in* the fire. " I am burning your child, Thea ! Your child and Eilert Lövborg's ! " Strickland ran away from Mrs S., not because he had ceased to love her—as a matter of fact he had never begun—but because he and his new mistress couldn't cohabit under the same roof as that icy virago. Art is an abstract subject, and women are not interested in abstract subjects. Listen to the average woman talking—clothes, hats, make-up, her menfolk, children, servants, rationing. No woman talking to me at supper after the theatre ever alludes to the matter of the play : her chatter is all about her adored Lilian and how wonderfully Ivor has kept his looks. Now every true artist of every kind I have ever met is entirely absorbed in his art, and never thinks about anything else, however much he may pretend. If people must chatter about art, let them do it intelligently. And as women seldom or never do this the artist naturally avoids the female prattler, and if he is married to one, sooner or later, provided he is not a moral coward, deserts her. Leo, to whom I am dictating this, interrupts:

L. P. It won't do, James. If you go on like this no woman will read your books or invite you to her house. They will all cut you, and then their husbands will cut you, and you will sit in the Café Royal like Mrs Allen and Catherine Morland at the Bath spa. It is absurd for you to think your attitude towards women is that of Johnson, or Walpole, or Swift. Where is your Mrs Thrale? Johnson adored her. Where is your Madame du Deffand? Walpole was fascinated by her, blind and old though she was. And your Stella? She was the one woman for whom Swift felt any affection.

J. A. I have my Gwen Chenhalls.

L. P. Your *Journal to Gwen* hasn't even started. I want you to realise that women are much more important in the social scheme than you admit. They make for the highest civilisation, they are an indispensable adjunct to manners and elegance. Hasn't it always been like that? Didn't Greek philosophers have to invite their Phrynes and Aspasias to make their parties "go"? What would Charles the Second's Court have been without the witty originals of all those Lelys and Knellers? And think of the women of the eighteenth century. Think of France. There was a time when women almost civilised Germany, though I suppose you would say that not even the Charlotte von Steins and the Henrietta Herz's and the Rahel Varnhagens could have accomplished *that.* Come to your senses. The cream of womanhood is the cream of humanity. Could anything be more boring than a world of men all talking about golf and cricket, racing and politics? Write an article on these lines. Say that the hand which rocks the cradle rules the world.

J. A. I'm damned if I'll put my name to such a lousy cliché.

L. P. Say, then, that you have always admired women, but that your misogyny is the result of an Unrequited Attachment. Say that all women have hearts of gold, say that they are generous, void of all spite and envy, sincere, truthful, and loyal.

J. A. Are they?

L. P. What the hell does that matter?

Feb. 9 *Tuesday.* Letter from Flight Lieutenant B. C. Hilliam ("Flotsam"), who was responsible for the Harrogate concert: "It was a long and lonely journey that Kligerman made yesterday, and this unit, from the C.O. down, is indeed grateful to him. He played exquisitely, and the ovation he received must have pleased him. Thanks indeed for the swift thought of having him play for us. Everybody here liked him personally, and he made an immediate hit."

Feb. 10 *Wednesday.* A depressing day. Spend the morning reading *Behold this Dreamer*, by Gerald Savory, the author of *George and Margaret.* All about a small-town idiot boy suspected of murder. Violent attack of indigestion brought on by combining a local café's roast beef (of the consistency of shoe-leather) with a Bath bun—the first ripple in a wave of economy which I proposed to inaugurate to-day. Spend the afternoon reading Gerald Kersh's *The Dead Look On*, a grim novel founded on the martyrdom of Lidice. At five o'clock screw myself up to the boredom of sitting through one of those quasi-musicals which consist of a Voice, a period plot, and, nine times out of ten, a fifth-rate re-hash of Viennese light opera. Arrive at the theatre, which is an out-of-the-way one, and dismiss taxi, to find that there is no performance, the Voice having contracted laryngitis. Where to go? I can think of no theatre that will bear a second visit, I have seen all the films, at the Club bridge is finished and they have started poker. There are no concerts. A restaurant? I have just had tea. A night-club? Not, I think, at a quarter past six. A brothel? I don't know any. Where in the devil's name can I go? It is pouring with rain, and bitterly cold. Shivering, I button my overcoat tightly around me, put up my collar and start on that most depressing of perambulations—a lonely pub-crawl. The hours drag, and at ten o'clock I arrive at the Café Royal—entirely sober! Leave at ten-thirty. Temper not improved when I compare my depression with the high spirits of some labourers I sit next to as I journey homewards in the Tube; they are starting their night-shift to repair some underground tunnel. And here my unfailing sense of logic comes to my rescue. For, I say to myself, there is no reason why they should be depressed, any more than a bank clerk should be depressed. One tunnel is not gayer than another, any more than one column of figures is jollier than another. Ninety-nine per cent. of men and women know their work for drudgery and don't pretend it is anything else. A doctor finds no fun in seeing his patient ill in bed. A dentist gets no kick out of drilling a hole in some one's tooth. But a critic—that's different—he deals with the very stuff of delight, and the only tools with which he works are his sense of enjoyment and his pen. I would rather move furniture or scrub floors than sit through a bad farce, because in the first case I need not pretend I am enjoying myself, and in the second I must. Does somebody say I should have gone home to-night and buried myself in a book ? I see. Having spent all the daylight hours in writing about books I am to waste the electric light reading them ? No. For the critic at a loose end I can see nothing but dissipation. And the man who can find dissipation in New Oxford Street in the early hours of a wet February evening has a more inventive mind than I can claim to possess.

Feb. 11 Letter from Ernest Helme :
Thursday.

Llangennith
Swansea
9.2.43

MY DEAR JAMES,

Many thanks for letting me see the Intaglio of *A la Recherche* [an article in the *S.T.* on the Theatre of 1882]. It may interest you to hear my recollections of the mighty past. Owing to the precocious education in dramatic, operatic, and musical art to which I was carefully subjected by my mother, aunt, and grandmother, I can recollect seeing and hearing the following artists actually in that year 1882, and of course frequently in subsequent years. Curiously enough in those subsequent years I never altered my first impressions. I fear this sounds conceited, but every play, every opera, every concert to which I was taken was meticulously discussed in detail on returning home, and I was never allowed to express criticism without giving my reason, which was then scrutinised minutely. Sir Claude Champion de Crespigny with Sir Evelyn Wood, both in Essex, had been admirers of my grandmother. Sir Claude was a magnificent sportsman, and won the House of Commons steeplechase at some amazing age. I believe over seventy. He rode in a steeplechase with three of his sons and finished in front of them. He was amateur boxing champion and used to don the gloves with my late soldier servant (formerly servant to Captain de C. in the K.D.G.) and when the old man passed away my servant, also from Essex, uttered this summing up : " 'E was a gentleman—brave as a lion, but 'e was frightened of 'er Ladyship."

Sarah Bernhardt in *Le Sphinx*—a most boring play and I seem to recollect her chained to a rock in the desert, after her eyes had been put out, taking about three-quarters of an hour to die and repeating at intervals " Je veux mourir ! Je veux mourir ! " every one devoutly wishing she would. I think even you, James, would have fallen into line. I do not think she retained this piece very long in her repertoire, and King Edward (then Prince of Wales) whom I saw in a box was reported to have expressed a wish (and he was a fine critic and enthusiastic admirer of Sarah) that she would never appear in it again.

Irving, Ellen Terry, and Mrs Stirling in *Romeo and Juliet*. Irving, alas, was too old and slightly doddering, but to anyone who can recollect Ellen Terry and Mrs Stirling as Juliet and the Nurse, no others really existed ; they were such perfect foils to each other. " Romeo, Romeo ! Wherefore," etc., was the most exquisitely spoken speech in English I have ever heard.

Lady Bancroft possessed " diablerie "—her consummate art clothed her art ; she was essentially a man's actress and was possessed of a wonderful magnetism. Her Peg Woffington in *Masks and Faces* was a milestone in stage history and, as her husband wrote, " No actress was ever on such wonderful terms of intimacy with her audience from the moment of her entry." I recollect her last appearance at the St James's Theatre at a charity matinée. The brilliant audience was dressed up to the nines. King Edward expressly attended and she was commanded to tea at the back of his box—some brilliant and witty talk I expect. Lady B. never to the end lost that marvellous allure or that " pearly " laugh.

Mrs Kendal was a woman's actress and never appealed in the same way to men. Her technique was perfect, but obvious —her elocution was a lesson—how I wish modern actresses could have heard her ! These two great actresses were utterly dissimilar and yet were always being very stupidly compared one with the other. Lady B.'s great successes were gained in London, Mrs Kendal's rather more in the provinces where her popularity was enormous. I always thought personally that age mellowed and improved Mrs K.'s art.

Tree I liked only in *Captain Swift*. His much advertised productions at His Majesty's never had the scholarly finish, or refinement, of Irving's at the Lyceum, and Tree frequently made himself ridiculous.

Mrs Bernard-Beere I thought a dreadful actress. She was the epitome of bathos, and tried to adopt Sarah Bernhardt's voice with fatal result—she was a wretched Zicka at the Haymarket with the Bancrofts.

Wilson Barrett was a very heavy actor—a mass of brawn: he always appeared broader than his height; he certainly laid on the entire gamut of emotion as Claud Melnotte and in *The Sign of the Cross*. His Hamlet and Othello were quite appalling, and being very short in stature he was always strutting about in cothurni to add height.

Marion Terry. What an exquisite actress in farce, melodrama, or comedy! Perfect.

Sembrich always unlucky *over here*: in her earlier days overshadowed by Patti and later, though not in America, by Melba, who was very inferior as an artist to Sembrich. Sembrich started her wonderful musical education by becoming a proficient violinist and pianist (studied with Liszt) and appeared in public as an instrumentalist at the age of twelve. She was always a first-class musician, which subsequently materially added to her brilliant success as a singer throughout a very long career. She studied singing under the younger Lamperti (son of the great Francesco L., the famous maestro) at Dresden. She was a real soprano sfogato and was the only perfect representative of the two great rôles of Astrafiamante (Queen of Night in *Il Flauto Magico*) and Constanza (*Il Seraglio*) that I have ever heard. I remember that at a Philharmonic Concert she gave a most brilliant rendering of the appallingly exacting soprano aria out of Spohr's *Faust*—now never attempted. Vocal difficulties did not seem to exist for Sembrich. She laboured under the disadvantage of having a pronounced squint. Curiously enough, about 1890 her voice lost its power (like so many Astrafiamante aspirants) and she in future wisely confined herself to soprano leggiero rôles.

Patti. I have so often written about her that I will confine myself to saying that her Zerlina was like Sembrich's Susanna—perfection, though on the other hand Sembrich's Zerlina fell far short of Patti's, as did her Violetta in *Traviata*, but Patti was blessed with natural advantages—a luscious and rich voice capable of unrivalled tone colour, an overwhelmingly lovely face and figure, and superb aplomb and magnetism. Her voice increased enormously in power as she advanced in years, but always retained its quality: she was no musician like Sembrich but had an unerring sense of phrasing.

Albani started as a soprano leggiero and made her début as Amina at Messina: she was a good musician, and Lamperti asserted that she took more pains than any pupil he had ever taught. Albani was an adequate actress with a charming face, but both her acting and singing lacked spontaneity: like all Lamperti's pupils, she possessed a perfect legato and I have never heard any rendering of "Piano piano" (*Der Freischütz*), "Dove sono" and "Porgi amor" (Mozart's *Nozze di Figaro*) equal to hers. She married Ernest Gye, the Covent Garden impresario, with the result that at the period of your *A la Recherche* the abonnés had rather an overdose of her. Her Church Scene in *Faust* was thrilling and superb with her great vocal opulence, but her garden scene unromantic and her jewel song slightly elephantine. She never looked Elsa like Nilsson, but I have never heard her Elizabeth, Isolde, Senta, or Eva equalled. Her renderings of "Dich teure Halle," the "Liebestod," and especially Senta's Ballad were inspired. Albani was a great *made* (entirely made) artist; even her voice, which originally was of small compass, she graciously admitted in her book she owed to Lamperti, and for some years after she had achieved fame she returned to him every summer for further study. Her success was confined almost completely to England, and she was the last great Festival Oratorio soprano.

Pauline Lucca, gifted with a fine voice and great personality, was a coarse unfinished singer; like all artists who have not studied sufficiently, her success was short-lived. I have never heard Mozart's "Voi che sapete" worse murdered. She was a good, a great Carmen, as her vocal imperfections could be glozed.

Yours aye,
ERNEST HELME

Feb. 12 *Friday.* Disappointed with the St James's revival of Turgenev's *A Month in the Country.* Like Pinero's Mlle Thomé, "over-gowned and over-hatted." Natalia's drawing-room was like Hollywood's notion of an antechamber at Versailles, with Norma Shearer in the offing. What I remember now of Rakitin is the glossiness of his beaver, and not the expression of a natural moral philosopher and a Russian one to boot. Would that shabby young tutor have had us concentrate so exclusively on his plum-coloured velvet paletot, like somebody out of *La Bohème* ? (I heard a man behind me whisper, " When does Tauber come on ? ") Why should the doctor's cheerful cynicism run the risk of being lost in the folds of his cravat ? Why should poor Michael Shepley be handicapped by an imposed nattiness of person and habit in his sincere attempt to portray a stable-haunting, pigsty-smelling Charles Bovary ? He came into the Café Royal afterwards in the clothes he ought to have worn ! Natalia sat among her geraniums looking like Malibran and wearing a creation befitting an Imperial Garden Party. Apart from clever little Isolde Denham, who was allowed to wear gingham, the cast seemed as much aware of its clothes as we were, thus breaking the first rule of period plays—that the characters shall not be period-conscious. I see from the programme that the settings were the work of Michael Relph, " by permission of Ealing Studios." They looked it. It is no defence that Natalia, a great lady as opposed to Tchehov's *bourgeoise*, would be a shimmer of silks and satins in a drawing-room whose marbles and lacquers hit the eye. Once more I resort to our old friend the *optique du théâtre*. It is possible for a piece to be so brilliantly acted that it makes no sense, as anybody must realise who has seen an all-star performance of *The School for Scandal*. That is not seeing the wood for the trees. At to-night's performance the characters were outshone by their settings. This is not seeing the trees for the wood.

Feb. 14 *Sunday.* The Sunday papers continue to be my favourite hunting-ground. Take this passage from Ivor's article to-day :

It needs but the slightest acquaintance with history and the arts which mirror history to appreciate the encouraging fact that nations, even nations of enormous size, can be radically altered in character and temperament within a few years. It is perfectly obvious, for example, that between Turgenev (1850) and Tchehov (1890) Russians changed very little : the mood of all, who had any chance to be idle, was one of graceful inertia and humorous fatalism. These people could hardly organise an apple-cart, much less a cherry orchard. Now the children of these lotus-eaters and of their feckless amusing servants have proved themselves able to achieve, after crippling losses, one of the greatest feats of organisation in all the history of war.

I wonder! The Revolution wiped out the lotus-eaters and replaced them by their serfs, the children of Lopahkin, possibly, but certainly not of Vanya, Sorin, Gayef, and others of the nostalgic brood. I cannot find argument here for the change in Russian nature Ivor is talking about; both kinds were in existence, and one superseded the other. It is like saying that the English nature changed under Cromwell. It didn't. For a short time the Puritan element came to the top, after which it was again superseded by the rakes. Or would Ivor maintain that the rakes became Puritans under Cromwell and changed back into rakes at the Restoration? On the same page William Glock quotes with approval Henry Boys's statement over the wireless: "Melody is a governing factor in Bartók's music." Moiseiwitsch, when I told him this at his recital to-day, said, "Yes, like hitting the piano-lid with walking-sticks." My best laugh, however, is provided by Tom Harrisson, who seriously suggests that the B.B.C. should follow up its broadcast of *War and Peace* with a full-length radio version of Proust's *Remembrance of Things Past*. What impression the Baron de Charlus would make on the London suburbs I hesitate to think.

Later. I heard to-night that the crowd besieging the St James's during the last two days has been so big that the management is about to set up a second box-office. Does Ivor really think that the public which has persistently stayed away from a masterpiece has suddenly become masterpiece-minded? Doesn't he realise that the motive is purely political and because the play is from the Russian, and that if Turgenev had been German, Italian, French, or even Swedish the piece would have played to empty benches?

Feb. 15 *Monday.* To-night's jamboree at the Regal in honour of the Free French made me ashamed of being British. It all goes back to something Henry Morley wrote in 1858 in his *Journal of a London Playgoer*. He was writing about the difference between the attitude to serious drama of the

French and ourselves. "There must be a deeper earnestness than plays can demand, in whatever serious thing Englishmen are to look at without exercise of that sense of the humorous which is part of their life; so natural a part that every man is in every grade of society regarded as a bore who lacks it; and the very phrase with thousands even among our educated men for not finding a thing acceptable is 'seeing no fun' in it." To-night's proceedings began with a superb news-film about Churchill's visit to the Near East, to be followed presently by a Workers' Choir and a first-rate 'short' depicting the recent activities of the French on land, sea, and in the air. All this constituted a dignified proceeding; and then the management, distrusting our ability to remain serious, thought fit to introduce a Donald Duck item which would have been inappropriate even if it had been amusing. But it was not in the least amusing. And it was received in complete silence by the highly distinguished audience, for once in a way ashamed of our national taste.

Then came the big thing of the evening, *To-morrow We Live*, a film about Occupied France which never moved beyond Surbiton except possibly for an excursion to Balham. I am getting tired of these schoolboy stories, a mixture of good Wallace rising to better Henty. And the Englishness of everybody! Godfrey Tearle as the French mayor led a party of martyrs to the place of execution with the unruffled suavity of an English country gentleman showing his guests the way to the dining-room. The only character who was convincingly French was the baker's wife, played by Yvonne Arnaud, who is French. The Nazis were much better because most of them were played by Germans. Why not use French players to play French parts? An English actor with his "Mossoo" this and "Madarm" that remains inescapably English; a French actor, however broken his English, remains ineluctably French. Our French guests were very polite about it all afterwards; what they thought is another matter.

***Feb.* 16 *Tuesday*.** According to Samuel Butler, man grows like the things he eats. If that is so, it has been going on a long time. A newer peril is that man may grow to resemble the things he looks at. It is an appalling thought that the minds of film critics should grow like the films they criticise. The normal film-goer never thinks about what he sees on the screen; it is seven o'clock when he goes in and half-past nine when he comes out, which is all that matters. But the film critic who has to make an article out of the wretched stuff must give at least some part of his mind to it. At least half the attention I give to any film is spent in trying to find a peg for an article about something else. To-night's affair at the New Gallery permits of a divagation so marvellously happy and so miraculously apt that I am grasping it with both hands. The film, says the preliminary 'literature,' is all about Marlene as a miner's doxy, and the action takes place in Pittsburgh. Now Pittsburgh is the town in which Duse died. "Yes?" says the reader. "What about it?" Only that it revives the old question as to how much of Duse was genius and how much guff.

I have been looking again at Arthur Symons's book. In this I read how she reached "a supremacy in art, so divine in her pure humanity, so mystic in the spiritual sense of the word, and so pathetic in her humility, which has rarely if ever been equalled, and which could never or rarely be surpassed." Symons quotes with approval another disciple: "She was doubly the chalice. To the mystery and exaltation of her art were added a strange element of aloofness, which made her a great person in the case of another drama which we call Life." Let us see now how Duse comported herself in that other drama which we call Life. On the same page I read: "A banquet was given after her last performance by the Italians residing in New York in Duse's honour, at which the whole company was present, but the guest of honour's place was vacant. She refused; she knew what a vexation it would be to hear the speeches, so she remained alone in the hotel with a book, which was much more to her taste." Is this grave discourtesy to her compatriots and hosts to be taken as an example of that spiritual mysticism and unsurpassable humility? Or is it an instance of the "strange element of aloofness"? Am telling readers of the *Tatler* that there is an element of aloofness in their film critic, who, knowing what vexation it would be to hear that film dialogue, decided to remain at home with a book, which was much more to his taste.

Feb. 17 *Wednesday.* A passage in *The Merchant of Venice* to-night (Frederick Valk at the New Theatre) struck me as a perfect picture of Leo :

> But hear thee, Gratiano :
> Thou art too wild, too rude, and bold of voice ;—
> Parts that become thee happily enough,
> And in such eyes as ours appear not faults ;
> But where thou art not known, why there they show
> Something too liberal. Pray thee, take pain
> To allay with some cold drops of modesty
> Thy skipping spirit ; lest, through thy wild behaviour,
> I be misconstrued in the place I go to,
> And lose my hopes.

" Skipping spirit " is exactly Leo. Many a time and oft I have taken the old thing to some pie-faced dinner party, promising myself that if he behaves properly at dinner he will be invited to play in the drawing-room afterwards. I generally arrange to sit within frowning distance of the old boy, after which I experience increasing agony. During the earlier stages of the meal he will sit like a model for Humpty Dumpty's Impenetrability, but I know that presently the dam will burst and something will be said which will blow the hostess out of the room. I remember one occasion on which the talk came round to Cora Pearl, and I told the guests how when she played in *La Belle Hélène* her abominable French set the audience on a roar. Somebody saying I was mistaken and that Cora had never appeared on the French stage, Leo could hold himself in no longer. He said, " Of course James is right. She appeared at the Variétés in 1867, and my dear aunt, who was a great friend of hers, sang in the chorus." At this revelation of low life some of the guests sniffed audibly. But Leo went on : " Some people have said that my aunt was a whore. I deny this. She was not a whore ; she had lovers, which is a very different thing. Sometimes one lover, sometimes two. I dislike over-statement. My aunt was never a whore ! "

Feb. 18 *Thursday.* George Harrap telephones me this morning that owing to a windfall he has got enough extra paper to print a small second edition of *Ego* 5. This paper shortage means that orders for books are pouring in with which publishers just can't cope. Taking what appears to be a short view, they don't seem even to want book notices. At least, I can see no other reason, unless they are boycotting me, for the extraordinarily small supply to hand during my term as book critic to the B.B.C. Not more than two or three a week. The result is that to-day I had to talk about something else, and I chose Quotation. Here are some bits which rather pleased me:

> When a man tells me that a good writer or a good speaker quotes either to show off or to save himself trouble I recognise the . . . well, unthinking mind. A few days ago we had an example of quotation at its finest—Mr Churchill in his speech to the Eighth Army congratulating them on their fourteen-hundred mile trek. He said that they had
>
> Nightly pitched their moving tent
> A day's march nearer home.
>
> Are we to think that the Prime Minister was flaunting his familiarity with the works of James Montgomery? Or that he could not have put the same thing in his own words? No. Mr Churchill is the greatest orator this country has possessed within living memory. He has a genius for coining apt, memorable, witty, and moving phrases. But he knew that no words which he could have invented would have stirred those boys like the words of the old hymn. Hearing them, lads from the fields, factories, and coal-mines, men from all walks of life, forgot the African Desert, and saw once again their native hills, beloved dales, and familiar city streets. . . .
>
> Say that I, a speaker and writer in a lower class, end a chapter on the Beauties of Nature with the words:
>
> To me the meanest flower that blows can give
> Thoughts that do often lie too deep for tears.
>
> It affords the educated reader pleasure to recognise the last lines of Wordsworth's *Ode on the Intimations of Immortality*; while the less instructed reader is presented with an exquisite thought beautifully expressed. If he is anything of a reader at all he will sense a quotation, and if he wants to know where that quotation comes from he must go to his Dictionary of Quotations and look it up. The reader who is not willing to go to this trouble is not a reader at all. He is putting books in the category of whist-drives or the pictures. . . .

No critic cares or knows whether one sort of twaddle is better or worse than another. No critic of music cares tuppence whether Nightingales in Berkeley Square are better worth listening to than Bluebirds over Dover. No critic of painting cares whether you prefer the picture of a perambulator holding up the traffic and entitled "His Majesty the Baby" to that one about a little boy measuring himself against a Newfoundland dog and saying "I'se Biggest." No literary critic cares whether you put the story of the mannequin who went into films and won fame in a night in front of that one about the manicurist who bestowed her hand upon the Marquis. Tripe is tripe all the world over, and in every art there is nothing to be said about tripe.

A good writer does not write entirely for the public. He writes in the first place to please himself, just as a good painter paints in the first place to please himself. A good writer is not going to be debarred from saying of Mr Shaw's passion for standing on his head that though this looks like madness yet there's method in it, just because the grocer's boy has never heard of Polonius whose phrase this is, or the play of *Hamlet* in which it occurs, and all he knows of Shakespeare is that "'e wos the bloke wot wrote the plot for that picture Norma Shearer was in . . . wot was it, naow? Rowmeo and Jewliette." . . .

Will the world want to abolish the aristocracy of birth? Perhaps. The aristocracy of wealth? Maybe. The one aristocracy which no war, no revolution, no change of government or constitution will try or want to alter is the Aristocracy of Art and Intellect. It is the only true Aristocracy in the world. I have no doubt that some of my listeners will find this unpalatable. But truth is truth, and a thing does not become untrue because it is difficult or unpleasant to believe, or true because it finds easy and agreeable acceptance. Anybody who stands before this microphone doing my job to-day is here to tell you what he, as writer and critic, holds to be the truth about books, not what he thinks it would flatter you to believe.

Feb. 19 *Friday.* Take, as Mrs Beeton would say, a Voice belonging to an innocent who behaves like Lamb's friend, George Dyer, but is a very Dr Pepusch at the spinet. Mix this, as Mrs Beeton would continue, with another Voice, this time a feminine one. Attire this organ in what Fielding describes as "Stays and Jumps," and let her that owns the Voice wear gauntlets and carry a riding-whip. To these add yet a third Voice, lighter and shriller than the last and belonging to a maiden niminy-piminising in white muslin and a corner but ready to take a hand in that waltz-time terzetto in which, in this kind of musical play, all emotional crises are ultimately resolved. Add some vanilla-flavoured, reminiscent Viennese music, bespeak dialogue without wit, see that the clowns are unfunny, dress the show well, keep the lights full on, allow to simmer for three hours, and your unsophisticated audience won't care whether you call the thing *Old Vienna* or *Old Heidelberg*. To-night's was called *Old Chelsea*. Actually these honey-coloured, jasmine-scented jamborees are not susceptible of criticism. " Methinks," said the Gauntlet towards the end of the second act, " you did wrong to come." Methought this was addressed to me. Metook the hint.

***Feb.* 22**
Monday. Lunched at Herbert Morgan's charming flat in Lowndes Close. Why they have to re-name these old mews I don't know. I left the Savage Club ten minutes before the appointed time and was twenty minutes late. Not only my taxi-driver but all those he asked failed to know the whereabouts of this Close. The other guests were Princess Marie Louise, Dame Lilian Braithwaite, my old friend Mrs Hudson, and H. E. Wortham. Herbert wanted me to organise some sort of celebration for Lilian, but she, with a very proper modesty, declined to have anything to do with such a proposal, adding that the honour she had recently received was more than sufficient.

***Feb.* 23**
Tuesday. It is nearly three in the morning and I am still trying to solve the riddle of *Itma*. Given that the desire to *épater le bourgeois* argues respect for bourgeois opinion, the basis of humour must be reason. Reason on its head, keeping strange company, moving in the wrong direction, produced Euclideanly to absurdity—but always reason. Groucho Marx, Peter Arno, Damon Runyon—all these are masters of a logic which they have made their own. I hold that the essence of farce is a commonplace background, since if this is lacking enormity ceases to have meaning. The jokes in *It's That Man Again*, the dreadful film with which the Tivoli reopened to-night, have no roots. They are fantastications of nothing. There was a moment when the " char " looked as though she might be going to do a funny thing. This was when

she shook her mop in the face of somebody bawling about melodee, and it seemed as if she might ram it down the singer's throat—a thing I have wanted to see happen to every musical-comedy heroine for the last thirty years. But nothing happened. The great difficulty is that there is nothing droll about Tommy Handley as there is about Bob Hope or Jack Benny. If to-morrow Tommy were to put up for Parliament I should have no hesitation in giving that forthright, sterling countenance my vote. No danger of any funny business there! I tried all possible expedients. I said to myself that if I had spent the previous twelve hours driving a ten-ton lorry I might find this film more entertaining than the road between Slopville and Sludgehampton. But, alas, I am not a lorry-driver. I reminded myself of the B.B.C.'s boast that last year twenty million people listened in to *Itma* regularly, and hurried back from their pubs and their clubs to do so. My one difficulty in believing that these twenty million people cannot have been wrong is that I do not believe that any twenty million people can be right about any matter concerning art. If this were so, then Charlie Kunz would be a greater pianist than Moiseiwitsch, and Vera Lynn a better singer than Gerhardt. Perhaps the solution I am trying to find is contained in a letter received this afternoon from a young woman in Bristol who writes, "I suppose you couldn't help me to like Shakespeare? I do try to, but when I read his plays my mind goes blank, and when I see them acted I go into a coma." To-night's film was certainly one for the cataleptic.

Feb. 24 From to-day's *Times*:
Wednesday.

> A young Indian seaman refused to be cross-examined by a woman barrister at Liverpool Assizes yesterday. "Mind your own business, I good boy. I no talk to girls," he said. The barrister tried again, but the Indian would not answer her questions, persisting that he "did not talk to girls." "You are a good boy," said Mr Justice Singleton, "but this lady is a good girl. You must answer her questions." "Oh! she good girl," said the Indian. "Very well, I answer questions."

I think the Indian was right the first time. The woman barrister looks and is ridiculous; and has been so since Portia. Neither should the sex sit on juries; no woman will believe that a witness wearing the wrong hat can be giving the right evidence. In the arts feminine activity should be strictly circumscribed. Novel-writing, yes ; play-writing, no. Acting, singing, dancing, yes ; painting, no. Conductor on a bus, yes ; on a concert platform, no. As for composing, the idea is as ludicrous as to suppose women capable of writing epic poetry. As executants, a little harp-playing, the Mendelssohn Violin Concerto, and the easier piano concertos of Mozart. I approve of women as nurses, governesses, cooks, laundresses, contortionists, typists. I disapprove of them as doctors, lawyers, critics, chauffeurs, butlers, and bar-tenders. They should not be allowed in public-houses except in that special department known as the Ladies' Bar ; nor in any man's club. Young women should not attend boxing matches or clutter up theatre foyers ; harpies and crones should not haunt snack-bars and brasseries, sitting around and looking, as George Mathew said to-night, like old tennis balls.

Feb. 25 *Thursday.* Dined with Sir Pelham Warner at the Conservative Club. A man of great charm and with enough modesty to go round a whole room. During dinner I contrived that the talk should all be about cricket. Among other things, P. W. said that he once asked Ranji who in his opinion was the world's greatest batsman. Ranji replied, " On a hard, fiery wicket, W. G., easily. But on all wickets, Charlo." (This was Ranji's name for C. B. Fry.) Warner talked a lot about Fry. How he saw him make his record long-jump, how the measurements were taken over and over again, and how the crowd shouted at the announcement of a world record. He remembered the famous match between Oxford and Blackheath. How Fry could run like a stag, and how if he failed to tackle his man it didn't matter because he could run after him, catch him up, and tackle him again. How in the match against Blackheath Fry outran and out-manœuvred the opposite backs and scored three tries, grounding the ball each time in the dead centre of the goal-posts. How after the match the crowd, cheering, followed him all the way back to Wadham. A lot more talk about the great cricketers of the past. In return for which I told him the story of how I bowled out W. G. Grace first ball. I was seven at the time, and the family was staying, I think, at either

Blackpool or Llandudno. I was playing cricket on the sands, and presently a huge man with an immense black beard offered to bowl to me. He did not seem much good at bowling on the soft pitch with a tennis ball, and I hit him all over the place. Being a well-brought-up little boy, I presently asked whether the gentleman would not like an innings, for which purpose I handed him my tiny bat. I bowled, the ball hit on a flat pebble, and instead of bouncing slithered between the two walking-sticks which were the wickets, the Great Man having played about two feet over it! (He would have ricked his back if he had done anything else.) I remember my father, who was sitting on the promenade pretending to watch, but actually reading the *Manchester Guardian*, laughing a great deal and telling me that I had bowled the world's greatest batsman. Which, let me confess, seemed to me a perfectly natural thing to do. After dinner we adjourned to the smoking-room, where I thought it only fair to exchange P. W.'s shop for mine, as he is very keen on the theatre. Wherefore I trotted out some of my best anecdotes, and the evening ended all square.

Feb. 26 Letter from Brother Harry:
Friday.

> I say categorically, *in toto*, *ab initio*, *ex officio*, and *pro bono publico*, that *Itma* is the funniest thing ever heard on the radio. I don't demand drollery from Handley. I demand, expect, and get unrelated surprises—a riot of utter nonsense. Wake up, my dear brother! Since *Itma* is inevitable, relax and enjoy it!!! I trust that this attack upon your wrong assessment of this funny thing DISCOMBOBULATES you. A good word used by Roosevelt recently at a Press Conference.

Also note from Howard Young, delightful fellow and part-author of *Itma*:

> MY DEAR JAMES,
> I have just read your attack on us all. You are a wolf in Charles Lamb's clothing.
>
> Bless you.
> H. Y.

And at lunch to-day Morris Harvey, Billy Leonard, Charles Heslop, and Reggie Purdell—comedians all—tell me that *Itma* is the greatest thing ever heard on the wireless, "provided," says Billy, "you listen to it seven or eight Sundays running. To anybody coming fresh to it, it would be meaningless." Unlike half the population of these islands, I have no use for delayed humour. "It's me noives," I suppose.

Feb. 27 *Saturday.* Have turned Kligerman over to Ibbs and Tillett. The transfer took place at Gwen Chenhalls's. Gwen is a really remarkable woman. After giving us lunch she announced that she was going to a matinée, leaving the port and cigars to me and a fair field for Alexis. Presently Ibbs and Tillett arrived and resolved themselves into a charming couple, John Tillett and his wife, formerly Emmie Bass. Alexis was in smashing form and tore into everything like a master, J. A. having taken care that he should play nothing below *molto vivace.* I laid great stress on his twenty-two years, and I. and T. were duly impressed, saying how refreshing it was to meet a young pianist who was something more than a virtuoso. At which I kept a perfectly straight face. "He will go far," chorused I. and T. And I replied, "In your hands, who can doubt it ?"

March 1 *Monday.* Letter from George Richards ends, "I must conclude now as the wireless is about to give us Hindemith's *La Chapelle Wesleyenne Engloutie.*"

March 2 *Tuesday.* I am tired of being told that the age is changing for the better. It seems to me that *plus ça change, plus ça* gets worse. A flight sergeant writing a fortnight ago to say that he had been given £10 to spend on books for his Mess and what did I recommend, I gave a list, in the *Express* of course, of sixty-six books in the Everyman series. Since when protests have poured in by every post. "For many months I have been running a library of about a thousand volumes in a military camp. Our shelves contain much of which you would approve. Scott, Trollope, Swift, Palgrave, Whitman, Southey, and even the egregious Gleig are there. I have consulted the 'issue book' and find that most of these volumes have never yet been borrowed at all." . . . "Our Mess has already got all Dickens's novels. I would say that it had no use for Dickens except that eight of the volumes are propping up the Mess piano, which is minus a leg." . . . "My two sons, who as flyers have both lost their lives in this war, would have shrieked at the notion of recommending Boswell's *Johnson*, *Gulliver's Travels*, or *Tom Brown's Schooldays*."

March 5 P.c. from Jock:
Friday.

DEAR JAMIE,

I've been re-re-rereading one of your *Contemporary Theatres* (in an unendingly agreeable search for your notice of *The Seven Who Were Hanged*), and it will interest you to know that, in spite of some recent bickerings and differences of opinion, I continue to think your dramatic criticisms transcendently superior in discrimination, gusto, raciness, poetical feeling, and power of language to any that appear in the other periodicals. That is sincere, but it is also second-hand. Word for word, from "transcendently" down to "periodicals." It was said, in the course of some differences and bickerings, to William Hazlitt by Wainewright the poisoner.

JOCK

March 8 To Brighton again on Saturday. Stayed at Charles
Monday. Smith's and spent the week-end revising and rewriting *Responsibility*, which Hutchinson's have offered to re-issue. Cut about one-fifth of the book, and am satisfied with the result. About one o'clock this morning there was some machine-gunning outside the window. As the Germans obviously know about the curfew for pedestrians, they must have been aiming at the motor-lorries lining Charles's street. Nobody hurt and no damage done. Coming up in the train I make one of my sudden decisions. This is to leave the Villa Volpone. I cannot get taxis, and the climb to the Tube kills me.

March 9 Have taken a flat of seven rooms, first floor with lift,
Tuesday. behind the Prince's Theatre, ten minutes from Piccadilly Circus, £250 a year. In accordance with my vow never again to live in a flat and move out of it at the same time, also take a suite at Kensington Palace Mansions for the next three weeks. Eighteen guineas a week and, I hope, an economy in the long run. Move in. As the rooms in the new

flat are enormous, swap some small pictures of which I am tired for a big canvas in the Modigliani manner by a young man aged twenty-three, one Adrian Ryan. Noticed this at the Redfern Galleries some time ago, and coveted it. To the Scala for a Jewish Jamboree: a review of Jewish Sailors, an indifferent performance of Andreyev's *The Seven Who Were Hanged*, an auction-sale, and a piano recital including "Rachmaninoff's Prelude in C flat minor" (*sic*)! In and between these activities find time to write a new preface to *Responsibility*.

March 10 *Wednesday.* Took "Plum" Warner—it would be affected not to call him this in spite of the short acquaintance—to the revival of *What Every Woman Knows*. He pretended that to be escorted by the critic of the *Sunday Times* was like being taken into the pavilion at Lord's by W. G. Grace. A crowd of snotty-nosed little autograph-hunters, finding nobody else to pester, fastened on me. Which, said Plum, reminded him of Bradman after a big score. And for the rest of the evening he called me Don. All rather old-worldly and pleasant, like the first act of *Mary Rose*. At supper I asked Plum which was the best innings he had ever played. He said, "One against Lancashire at Old Trafford in which I scored 6. The next best was 24 in the second innings of Gentlemen v. Players, at Lord's, in 1913. The wicket was extremely difficult—very hot sunshine pouring down on a pitch which had previously been saturated by rain—and the bowlers one had to face were Barnes, from the Pavilion end, and Tarrant, from the Nursery end. I remember saying to Barnes on the fall of a wicket, 'You know, Barney, it's an intellectual treat trying to play you on this wicket,' and he smiled and said, 'How long are you going to stay in?' and I replied, 'That depends on you.' I have a distinct recollection of almost every ball. Barnes was getting so much spin that he literally tore pieces out of the turf. In the end I was caught at the wicket off him—a most magnificent catch by E. J. ('Tiger') Smith, of Warwickshire. The ball off which Smith made this great catch was a leg-break of perfect length, which jumped very quickly and just touched the thumb of my right-hand glove. Tiger, standing at his full height, caught the ball in front of his right eye, and I remember saying to him afterwards, 'I think I was a bit unlucky because most wicket-keepers would have ducked, and I should have scored a four.' In his description of the match the *Times* correspondent was kind enough to make some very complimentary remarks about this innings of 24 of mine, and finished by saying, 'Had Mr Warner not been playing so extremely well he would not have touched that beautiful leg-break from Barnes, off which Smith made his great catch.'"

March 12 *Friday.* Delivered the revised *Responsibility* to Hutchinson's. Should like to think that my first novel was "a piece of the headlong felicity sometimes brought off by writers when young, just because they are young; their spirits are high; their delight in the way others write is so fresh that they copy with gusto, not tamely; they are not yet dulled by finding they scarcely know anything." Montague, of course.

March 13 *Saturday.* Apart from Nervo and Knox, absolute drolls now in their heyday, to-night's show at the Coliseum, *It's Foolish but It's Fun,* was below standard. Some fairish dancing. Bruce Carfax sang an empty ditty about an empty house, which turned out not to be empty but to contain a young woman, alone in a drawing-room, reciting for her private edification the last speech in *Cavalcade.* The female singers had either no voice, or, when they used the microphone, too much.

March 14 *Sunday.* A trifle homesick for the Villa Volpone. Strange how one can have a hankering for places one has hated! Cheered up as soon as my houseboy came in with the papers. William Glock in immense form:

> Kreisler and Toscanini could play Berg's violin concerto to a factory audience and give maximum pleasure.

And again:

> The demand for Tschaikowsky's first piano concerto and other favourites has been created, to some extent, artificially. Programmes, broadcast talks, popular books on music have misled millions of listeners into believing in one basic kind of musical thought. We feel at home with the drama of themes and tonalities, but hopelessly lost in the spiritual climate, say, of the sixteenth century. Such a climate could help to teach us that the purpose of music is not to play upon, or even to express for us, our emotions.

I see. But in what order is the factory audience to be *extasiè'd* ? Berg first and then Byrd ? Or vice versa ? If the factory hands of to-day are anything like those I knew at Nelson, Berg will get the Byrd all right.

Saw the new Orson Welles film, *The Magnificent Ambersons.* Lovely photography, half of it pure Cecil Beaton, the other half so Renoir-ish that you can't tell whether the dying mother is passing away in a bedroom or a conservatory. Muddled, aggressively dull story, with a couple of sisters carrying on *à la* Gunhild Borkman and Ella Rentheim. A strange jumble of Ibsen and Eugene O'Neill with a dash of Euripides. And does Welles really think that a high-mettled hackney could be driven past the new spitting, hissing motor-car without going over the hedge and taking the gig with him ?

March 15 *Monday.* Talking the other night to X at the Club about De Quincey, and remarking that I really knew very little about him, this morning I received David Masson's excellent Memoir of the great essayist in John Morley's " English Men of Letters " series. This sent me to J. R. Findlay's article in the *Encyclopædia Britannica* (9th edition). Several passages in this seemed to me to strike very near home, substituting " less than genius " for " genius." I quote :

> He was careless to recklessness in the use of money, and debts and pecuniary difficulties of all sorts hung about him through the greater part of his life. There was, indeed, his associates affirm, an element of romance even in his impecuniosity, as there was in everything about him ; and the diplomatic and other devices by which he contrived to keep clear of clamant creditors, while scrupulously fulfilling many obligations, often disarmed animosity, and converted annoyance into amusement. . . . It is useless to complain of his having lavished and diffused his talents and acquirements over so vast a variety of often comparatively trivial and passing topics, instead of concentrating them on one or two great subjects. The world must accept gifts from men of genius as they offer them ; circumstance and the hour often rule their form. . . . To the appreciation of De Quincey the reader must bring an imaginative faculty somewhat akin to his own—a certain general culture, and large knowledge of books, and men, and things. Otherwise much of that slight and delicate

allusion that gives point and colour and charm to his writings will be missed. . . . He was a born critic, a logician by instinct and culture, a student by choice, a scholar by right of conquest of the stores of many minds. . . . Habits of study the most lawless possible in respect of regular hours or any considerations of health or comfort, the habit of working as pleased himself without regard to the divisions of night or day, of times of sleeping or waking, even of the slow procession of the seasons, had latterly so disinclined him to the restraints, however slight, of ordinary social intercourse, that he very seldom submitted to them. . . . The natural bent of his mind and disposition, and his life-long devotion to letters, to say nothing of his opium-eating, rendered him, it must be allowed, regardless of ordinary obligations in life—domestic and pecuniary—to a degree that would have been not only culpable, but very highly so, in any less singularly constituted mind.

March 16 *Tuesday.* Adjudicated at the R.A.D.A. annual performance, the other judges being Athene Seyler, Hilda Trevelyan, and Owen Nares. The general level of acting poor, and except for the Shakespeare a wretched lot of plays, including a wholly unfunny farce by the Sierras and a long and dull slab from *St Joan.* We awarded the Gold Medal to Jacqueline Maude for her Queen Margaret in *Richard III.* (Robert Atkins said afterwards that he was willing to give this young woman a job to-morrow, and Cochran told me that he looked in his programme to see what professional actress they'd got to eke out the amateurs.) Nevertheless our decision was highly unpopular, the audience wanting Woolfe Morris, a seventeen-year-old with a pronounced squint which did his Richard Crookback no harm and will help him in more modern gangster parts. His Richard was lively, amusing, and well thought out, and the boy showed more promise than anybody else. But the terms of reference said "best performance," not the most promising one. It was hinted by Authority that we might like to change our minds, but I refused and carried the others with me. If the R.A.D.A. wants us to guess who will be the best performer in five years it should say so. The Queen attended the performance, there was tea afterwards, and I was presented.

Playing bridge to-night at a club of which I am not a member,

I drew as my partner a refugee whose manners were ruder than the laws of sanctuary permit. The game hadn't been long in progress when he said, " Partner, to me it appears you do not know a heart from a spade ! " I replied meekly, " Partner, how right you are ! " I then dealt, and, picking up an amazing hand consisting of eight top spades, Ace, King of diamonds, Ace, Queen, ten of clubs, and no hearts, unhesitatingly bid *six hearts*, vulnerable. This was doubled on my left, my partner re-doubled, and I proceeded with every sign of satisfaction to go down six tricks : which, at five shillings a hundred, cost me £8 10*s*. 0*d*. I couldn't afford this, but it made the other fellow lose £8 10*s*. 0*d*. as well, which served him right. I said, " Sorry, partner, but that comes from not knowing a heart from a spade." He apologised, and for the rest of the evening refrained from criticism.

March 17 *Wednesday*. What a very odd fellow Labouchere must have been! I have just come across an interview given by him to a prominent newspaper on December 23, 1888 :

> In my theatre I trained all the celebrated actors and actresses of to-day—Ellen Terry, Irving, Lionel Brough, Beerbohm Tree, Mrs Bernard-Beere, Charles Wyndham, Brookfield, Kate Vaughan, and the present idol of Australia and America, Nellie Farren.

For which Labby was sharply rebuked by a writer in a rival paper :

> Mr Labouchere seems to be under the impression that if he had not gone into the theatrical business, we should never have had some of our best actors and actresses. It is quite true that Mr Henry Irving, Mr Charles Wyndham, Mr Lionel Brough, Miss Ellen Terry, and other present notorieties appeared at the Queen's Theatre, but they had acted before. If the proprietor of *Truth* really told an interviewer that " in my theatre I trained all the celebrated actors and actresses of to-day," his invention must be pretty well on a level with his impudence.

" They had acted before " is a gem.

March 18 *Thursday*. To Watford with Michael Redgrave, Richard Attenborough, and Peter Noble to decide who should be the town's Beauty Queen. Enormous hall. Jazz-band never stopped making the filthiest noises. Film cameras. Lots of perspiring, fulsome little Jews manning both. No fee, and no sign of a drink. Why I do these things beats me; I suppose I think it's a contribution towards winning the war. Back about 1 A.M. and sit up till four listening to Michael and trying to keep up with him intellectually.

March 19 *Friday.* That nimble, irrepressible, but withal quiet wit, Spike Hughes, was in great form at the Club to-day. The conversation turning on J. B. Priestley, he murmured, "Post scriptum homo tristis est."

March 20 *Saturday.* Went to the St James's Club and played piquet with Dickie Rivière, now a major in the Grenadiers, a delightful man whose grandfather fought against us at Waterloo. Won 17*s.* 6*d.* at half a crown a hundred. Afterwards to see Peter Page, laid up with gout and saying, "I wish I had the pluck of old Lord K——. I met him just before the last war, hobbling up the Haymarket. I hailed a cab and helped him in. He said, 'Thankee, m' boy. Tell the fellow to drive to Hyde Park Corner and stop at the first blonde.'"

March 21 *Sunday.* Cancelled to-day's Brains Trust engagement at Wendover. Seizing a moment to look at my instructions, I find:

> At the completion of the Session you will be able to catch the 9.02 from Wendover, which arrives at Baker Street, 10.17 P.M. To catch this train will be rather a rush. . . .

In plain English, I shan't catch it. Even if I do, the train will be late, which means that I shall be stranded at Baker Street with no way of getting to Kensington except on foot. The other members booked to go down are Bill Barrett, P. P. Eckersley, Edwin Evans, Norman Ewer, Walter Legge, and A. G. Street. And I decide that if E.N.S.A. can't get the petrol to take these brains to wherever they're wanted and bring them back, it must get along without mine. I remember on the last occasion, also a Sunday night, arriving at Waterloo late, running up the stairs and being dragged into the last train in a state of semi-collapse. It isn't good enough. I will go anywhere and do anything for anybody provided there's transport and drink. If not, then not.

Fatras. From a letter. "You should know better than to try to teach a politician what he doesn't know. It's a whole-time job and hopeless. Like teaching a snake to walk. Even if willing to learn he is unlikely to have the necessary apparatus."

March 22 *Monday*. From Tom Harrisson's Radio article in yesterday's *Observer* :

> Then Schubert's Trio in B flat, quite neatly played, until James Agate took the air for the Thursday book talk. I prefer my Agate written ; his jerky voice fails to make the ear feel friendly. I'm glad Frank Swinnerton takes over this series again as from next Thursday. After Agate, half an hour of soft-syncopater Geraldo and his team of no less than a dozen crooners.

Let's hope they made the Harrissonian ear feel friendly !

Contrast this letter from my old friend, Eiluned Lewis, author of *The Captain's Wife* about which I talked last Thursday :

> *Rabbit's Heath Cottage*
> *Tilburstow Hill*
> *Bletchingley*
> *Surrey*
> *March* 19*th*
>
> DEAR MR AGATE,
>
> I rather think that you have been saying some very pretty things about me and *The Captain's Wife* this week, but it is difficult to be quite sure. A press-cutting agency has sent me a small slice of the *Daily Express*, carefully excluding the name of the writer, but no one, I feel certain, save yourself would be so reckless and so generous as to mention Miss Mitford, Mrs Gaskell, Miss Austen and me in one breath. Then there was yesterday afternoon when my little housemaid of fifteen came running breathless to tell me : "They're talking about your book on the wireless !" Alas, the talk was almost ended ; I was just in time to hear a quotation, but a quotation from my own words read in a voice that I think I should recognise in the middle of the Sahara ; your voice, bringing back so many Saturday afternoons in Fleet Street, and the burning question of cross-headings.
>
> I write from, of all astonishing places, the Bedford Hotel, Brighton, where Graeme and I have come for the week-end. The reason for this is that as well as possessing the observation

of Miss M., the tenderness of Mrs G. (I liked that bit especially), and the accuracy of Miss A., I also have a cough like Emily Brontë's.

Yours sincerely and gratefully,
EILUNED HENDREY

Here is one ear that feels friendly !

March 23 *Tuesday.* Coming into the bar at the Savage, I heard somebody say, "My dear fellow, he's as movable as Easter!"

They were talking about my new address and my migratory habits in general. Since 1918, when I first came to live in Kensington Gardens Square, I have changed my abode seventeen times—including country houses and seaside bungalows—eighteen if you count the little general shop in South Lambeth. What fun that shop was—at the beginning at any rate. As the place was called Warren's Stores, I commissioned a large weather-proof oil-painting to hang outside over the door, showing Mr and Mrs Rabbit and their little bunnies trooping back to the warren. I never saw anybody raise his eyes to it! My brother Harry, who had the flat over the shop and used to help behind the counter on Sundays, had an idea to attract passers-by after the place was closed for the night. This was an illuminated toy theatre with films and legends changed weekly, all charmingly boxed in and lit. We stood together on the other side of the road to watch the result. Not a soul took the slightest notice! It was then that I made the discovery that the masses cannot be educated, that there is nothing to be done about them, and that all time and effort in that direction are wasted. Until I gave up the shop I lived in Warwick Street, Pimlico; Hogarth Road, Earl's Court; Great Ormond Street; Portsdown Road, Maida Vale; and Ladbroke Gardens, though in what order I cannot remember. What I do remember was an evening in the last place. I was consuming a frugal meal of kippers and green Chartreuse when my landlady announced that a "gent 'ad come to dinner." And in walked Joe Beckett, the boxer! He had, of course, mistaken the house. Then came the flat in West Street, over the chapel of John Wesley. It was here that Leo Pavia first came to see me. In those days he was for ever fetching and carrying, always provided the stuff to be fetched and carried was liquor. And many were the quarts and quarterns he wheedled out of the landlord at the corner on occasions when my credit was over-strained. It was here that Sybil Thorndike came to tea, and the tea for some obscure reason was a deep violet, and Sybil insisted on going out to procure some more condensed milk. A frequent visitor at the time was Gerald Barry, who wrote in his review of my first *Ego* :

> When I first knew him (which was when he first invaded London, seeking fame and tempting fortune) he looked to my inexperienced eye much more like a successful coachman than a would-be dramatic critic. He might have had all Hazlitt and Balzac at the end of his pen, but what he had on the end of his nose was pure Tony Weller. The champagne was to come later ; in those days it was coffee essence out of a chipped mug with condensed milk and no spoon. The coffee, poisonous at any time, would be doubly undrinkable on Tuesdays, for that was the day on which his theatre article had to be finished, and this meant ardours and endurances prolonged throughout the day and on into the small hours, labouring portentously to produce twelve hundred words of sparkling spontaneity while the coffee congealed, turned green.

Then I moved to 55 Doughty Street, and anybody who has read *Gemel in London* will know what life there was like. By this time I had begun to collect some furniture, and it was here I took the first of my long line of personal attendants—to wit, one Freddie Webster. For years Freddie was the spearhead of my defence against duns—which may not make military sense, though debtors will know what I mean. I also owe to F. something I can never repay—his insistence that I should receive in audience a young tousled tramp who had walked and hitch-hiked three hundred and fifty miles from Scotland to see me, and whose name was Alan Dent. But I have written of all this in *Ego*. Then I became rather grand, and moved to a really handsome flat in Palace Court, Bayswater, where I gave considerably better parties than I could afford. The usual financial crisis cropping up, I retired again to Kensington Gardens Square, and later to a tiny flat, again in Doughty Street, in the house in which Sydney Smith lived. Things looking up once more, I moved to Antrim Mansions, N.W.3, and this I left to take up residence at the Villa Volpone. In and among all these I have had houses at Beaconsfield and Barnet, and bungalows at Westcliff and Thorpe Bay. In my wildest moments I have never contemplated the affixing of more than one plaque to mark the location and duration of my residence. But I should like to put it on record, for the benefit of the L.C.C. when the time comes, that it was at my first address in Doughty Street that I did my best work and was happiest.

March 24 *Wednesday.* Letter from that good and unassuming actor, Barry Jones :

48 *Campden Hill Square*
W.8

March 23*rd*, 1943

DEAR MR AGATE,

Writing you will not I/you hope become a habit. I've wanted to send you the enclosed for some years, as a matter of fact. It has always been a sort of standard for me, and whereas throughout my career in various countries, and from *Hamlet* to *Charley's Aunt* as might be said, I have only ever had the kindest treatment from critics—I have always felt " Well, whatever may come some day, nothing can beat this, and Kean should worry ! " I may say that the review being a Guernsey one has also always warned me never to appear on my native heath. I have no English, Scottish, Welsh or Irish blood in me, it's all Channel Island, but at that, I'd hate to appear before them. I can expect no one not from the Islands to realise how the local character shouts through the notice, any more than I have found anyone beyond a sister of mine who realises and enjoys the tremendous and affectionate leg-pulling of Victor Hugo in *Toilers of the Sea*.

We are not, as a rule, " amused " in Guernsey ! Nor have I found in my beloved and bloody profession much humour about bad notices. And no interest from them in the enclosed.

But I thought it might interest you if you did not already know it. If it is old history—apologies.

Kind regards,
BARRY JONES

CRITICISM OF EDMUND KEAN IN AN UN-NAMED GUERNSEY PAPER IN MARCH 1813

Last night a young man, whose name the bills said was Kean, made his first appearance as Hamlet, and truly his performance of the character made us wish that we had been indulged with the country system of excluding it and playing all the other characters.

This person has, we understand, a high character in several

parts of England, and his vanity has repeatedly prompted him to endeavour to procure an engagement at one of the theatres in the metropolis. The difficulties he has met with have, however, proved insurmountable, and the managers of Drury Lane and Covent Garden have saved themselves the disgrace to which they would be subject by countenancing such impudence and incompetency.

Even his performance of the inferior characters of the drama would be objectionable, if there was nothing to render him ridiculous but one of the vilest figures that has been seen either on or off the stage. And if his mind was half so qualified for the representation of Richard III, which he is shortly to appear in, as his person is suited to the deformities with which the tyrant is supposed to have been distinguished from his fellows, his success would be most unequivocal.

As to his Hamlet, it is one of the most terrible representations to which Shakespeare has ever been subjected. Without grace or dignity he comes forward ; he shews unconsciousness that anyone is before him, and is often so forgetful of the respect due to an audience, that he turns his back on them in some of those scenes in which contemplation is to be indulged, as if for the purpose of shewing his abstraction from all ordinary subjects.

His voice is harsh and monotonous, but, as it is deep, answers well enough the idea he entertains of impressing terror by a tone which seems to proceed from a charnel-house.

Edmund Kean, the greatest of English tragedians, made his all-conquering first appearance in London on January 26, 1814, less than a year after the notice in the Guernsey paper. The Guernseyites had no reason to love Kean, who left them in disgrace. Cast for Charles I in some impossible melodrama, Kean, who hated both part and play, got drunk, sent word that "King Charles had been beheaded on his way to the theatre," and sat in the auditorium hurling insults at his substitute. Everything about Kean—his drunkenness and debauchery, his pride and his bad manners—tells me that he was a six times better actor than Macready, "moral, grave, sublime."

March 25 *Thursday.* George Robey and his wife gave me lunch at the Ivy. Both in great form. The occasion was the presentation to me of George's famous cane. To match the Chaplin one. Am having both mounted on royal blue velvet and glass-cased. During lunch George recited *sotto voce* the Ghost's speech in *Hamlet*, Act I, Sc. 5, beginning " I am thy father's spirit " as far as " List, list, O, list ! " and taking up again at " Sleeping within mine orchard " down to " remember me." Word-perfect. I asked him when he had studied this. He said, " Before I went on the stage. It is to this speech that I owe my enunciation." Like Barry Lupino, George complained that the modern audience is radio-conscious. " They don't laugh at one joke for fear of missing the next." Manifest nonsense : they laugh as much as ever when they're really tickled. I cannot tell these old dears that the ageing " comic " is a tragic figure. Why this should be so I do not know, unless it is that all low comedy is a sowing of wild oats which embarrasses at sixty and disgusts at seventy. Or does there come a time when the natural humour in a man evaporates ? It was so with Harry Tate, who had become quite unfunny long before he died. So, too, with Arthur Roberts ; and I remember Little Tich at the old Alhambra leaving the stage with hardly a hand. Yet in his heyday he was wont to send the house into delirium. There is melancholy here.

A firm which boasts of having removed pianos for sixty-five years reports that owing to the narrowness of the stairs and the too-sharp right-hand turn, the big Broadwood that Princess Marie Louise asked me to take care of for the Three Arts Club won't go in.

March 26 *Friday.* *Strike a New Note* at the Prince of Wales's brings to town Sid Field, a really first-rate comedian whose material is clean throughout—a change from the modern sort which relies almost entirely on dirt. The new man is very, very funny—a mixture of George Carney, Billy Bennett, Adolphe Menjou, and Harry Tate, with a dash of Ouida's guardee. The rest of the show—all juveniles—is poorish. And what would Vesta Tilley have thought of a young woman impersonating a Piccadilly Johnny in evening dress with a top hat and her golden hair hanging down her back ?

Broadwood's telephone that they have been moving *their* pianos a lot longer than sixty-five years and that my instrument *will* go in.

March 27 A letter concerning Amanda Ros :
Saturday.

As you have so frequently mentioned Amanda in previous *Egos*, I have often wondered how much you know about her—apart from her masterpieces ?

My knowledge of her dates between the years 1891 and 1895. Her maiden name was Annie McKittrick. She was of very humble origin. Her husband was station-master at Larne Harbour for many years. My own age at that time was between 11 and 15. My eldest brother was a classical master in a Belfast school ; we lived just outside Larne, and so made the acquaintance of John and Amanda by reason of daily train journeys.

Now, this brother had journalistic leanings and a very flippant pen, and had a local reputation for being a most erudite literary gent—which in fact he was. It was natural, then, that Amanda should bring her manuscripts to him to read and touch up where necessary. Fortunately his sense of humour overcame his scholarly criticism. He read them, and after nearly passing out through sheer amazement concluded that there never was and never would be anything like them. When she asked him for his opinion he gravely assured her that her literary talent was superb, and that it would be presumption for anyone of his humble limitations to attempt to paint the lily or alter half a line of it. The question then arose as to finding funds to publish, and here my brother came to Amanda's aid together with another friend of his—and they put up the money. Both of them are referred to under different names in complimentary words in the books. Now, in *Delina Delaney* there is a long preface in which she quotes at full length a critique written by Barry Pain which appeared, I think, in the *Ill. London News*. My brother bought up a lot of copies, ostensibly to assist sales, but in reality to circulate to his friends—and it was he who sent it to Barry Pain—with the results you know.

Amanda was a great big ombompom-bosomed virago with a vitriolic tongue—which brings me to ask whether you have read her *Poems of Puncture* ? The subject-matter consists of her idea of de-bunking her local enemies by pouring out bucketsful of vitriol on them under disguised names. The village solicitor, the grocer, certain farmers, an auctioneer, and many others come under her lash—all duly and finally "punctured." Incidentally, she wrote a magnificent fist—which indicates her character and forcefulness. She fancied herself among the immortal novelists, and posed accordingly.

To see her stately walk up the aisle in church on Sundays was a week's entertainment—especially as she always made a point of being very late, so that all would be in their seats to admire her. Have you ever heard the local Antrim accent ? Raucous and harsh and scarcely understandable by, say, an Englishman ? Well, that was her native tongue, but she took steps to improve her accent, and tried to talk like the gentry—with results as outlandish as her books.

I have reason to remember her. I am deaf in one ear. It happened thus : I was a polite little boy who took off my cap to the Rectory ladies and others who might be ranked as our local middle class ; but we just didn't cap what we called "common people"—and the station-master was in this category—he took a tip from my father at Christmas each year. Well, one day I was passing her cottage, when she was airing her bosom at the gate. I passed without looking at her. She called me back ; "Young man, don't you know who I am ?" I allowed diffidently that I did. "Then why don't you take off your cap to a lady ?" In the innocence of my young heart and as the result of my (snobbish ?) upbringing, I blurted out, "But *you* aren't a lady." My meaning was obvious, *i.e.*, to *me*, but what I got in reply was a stunning left to the ear which sent both me and my cap into the middle of the road. And that ear has never functioned since. We never solved the question of her pre-marital antecedents—whether she had been a maid in a gentleman's house, or where she picked up her intimate acquaintance with the lives and doings of the titled folk for her books.

My second brother acquired Amanda's entire output from my eldest brother's library—all autographed by her to him. My nephew has the whole range, inherited from my brother, but he realises their monetary value and won't part with them to me.

If you were to over-hit your third stroke at the twelfth hole here, your ball would come slap into my den, so may I look forward to that happy event, in the hope that you will come and retrieve it—and we'll have a drink on the strength of it.

The only thing I enjoy about moving is re-hanging the pictures and seeing how well they look in their new setting. Spent most of to-day re-arranging the books—a nerve-racking, back-aching business. Do I keep or throw away Pope's translation of the *Iliad* ? In addition to Charlie Rogers, up on leave, had a small army of helpers during the last three days. One of them threw an epileptic fit, and had to be held down and so on. Lasted about ten minutes, throughout which Leo went on typing !

Extraordinary man! Has been pestering me lately with drafts of letters to his landlord suggesting that if he is let off his arrears he will pay the rent regularly in the future. "The thing, James, is to come to an arrangement. Once you've come to an arrangement, you can decide whether to keep it or not."

March 28 *Sunday.* The highbrow at his most riotous. A fortnight ago William Glock was advocating Berg's violin concerto for factory audiences. This morning he writes:

> The violin concerto is based upon a twelve-tone series which is so arranged that it forms minor and major triads and also anticipates the opening phrase of Bach's Chorale, "Es ist genug," which is used at the end of the concerto.

Unless my old county has completely changed during the last forty years some juicy Lancashire equivalent of "Es ist genug" will be forthcoming about two minutes after the start of the concerto!

Find Hutchinson's cheque for *Responsibility* waiting for me at the Club—£150, of which Stanley Rubinstein gets half. As the work of revision took less than a week, this isn't too bad. Yesterday I sold Hutchinson's another book, based on Clement Scott's Newspaper Cutting Book (*Ego* 3, p. 232). 70,000 words. £150 down, of which I am giving Leo £25 for copying and typing. S. R. takes half the rest, leaving me with £62 10*s*. 0*d*. *and the book to write*, which is the snag. Without these two books I must either have remained moored at Swiss Cottage or been financially sunk. Once again I have proved that Demand creates Supply (*Ego*, p. 23). Which reminds me that last week I parted with my little horse. Before the war I refused £1500 for him; last week, on Stanley's urgent recommendation, I accepted an offer of £100, which just about pays for his keep during the last three and a half years. I am enough of a mathematician to realise that it is exactly as though, on the day the war started, I had taken Ego out of his box and made a present of him to the first passer-by. "Champagne and ponies give me the zest which I give back in my work. When the day comes that I cannot indulge the second of these passions—for at a pinch I can give up the first—that day and every one which succeeds it will be a *dies non*." So ended the first chapter of *Ego*. Fortunately I still have my filly, Lady Viking.

March 30 *Tuesday.* The piano goes in.

March 31 *Wednesday.* My houseboy departs. This leaves Leo and me with seven rooms and two sets of offices to quarrel in. However, such curtains and carpets as I possess are now up and down, the books are sorted and the pictures hung. And Leo has promised to doss here until I get somebody else. Wherefore I wander round the flat feeling fairly cheerful and repeating to myself Ambrose Bierce's

> Spring beckons! All things to the call respond;
> The trees are leaving, and cashiers abscond.

April 1 *Thursday.* Yesterday afternoon I ran into Freddie Gibson, an intelligent young man and book-lover who, some years ago, looked after me for a time and left to take a job with a publisher, which he still holds. On his telling me that he was not too comfortable in his lodgings, it was arranged that he should take one of my too many rooms. This should settle the loneliness problem. All I ask now is that people will stop picking quarrels with me, and that my phobias will leave me alone for a bit.

Fatras. Was shown the MS. of a highbrow play about Chopin. "The curtain goes up and reveals an empty stage. Enter George Sand, unperceived."

April 2 *Friday.* Am in love with the new flat, and particularly the entrance-hall. It is here that I have established the Musée Sarah Bernhardt, consisting of the two immense photographs, some smaller ones, a framed holograph letter to my brother Edward, and a tiny picture of Rachel to keep Sarah in her place. The 40-foot length of the hall has this further advantage, that whenever I get embroiled with Leo I shall be able to quote Filmer Jesson in Pinero's *His House in Order*: "Shall we choose another topic—or would you prefer to walk?" But what I am most enjoying is my regained freedom. I am without a servant for the first time since West Street in 1921, and the relief is immense. I am not clever with dependants and the fault is mine. I think of them as equals; what they want is to be treated like hirelings. I remember one of my chauffeurs saying on the day he left: " Look here, sir, let me give you a tip. Don't ask your next chauffeur if he minds driving you to such-and-such a place. He *can't* mind! Tell him where you want to go, and to be bloody quick about it. The bloke knows what to do, and there's no argument!" Am promised a charwoman in the near future. Perhaps I am not yet quite adept at or with the electric cooker. Told Billy Leonard something of my troubles with it. He said, " Yes, I know. You turn the wrong knob and get *Itma*."

April 4 Sunday. To the Dorchester for an Interim Austerity Dinner of the Stage Golfing Society. In the absence of the First Lord of the Admiralty responded for the guests. Sat between Basil Cameron and Dickie Rivière. Both in good form, Dickie telling me how, motoring with Peter Page from Bath to London just before the war, they betted on whether they would encounter more beards or traction-engines. The traction-engines won! Peter, by the way, is in a nursing-home. Clifford Mollison made a witty speech, and I don't think I was bad. Much of the pleasure of the evening was destroyed when, at the end, I had to hang about outside for over an hour waiting for a taxi.

April 7 Wednesday. One of my favourite passages in Marlowe is the one in which Tamburlaine, parading his sons before him, addresses them as follows:

> But now, my boys, leave off and list to me,
> That mean to teach you rudiments of war;
> I'll have you learn to sleep upon the ground,
> March in your armour through watery fens,
> Sustain the scorching heat and freezing cold,
> Hunger and thirst, right adjuncts of the war,
> And after this to scale a castle wall,
> Besiege a fort, to undermine a town,
> And make whole cities caper in the air.

But I am tired of that film in which the leader of a Commando returns from a raid on board a destroyer cheek by jowl with his Allied sweetheart while the crew sings the *Marseillaise* to a background of capering gasometers and dancing town halls.

April 8 *Thursday.* I am indebted to an unknown friend for this

EPITAPH ON A PROUD LADY

Underneath this leaning stone,
Moss and lichen overgrown,
Lies her body, still and straight,
That was ever passionate.
The bright mind, her flashing wit
Unto quietness submit;
And her wilful hands are laid,
Trustfully and unafraid,
Where no passion troubleth—
In the steady hands of Death.

The author is Ronald Charles Scriven, of the *Yorkshire Observer.*

April 9 *Friday.* Years ago Francis Perrot, of the *Manchester Guardian,* 'covered' a poetry reading by Edith Sitwell at the Ashburton Club in Red Lion Square:

For one ordinary man who had wandered in it was all sufficiently surprising. . . . One heard of such remarkable things as "fruit buds that whimper," and "skies like potting shed," and also of the "sensual aspects of the hairy sky." Even if it had been in tune with the proceedings the intruder would not have dared to indulge in what Miss Edith Sitwell calls "harsh and crackling rags of laughter," or even in "saturnine cold laughter," or, again, in "wood-green laughter." A Philistine might have burst into Golder's Green laughter, but there would have been a riot. At the end one retreated into the "old pig-snouted darkness" in Red Lion Square, having had a good mixed time.

Wonderful stuff! To-day's black-out is "pig-snouted."

April 11 *Sunday.* Here is some of what I say to-day in the *S.T.* about the Henry James centenary:

"If there be such a thing as a mere bun." If there be such a thing as mere birth Henry James was born a hundred years ago next Thursday. Whether his books are dead, or were ever really alive, is not for me to determine. But there can be no doubt about the birth, the still-birth of the plays. The story of the disgraceful reception of *Guy Domville* (St James's, January 5, 1895) has been told too often to need repeating here. G. B. S., newly seated in his chair at the old *Saturday Review,* declared James's dramatic authorship to be valid and his plays *du théâtre* " when the right people are in the theatre." My impression is that the first and third acts were good, with a very poor middle act. Some years later, under another sovereign, James had what it is permissible to call another go. The piece was a comedy called *The High Bid*, and it was produced at His Majesty's Theatre. I have before me a plain account—if there be such a thing as a plain account—of the proceedings by the London correspondent of the *Manchester Guardian*. It tells me that the thing put up for auction was the heir to an English title, and that the bidders were a young Englishwoman " of fluttering commonness " and a young American lady. (Here I am reminded of Bessie Alden in *An International Episode*.) " She finds herself at the end of the play bright, high-voiced, and so inimitably expert, getting the whole thing, but also indubitably ' got ' herself," continues the London correspondent. The house was so full that the critic thought Mr Forbes-Robertson might put on the play for a run. Mr Forbes-Robertson thought otherwise. Whenever I think of James's plays I recall his Mrs Highmore, the popular authoress in the story called *The Next Time*. This absurd lady had *views*. " A success was as prosaic as a good dinner : there was nothing more to be said about it than that you had had it. Who but vulgar people, in such a case, made gloating remarks about the courses ? It was by such vulgar people, often, that a success was attested." Mrs Highmore yearned to be, but, of course, only once, an exquisite failure like the great Ralph Limbert. " There was something a failure was, a failure in the market, that a success somehow wasn't." Poor James, like Limbert, had no difficulty in obtaining the thing a later age has called the *flop d'estime*. " He'd be vulgar, he'd be rudimentary, he'd be atrocious : he'd be elaborately what he hadn't been before," resolved Limbert, who, however, couldn't keep to his resolution. Neither could James. Did the author of these two plays ever reflect, I wonder, that a success in the theatre is something a failure somehow isn't ? Did his dramatic soul come to know Keats's Melancholy ? Or was it among his cloudy strophes hung ?

April 13 A lady in Campden Hill Square writes :
Tuesday.

As you were always the companion of a drawn-out Sunday breakfast, perhaps you will forgive the informality of this address. If you can bear to read further I think it will interest you. Plump Mrs Green of Hillgate Place, having fought for fish in Billingsgate, was cleverly frying it behind her counter. Plomp! into the batter-trough. Hiss-s-s into the cistern of boiling fat. Slight pause for conversation. And out the fish comes on to the dish in the basket to take home. From the large handsome book at her side she tears out a page—"I can't read French," she says, and covers up the golden booty. I send you the rescued leaf from the 1849 *Courrier de l'Europe*, which wafted me into an atmosphere of the Royal obsequies of Victoria's Aunt, into the tears of poor Marie pleading for the life of the clockmaker's assistant who made a half-hearted attempt on her throat—I must get some more fish to learn the fate of Louis—and then carried me along to the red carpet, the satin shoes and white gloves of the theatre where Rachel makes her return.

Leo says: "I suppose this means you'll fill your space with a lot more French which you'll be too lazy to translate?" Me, stiffly: "I prefer to give it in the original." Leo: "Why do you insist that your readers can speak French? I don't suppose half of them can speak English!" Whereupon I decide to give neither the French nor the English. The omission will be the reader's loss, not mine. The article they will never read is signed "Théophile Gautier"!!!!

April 14 *Wednesday.* The talk at the Club turning on clichés, Constant Lambert bet me five pounds I wouldn't begin a *Sunday Times* article with "Much water has flowed beneath Thames bridges." . . . This was too good to be missed, and I have begun my article for Sunday, "Much water has flowed beneath Thames bridges since at the Scala Theatre I saw my first performance of *Abraham Lincoln*." Not a large audience to-night for the revival at the Playhouse. Reading Hazlitt in bed afterwards, I came across this passage in the essay *On Egotism*: "The only great man in modern times, that is, the only man who rose in deeds and fame to the level of antiquity, who might turn his gaze upon himself, for on him all eyes were fixed as his majestic stature towered above thrones and monuments of renown, died the other day in exile, and in lingering agony; and we still see fellows strutting about the streets, and fancying they are something!" But, bless me, how little the Corsican looks to the eye of to-day when measured against the backwoodsman! I thought Herbert Lomas's Lincoln

Photo Sidney W. Newbery

Willie Clarkson

Photo Tunbridge-Sedgwick

Bust by Sarah

(*See p.* 195)

magnificent, and that he got right down to what Whitman calls "the invisible foundations and vertebra" of Lincoln's character. After describing these as mystical, abstract, moral, and spiritual, W. W. goes on to say that "upon all of them was built, and out of all of them radiated, under the control of the average of circumstances, what the vulgar call *horse-sense*." Lomas hit this note perfectly in the middle. Guthrie had the tact to get rid of the two Chroniclers, major bores who used to talk too much before the play began, too much while it was going on, and too much when it was over.

April 17 *Saturday.* On Monday last I opened the door to the incarnation of Miss Skiffins, complete with green gloves. It announced in an excessively genteel voice that it was the lady who was going to "do" for the gent on the first floor. Meaning me. Since I hate people who are above their jobs I took an instant dislike to the incarnation, but, discovering that its husband had been blind from birth, struck a bargain at 5*s*. 6*d*. a morning, two mornings a week. Whereupon it vanished, and has not been since seen.

April 18 *Sunday.* The flat being empty, I practise the piano for an hour—a thing I have not done since I was a boy. Afterwards cook my own lunch—a thing I have not done for twenty years. Pork Chop. Looking for guidance in my Electrical Cookery Book, I turn up the letter "P," and find any amount of instruction about Peach Gâteau, Petits Fours, Pineapple Souflée, Pound Cake, and Prairie Oysters, but not a word about Pork Chops. Look up Chops Mutton and Chops Pork and again draw blank. However, I manage somehow, and a chunk of cheese crowns a meal as good as any to be had in the West End.

April 19 *Monday.* Pity the old player who clings to the stage long after nature, propriety, and his best friends have hinted that he should retire. You take some young person to see a woman who, only a brief twenty years ago, was a great actress and a famous beauty. The curtain rises, and there is exposed an aged, wrinkled puppet meaning and looking nothing. And the chit by your side is plainly asking herself, "Is *this* the face. . . ." Or you take a schoolboy to see some once-great actor whose gestures might have been limned by Michael Angelo and whose voice you remember as having the surge and swell of some cathedral organ. And what do you behold? An old pantaloon with a sagging paunch and " most weak hams." And you wonder—or do you?—at the schoolboy who wishes you had taken him to the pictures instead. This afternoon I spent an hour and a half of exquisite melancholy looking at Duvivier's *La Fin du Jour*. This film is about a Home for Retired Actors and Actresses. All these Bajazets and Polyeuctes, these Alcestes and Don Diègues, these Andromaches and Paulines, Célimènes and Angéliques—all the cast have the heads and masks of actors and actresses. See one of these *cabotins* pacing a boulevard and you will say to yourself, " Aha, an old trouper." The women, too have that undeniable actress-look; you would never mistake them for dressmakers, or procuresses, or even *femmes du monde en décadence*. Bad actors too, *tragédiens de province*, stars in Lyons or Marseilles, players who have borne the brunt of a great art with nothing to support them except their love and their loyalty. Figures in a dream-world who in their heyday lived on and in their dreams, and who, now that their sun has set, continue to subsist on the recollection of those dreams. How well we know Jouvet's St Clair, that matinée idol of some forty years' standing, now in the unconcealable sixties. Is his luxuriant hair dyed? We think it must be. Are his eyes a little strained? We feel that he is beginning to need that monocle he has used with such dashing effect. Is his step a little less springy? Yes, and we would hazard that the throat, were we allowed to see it, has become a little more stringy. Is this would-be embodiment of youth and romance as jaunty as of yore? Yes, but pitifully so. And therein lies his tragedy. There is a fine sensitive performance by Victor Francen of a sincere actor called Marny, the equivalent, one feels, of our own Hermann Vezin, whom every one admired and nobody went to see. Cold, unimpassioned, perfect in technique, Vezin could have met—and defeated—any argument advanced against his acting. The only difficulty was that when Vezin was the leading player no one seemed to want to visit that particular theatre. Duvivier alleges some private emotional sequence as the explanation of Marny's failure. But we know better. He is just the correct, unsuccessful player. In the centre of the picture is Cabrissade, grandly played by Michel Simon. Here is that well-known phenomenon, the man who is an artist to his finger-tips *off* the stage. What fire! What *fougue*! What temperament! What a finished and consummate comedian! And all who know Cabrissade know also that nothing happens when he is *on* the stage. But nothing at all! *For the man can't act.* And therein lies his tragedy. It is these failures—Duvivier stresses the point—who are most in love with their calling. The stage is their world and without it they cease to exist. They spend their working years rehearsing for the success they are never to have, and their years of retirement lying about the triumphs they never had. Of such is Cabrissade, a buffoon with the mind of a monkey, but, alas, without the monkey's power of mimicry. He is your *bon enfant* possessed of the traditional *cœur d'or*, and it is this which is remembered in the speech at his graveside. "No," says the failure Marny, "no, my good friend Cabrissade, I will not, in this funeral oration which you penned yourself, proclaim you to have been a man of talent. You never possessed one shred of talent. But you loved the theatre passionately, and it is for that that we mourn you."

April 20
Tuesday. Letter from John Byron, who, some months ago, badly ricked his back while acting as P.T. instructor in the R.A.F.:

c/o Playhouse
Oxford

18*th April*, 1943

MY DEAR JAMES,

Many thanks for your card—though I should have liked it better if you had told me more about yourself—but I was touched that you should have written when you were so busy.

I have spent the last few months seeing specialists about my back. Interviewing Service doctors is as satisfying as carrying on an intimate conversation with somebody who is at an upstairs window when one is in the garden. "They" have now decided that they can't cure me, so they are going to invalid me out of the Service.

I shall go to Oxford that you love so much—and collect my things—also my scattered wits. Then I shall see if I can get work with Guthrie or Casson—it's hard to know where one can learn one's job these days. That's all my news.

By the way, here's a new and true story. A chap here used to work in a draper's shop in Chester. One day a lady came in to buy some material for a dress. She eventually chose mauve georgette. Taking up a large piece she draped it round the shoulders and over the head of the startled young shopman, saying, "And how do you think you would look in *that* at six o'clock in the morning?" He discovered later that the lady was Mrs Patrick Campbell.

Take care of yourself and let me see you when I come to London.

Yours as ever,

JOHN BYRON

To the Arts Theatre to-night to see a new comedy by Hugh Burden, *The Young and Lovely.* All about a modern hussy whose commonness of mind negatives all sympathy with, and interest in, the complicated movements of her heart and thighs. Good performances by Joyce Heron and Catherine Lacey as the baggage and the wife, but the evening saved as a whole by Margaret Scudamore, mother of Michael Redgrave and a good actress in her own right (school of Mrs Kendal), and Denys Blakelock, who gave a wonderful performance of Leo Pavia in a make-up half-way between Verlaine and W. G. Grace.

April 22 *Thursday.* J. B. Priestley's *They Came to a City* is that boring thing, a propagandist play. In this city they have, it seems, abolished capitalism. The happy workers—the upper classes have, of course, been done away with—spend their playtime dancing and singing in sunny public parks. Like the underground at Piccadilly Circus on Saturday night after the pubs close.

April 23 *Friday.* "Times change," as some antique or mediæval josser observed. And went on to say that we change with them. This does not apply to the English, who are unchanging, except in one respect. Sixty years ago W. S. Gilbert was pouring scorn on

> The idiot who praises, with enthusiastic tone,
> All centuries but this, and every country but his own.

Gilbert could not write this about the Englishman of to-day. Certainly not about our young intellectuals who have a flair for knowing all about to-day and nothing about yesterday, all about Bing Crosby but nothing about Byng the Admiral; who can jabber about Hindemith and have scarcely heard of Haydn; who go into surrealist raptures over some daub representing a sardine-tail coming out of a daffodil and cannot tell the difference between a Raphael and a Rowlandson; who wallow in Eliot (T. S.) and have never heard of George. "Art," says Gilbert's Bunthorne, "stopped short at the cultivated Court of the Empress Josephine." The young man, and, for that matter, the young woman, of the moment holds that art began with Noel Coward and will end with Noel Gay!

Easter Monday. War-time meals remind me of the Duchess of Berwick in *Lady Windermere's Fan.* "Mr Hopper's father made a great fortune by selling some kind of food in circular tins—most palatable, I believe—I fancy it is the thing that servants always refuse to eat." If only the makers of food substitutes would stop trying to render them palatable! One will probably never know what it is that gives everything one eats to-day that taste of O-Cedar Mop with a soupçon of Flit.

Jock called, partly to see the new flat and partly to borrow a phrase. He is giving up his job on the *Listener*, where he was critic of radio drama, and wants to use Karen Bramsen's farewell to the cliffs of Dover which I was the first to quote: "I quit you wiz despise!" Asked us what our programme would be if we knew we were going to drop down dead at the end of the concert. Leo said the Missa Solennis. And here is my choice:

Overture. *Cockaigne* . . Elgar
Violin Concerto . . . . . Mendelssohn
Symphonie Fantastique . . Berlioz
Interval
Ein Heldenleben . . . . . Strauss

The Hallé Orchestra
Soloist: Norman Neruda
Conductor: Hans Richter

The first piece because I am English and at heart a Londoner. For the second item see *Ego* 5, p. 118. The rest needs no defending.

Finally Jock presents me with the very rare *Theatrical Notes* by Joseph Knight. This begins, to my great delight, with Irving's 1874 production of *Hamlet*, and ends with Tennyson's *The Falcon* (1879) with the Kendals. I am, of course, enchanted with a criticism of Sarah's *Phèdre* which, beginning with one of the flattest pieces of assertion in all criticism, suddenly finds wings :

> What in most members of the company is fine and highly cultivated talent is in Mdlle Bernhardt genius. We are not disposed to plunge into the sea of troubles that awaits those who attempt a definition of the quality thus named. We content ourselves with a bare assertion that the powers of dramatic exposition possessed by this lady reach this point. . . . What the Comédie Française, if it consults its own interests, will do, and indeed does, is to take the gifts the gods provide, and maintain as long as it can a connection that may in time become impossible. [It did.—J. A.] Genius is an uncomfortable and unmanageable thing, and in its association with mediocrity or even with excellence it brings endless confusion and discord. The world seldom knows how to treat it, and still more seldom does it know how to treat itself. None the less it must be left to itself. It is impossible to chain it as a watch-dog to a kennel, or to shut it like domestic cattle in a pen. It is often inconvenient and ridiculous, resembling, as Baudelaire says of the poet, the albatross:
>
> Prince des nuées
> Qui hante la tempête et se rit de l'archer ;
> Exilé sur le sol au milieu des huées,
> Ses ailes de géant l'empêchent de marcher.

May 2 *Sunday.* A busy week. On Tuesday morning I found the title for the book I am doing on Clement Scott's newspaper cuttings—*These Were Actors.* Needs must that I then complete the book within forty-eight hours—which I did ! This precipitancy is an obsession and a mania with me. Anyhow, by three o'clock on Thursday morning I had looked through some four thousand cuttings, made my selections, drawn up a rough draft of the connecting links, and written the preface, though I have no doubt I shall do a lot of titivating later on. Was taken by Dickie Rivière to lunch at the Guards' Mess in St James's Palace ; the Captain of the Guard and my host was Major Craigie, the son of "John Oliver Hobbes." Extraordinarily interesting. Things to be seen which would tease a civilian out of thought. The Lock of the Principal Gate of Hougoumont Farm defended by the Brigade of Guards at Waterloo! Half a dozen officers present at lunch with their womenfolk. Spartan food, not-so-Spartan drink. The ladies departed, we settled down to port, and bridge at which I won 34*s*. On Thursday and Friday nights went to the premières of Noel's two new plays. Worked at my *S.T.* notice all Friday, sitting up half the night, and yesterday up to going to press. The difficulty is the shortage of space and the nécessity of packing the stuff tight so that the reader gets as much for his money as if one had the old couple of columns to splash about in.

May 4 *Tuesday.* Letter from "somewhere in the Midlands."

LEARNED MAESTRO.—After your very high appreciation of Boswell's *Johnson*, I was encouraged to buy the three volumes, fondly imagining that my comrades and self had a rare treat in store! But after wading through half the first volume, best described in the words of Rudyard Kipling as "A coruscating Niagara of Blatherumskite," and enduring the hearty and well-deserved curses and groans of said comrades, I have been forced to hide said volumes, which are now propping up rabbit-hutches at end of garden!

In fairness to others needing 'advice' in their choice of 'nice bright literature' for the troops, the bulk of whom are young and unsophisticated, will you dare to insert this in your column, or a *résumé* thereof?

Yours in frenzied anticipation,
(*Acting-unpaid*) L/Cpl. NOBBY CLARKE
("The Death and Mustards")

May 6 *Thursday.* From the latest novel:

The younger man, dark, martial, and suavely arrogant, bowed over the archducal ring, and rested his great plumed hat on the polished footstool that stood near the chair placed for him. Then, with eyes staring past the Archduke at Messire Tiziano's portrait of the Emperor Charles, he stated briefly the burden of his visit. "I have received messages from Madrid," he told the grave listener in an arrogant tone, "concerning the Prince de Condé."

I look up at my portrait of Willie Clarkson in fancy dress, and note that whether as the Prince de Condé, or *Traviata's* Alfredo, or just Puss-in-Boots, Willie also looks suavely arrogant with his great plumed hat, scarf, top-boots, and lace-frilled knickerbockers. And it flashes across my mind that while most historical novels are more or less absurd, none of them is as exquisitely absurd as Willie.

May 9
Sunday. The Editor of the *Bristol Evening Post* having wired me for 1400 words in connection with the re-opening of Bristol's old Theatre Royal as the First National Theatre, I spend the morning dictating some reminiscences to Leo. Rather pleased with " Manchester, that centre of life and art, civic culture, Hallé concerts, and all the rest of it, has allowed its Theatre Royal, where Irving played Jingle and Robert Macaire, to fall into the slough of picturedom. My admiration for Bristol is the measure of my disappointment with my native city."

May 10
Monday. My old friend B—see *Ego* 3—having moved up from Cairo, writes, " After all, Tripoli is 1500 miles nearer the Tottenham Court Road."

Wrote 2000 words on *Venice Preserved* for *These Were Actors*, dutifully gazed at a rubbishy picture at the Empire, and traipsed out to Holloway to open a civic exhibition of paintings ! The last a *corvée* accomplished with, I think, reasonable grace.

May 12
Wednesday. Wrote *Tatler* article on Monday's silly picture, and then trundled down to Bristol for the re-opening of the old Theatre Royal. Pious aspirations by Lord Keynes that this may be the first step in decentralising the drama. (Lord's cricket will always be better than village.) Performance of *She Stoops to Conquer* with Sybil, who has this in common with Mrs Siddons—she is not a comic actress. Clowned Mrs Hardcastle to-night like an adenoidal—always her refuge in comedy—amalgam of Hermione Baddeley and George Graves. Bristolians giggled and Londoners goggled. But then I suppose Sybil couldn't resist being in at a " do " like this, seeing that it is so praiseworthy a " do." She has the heart of a fire-engine, and should be protected against herself.

Sat up late arguing with Bertie Farjeon and Leo, who both want the wireless to be wholly cultural. To me the idea that a man who has been working for twelve hours on a demolition squad to make the street safe for me to walk in shouldn't be allowed to laugh at Arthur Askey after his bit of supper, is intellectual snobbery of the worst type. I asked the conductress of the bus which took me to Holloway on Monday whether she found her hours long.

"Not too long."

"How long exactly ?"

"Five till eleven."

"Do they make arrangements to get you home ?"

"Not what you might call arrangements. Have to wait till just after midnight, and then a bus puts me down twenty minutes from where I live. It's not too bad, reelly."

What would be "reelly" too bad would be to prevent this valiant little lady from having half an hour of Bing Crosby before she starts work. Farjeon said he would forbid all crooning, and Leo insisted on compulsory Haydn and Mozart. I think both view-points are insane, and had great difficulty in not telling their holders so. Indeed, I lost my temper, though I hope I didn't show it. (Is this the same as keeping it ?) Cooled down by going over to Cookman and Darlington and telling those august representatives of *The Times* and the *Telegraph* the more recountable of my experiences in Harlem. Had been feeling wretchedly ill and nervy all day, and was afraid I shouldn't sleep. I did, though, like a top. On the way from the station this afternoon called at my assistant typist's for 20,000 words of *These Were Actors* promised me for to-day. Found only 2000 words done. Excuse—a baby at the breast. Was about to fly into a rage when I thought of Mrs Micawber, and wondered how much that harassed, over-encumbered lady would have got done.

May 13 *Thursday.* Lost my temper at the Café Royal. I will not be buttonholed by dirty, intoxicated poets. A man cannot help being a poet. But he can help being unwashed, drunk, and offensive. My intolerance in this matter of drunkenness has a logical basis. I object to giving my attention and receiving in return crapulous, incoherent maunderings. I am not getting my attention's worth. Composure restored when a well-known artist and member of a famous club—which indicated, on my putting up for it, that I should be black-balled—offered to paint my portrait " in the spirit in which Reynolds painted Goldsmith."

May 14 *Friday.* Mrs Micawber being still preoccupied, the typescript of *These Were Actors* doesn't arrive, and I spend the afternoon at Lord's watching some dull cricket. Supper with Michael Shepley, who, as always, restores my spirits.

May 16 *Sunday.* How I hate week-ends ! The typescript arrived late last night, Mrs Micawber having made an effort. To my horror the book runs out at a bare 48,000 words, whereas I have contracted for a minimum of 60,000. This means that I have to go through the material again to cull more extracts. Spend the morning doing this, and am now on fire to have the result typed. Realising that no one works on Sundays except me, and my friends all being engaged, I spend the afternoon and evening going through my old clothes, making tea, and pretending I'm not lonely. To the Café Royal for supper, where I get fuddled. Justifiably, because I am willing to work, and there is no one to work with me.

May 19 *Wednesday.* Pinero's *The Second Mrs Tanqueray* will have its fiftieth anniversary to-morrow. Spend the day writing about this for the *S.T.* There is a lot to be said, and it is the devil's own job compressing it into 800 words.

May 20 *Thursday.* Revise and deliver the Pinero article. Sitting in the pictures I realise that I have left out the most important thing I wanted to say. Leave the cinema and hurry to the *S.T.* office, rescue script, start revising, only to discover that the whole thing will have to be re-written. Take it home and work on it till 4 A.M.

May 21 *Friday.* Have misgivings about the pronouncements by two music critics to-day. For instance, the *Times* man has been to the Albert Hall to hear a programme consisting of Busoni's Comedy Overture, Brahms's Third Symphony, and Holst's The Planets. And I read : " One came away astonished at the imaginative power of sound, and glad that those more personal factors involved by a concerto and its soloist were absent. The orchestra and the music were all-sufficient." Then how does the fellow manage to put up with the conductor and the players ? Why not a dark room and the wireless ? Are we to believe that in such a programme Schnabel in the Emperor, or Myra Hess in the Schumann, would be merely good taste misplaced ? Next the *Radio Times*, where I find Ralph Hill saying about the late Leslie Heward : " Although unspectacular in his methods, he was a great musician and a sensitive artist, and it was no doubt owing to these qualities that he passed comparatively unnoticed by the public at large." But Toscanini and Beecham are both great musicians and sensitive artists. Have they passed " comparatively unnoticed by the public at large " ? Just loose expression, of course, because what Ralph means is "In spite of being a great musician and a sensitive artist Heward was unspectacular in his methods, and it was no doubt owing to this that he passed, etc., etc." Poor Heward ! He used to come on to the platform looking as though he had left Moscow in flames behind him. How on earth could the public be expected to know that at that morning's rehearsal he had won the battle of Borodin(o) ! !

Lunched to-day at the Club and was introduced to Hesketh Pearson. Has the air of having acted with George Alexander, and told me he had in fact done so. An amusing fellow. Said of Conan Doyle's two sons, whose permission he had to get for his *Conan Doyle*, that they were " both extremely pleasant. Or rather one was. The other one is in America." About a friend of his, a well-known reviewer, " But of course, my dear chap, he misquoted you. He would misquote anybody, and bear him no malice for it."

May 23 *Sunday.* Wrote 2000 words for a book in connection with Cochran's jamboree at the Albert Hall, *Seventy Years of Song*. Am seizing the chance of pointing out that just as Victorian women had infinitely more grace than the perky, tight-skirted little baggages of to-day, so even the comic songs of the period had a fragrance about which the modern dance-band leader knows nothing. I relate how, between the two wars, I used to spoof even accomplished musicians by playing the tune of " Is yer Mammy always wid ye ? " very slowly, using German words, " Bleibt die Mutter bei Dir immer ? ", and making them believe that this was another Cradle-song by Brahms, a copy of which I had discovered lining a drawer in my bedroom in the Tiergarten Hotel in Berlin.

Lunch at the Savage Club to Pare Lorentz (see *Ego* 3), now a major in the U.S. Air Force and passing through London on his way home from North Africa. Tells me that since the black-out New York has suffered a recrudescence of the old-time " mugging," or robbery with violence. Some twelve to fourteen fatal cases already. George Jean Nathan was attacked on Fifth Avenue some little time ago and got his skull fractured. Very ill, but recovered. P. L. also told me that every cable sent from North Africa to Roosevelt is received by Hitler first, the forwarding agents being charming people who, under the cloak of neutrality, are active belligerents. Told us a story of sitting in the train opposite an Englishman who was so bored with a novel that he tore out each page as he read it and threw it out of the window !

In the afternoon comes Kligerman to play to us the programme of a recital he is giving next week at Hampstead. This runs :

Variations in F minor . .	Haydn
Sonata Op. 57 (Appassionata) .	Beethoven
Nocturne F sharp Op. 15 . .	Chopin
Four Preludes Op. 28 . . .	,,
Ballade F minor Op. 52 . .	,,
Polonaise No. 2	Liszt

" And, when I ope my lips, let no dog bark." When my opinion of an actor is asked I give it, and there's no more to be said. But about pianists I am no Sir Oracle, nor do I pretend to be when Leo Pavia is around. So after Alexis had departed I asked him what he thought. He said, " He hasn't improved in the interval : he's gone back a bit. But I'd rather have a temporary deterioration than that boring level of static excellence one hears among most of the famous people nowadays. His touch is harder than ever : at times one thinks of him as a boxer *manqué*. Shall we ever give him wit, humour, lightness, delicacy, romance, and all the outfit one needs for Chopin and the best Mendelssohn and Schumann? Will he always be a virtuoso and hardly ever a musician? Will he always play Beethoven as if he had a grudge against him, or Liszt as if he were advertising a travelling circus? I despair," said the old creature, absent-mindedly filling his pipe from my pouch, "I despair sometimes of so much immaturity ripening, so many faults being corrected, so raw a recruit becoming an artist—well, in a way he is an artist already, but you know what I mean—the artist both learning and teaching, inspired and inspiring, shedding and acquiring, in a perpetual state of intellectual and emotional progress." To which I replied, "I concur, *mon ami*."

May 24 *Monday.* Finished titivating *These Were Actors*. The book now runs to 60,000 words, of which my share is roughly 12,000 words. I should not have written even these except that I once had a bitter experience in connection with my anthology called *The English Dramatic Critics*. In this book I took selections from some forty practitioners of dramatic criticism between the years 1660 and 1932. "You must string the pearls," wrote Max Beerbohm, and I replied that I had strung them with invisible thread. This, alas, meant that there was nothing for the reviewers to get hold of except the criticisms themselves, which naturally they didn't want to be bothered with. The result was that the book was meagrely reviewed, and, as far as I remember, had a very small sale. Arthur Barker had got it up in grand style with handsome type and beautiful paper. But it fell stillborn from the press, and I have never set eyes on the comely thing since; have ransacked the twopenny boxes in the Charing Cross Road in vain. I suppose what I ought to have told readers was that Addison was an essayist and ditto Steele, Goldsmith the author of a good novel and a popular comedy, Boswell famous for a biography, Leigh Hunt notorious because he went to gaol, Lamb afflicted with a semi-lunatic sister, and Hazlitt the victim of a slut. Then, that Forster was the great authority on Dickens, George Henry Lewes lived in sin with George Eliot (explaining, of course, that G. E. was a female), Henry Morley must not be confounded with John, Joseph Knight had a beard, Clement Scott wore a moss-rose in his buttonhole, William Archer had a sense of humour tucked away somewhere. That G. B. S. is still a vegetarian, Montague was the critic who, on the outbreak of war in 1914, dyed his white hair black, that Grein and Walkley are dead but that Max is still very much alive, and that Allan Monkhouse had a paralysed father to whom he read Walter Scott's novels every night. Had I given the reviewers these tit-bits to get hold of, the book would doubtless have had columns of reviews and reasonable sales. This time I shall not make this mistake.

People who relate their dreams are bores. Nevertheless, here is an old one of mine. It dates back to the time when my mother first took me to London. I enter a chemist's shop to inquire the price of a magnificent piece of old brocade in the window, leaving my mother sitting on the doorstep. The melancholy proprietor bows and says, "Good morning, young gentleman, I am Hermann Vezin." Abashed, I quit the shop in haste, stumbling over my mother, who rises and points to the street. There I behold a procession of grooms in Lincoln green, with cockades in their hats, leading a string of white and dappled palfreys. From wallets slung at their sides they take handfuls of gay-coloured butterflies and launch them in the air. "That," says my mother composedly, "is the new way of advertising croquet on the Thames Embankment!"

I thought of this dream when, in the Café Royal to-night, a total stranger came up to me and said, "Mr Agate, permit me to tell you of a dream I had last night. It was about you. You were sitting on the grass in Regent's Park surrounded entirely by wicker-work and leather straps. I said, 'What caper are you up to now, Mr Agate?' And you replied, 'No caper at all. I am making a luncheon basket for Dame Madge Kendal!'"

May 25 *Tuesday.* After Titivation comes Tinkering. But even this must have an end sometime. Which means that I have finished *These Were Actors*.

From a letter:

> How does one become an Agate "fan"? Concrete and steel girders and jungle-pioneering and big-game would seem to have little in common with dramatic criticism. In other words, I left home in 1902 (*æt.* 22), to go out to Burma. I did not see England again until 1926. Obviously, therefore, the

Theatre did not loom large in my diversions. *Florodora*, *The Country Girl*, and Gilbert and Sullivan were about the extent of my memories. On my first home leave in '26 I just had to go to see *Juno and the Paycock* and *The Plough and the Stars*. I think that it is to these two plays that I trace my first seeds of Agate fever; though you will find it difficult to trace the connection until I explain.

Envisage me, an Engineering Student in Trinity, sitting in Mooney's opposite the Rotunda Maternity Hospital, up to closing-time, in company with James Joyce and Oliver Gogarty. (Joyce doesn't otherwise come into the picture.) Oliver was a medico; he should have been sitting in the students' waiting-room, awaiting his turn for a call to go down to the slums to a "delivery." You know already the fame to which Gogarty has since risen as a writer and Senator in the Irish Govt.

Well, as it wasn't safe to go alone to the appalling slums of Hell's Gate and Tyrone Street, the two of us, armed with our little black bags, sallied forth to the dirty work. (James Joyce has nothing on me in *Ulysses* which I can't locate and verify, yet he never gets down to the appalling scenes which we had to visit.)

Which brings me to *Juno*. When I saw it I sat gripping my toes and with a lump in my throat all the time, and saying, "Those people aren't acting; they are IT." The slums and the poverty and the life of the people all came back to me, and I thought I was gulping and crying and drinking porter out of a broken bottle in a roomful of drunken Dubliners of the lowest order—and that's saying a mouthful—while we drank the health of a husbandless mother and her newborn waif; and I was dazed when I woke up to the fact that I was in a theatre in London going presently to Kettner's for supper.

Yes, *I* got the full flavour out of Juno and Co. but my puzzle is to know, How the hell does James Agate get it, who has probably never seen the real thing as I have seen it, or known the people as I have known them? The answer must be, Those people aren't acting; they're IT.

I won't pretend that I am not flattered.

May 26 *Wednesday*. Feliks Topolski sends me the original of his "Richmond Horse Show," which I admired so much in his last collection of drawings. Whether he knows anything or not about horses I don't know. But he has perfectly caught their spirit and movement. I thought I had forgotten all about shows and showing, and here is the old nostalgia revived.

May 27 *Thursday.* Disappointed with Paul Vincent Carroll's *Shadow and Substance*, the play of which the American critics thought so highly. Turned up what Jock wrote about the Dublin production and find he called the play "a luminous and *nitid* piece of work." As though Gertrude should say, "Good Hamlet, cast thy nighted colour off, and put thy nitid favour on again"! To me the piece is the very opposite of nitid, which, according to my dictionary, means "Bright, lustrous, shining." I find it dark, clouded, and obscure. The subject—whether a man should hold office in a Church who is not a hundred-per-cent. believer in that Church—is of course very difficult. Which brings me to a rule I have always tried to observe—this is, that the more complicated the subject, the simpler must be the way one writes about it. Elaborate writing is permissible only when the subject is daylight-clear. It is permissible to be worried by the implication of a master-dramatist's message, but not by its decoding. One may, or may not, agree that elderly gentlemen should climb steeples at the cost of falling off them. But who doubts that, in *The Master Builder*, Solness does in fact climb a steeple, and does in fact fall off it? The fault in the Carroll play is that one never knows exactly what steeple the Canon is attempting. Joyce Redman exquisite as the little servant. Malcolm Keen can touch nothing without adorning it. But I think he over-ornaments that hollow vase—Candida's Morell plus Stalky's King—which is the Canon. Shouldn't he make us suspect that a man who has about as much spirituality as a parched pea has no right to be in the Church at all?

May 28 *Friday.* Half-way through *Magic Carpet*, the new extravaganza at the Prince's last night, I decided that my notice of Carroll's play wouldn't do, although I had wrestled with it all day. Went down to the *S.T.* office, rescued the script, took it to the Café Royal, wrestled further with it, took it back to the flat, and sat up till four still wrestling. The trouble with the thing was that there were too many words and too few ideas. Too much shadow and too little substance. Had

Richmond Horse Show
Feliks Topolski

Photo Tunbridge-Sedgwick

The Book
(*See p.* 166)

another go at it this morning in the intervals of reading the week's books for the *D.E.*, and writing about them. Shall doubtless have another go when the proofs arrive to-morrow. Who says I am not a spontaneous writer ?

May 30 *Sunday.* Reasonably satisfied with my *Shadow and Substance* article in the *S.T.* to-day. Turn to the *Observer* to find confirmation of my views—and discover Horsnell with less than three inches about the play, and the man replacing Ivor Brown, who is away ill, writing about amateurs at Bradford in yet another tract by Priestley. I don't suppose Bradford amateurs are worse than any other amateurs. But who wants to read about them ? These Theatre-and-Lifeists—Ivor's remarkable name for his column—mean death to any playgoing I care about.

And here is something from Ernest's column in the *S.T.*:

> Score-reading is absolutely indispensable, in more ways than one, to anyone to whom listening to music in the concert-room is something more than a sort of ear-bath, anyone who really wants to know what, so to speak, the composer is talking about. The disparagers of score-reading seem to imagine that the pure essence of a work is embodied in the sound of it, with the corollary that when we have heard the sounds we have necessarily heard the work. I propose to try and show that this is pure delusion, that we can hear a given piece of music a hundred times and yet, if we do not know it also from the sight of the notes the composer has put on paper, get no further than the outer rim of his thought.

Which has inspired me to the following one-act drama :

ERNEST AND HIS COOK

Play in One Act

SCENE : *Ernest's dining-room. Evidence of cerebration everywhere. Over the mantelpiece a portrait of " Béla Bartók's Musical Make-up " by Twerpp. On the piano, whose keyboard has been removed, is the score of Jacob Britain's Concertante for bagpipes, foghorn, siren, road-drill, and Wurlitzer, with a marker to tell Ernest where he left off reading. It is lunch-time.*

ERNEST. An excellent pudding, my love.

MRS N. I'm glad you like the flavour.

ERNEST. Flavour? What has flavour to do with it?

MRS N (*mildly*). Then what is it you like about it, dear?

ERNEST (*testily*). Flavour is mere mouth-wash. [*Correcting himself*] I should have said tongue-bath. What interests me is the thinking behind the pudding. Pray ask cook to write out her recipes for me in future. I hate getting no further than the outer rim of her culinary thought!

CURTAIN

June 1 *Tuesday*. Get up feeling wholly miserable. Spend the morning writing letters. Take George Mathew to lunch at the Club, where Moiseiwitsch joins us, and while he talks I feel better. Back to flat feeling worse. Then says Leo, "Sit down, James, and I'll play to you." And he plays that agonising slow movement from the Hammerklavier Sonata, followed by the Chopin Valse, Opus 64, No. 3—and if the reader doesn't think these two pieces go together he should get somebody to play them both in succession. Like turning from a *Crucifixion* to some exquisite flower piece. (I suppose Ernest Newman would say that a blind man wouldn't be able to appreciate the grace and beauty of the Valse unless he had read it in Braille beforehand.) Then, remembering how Sarah, when she felt faint, used to run up six flights of stairs and go through her wardrobe, I rouse myself and dictate some twenty-six letters, advising young men what to do with their manuscripts, informing widows at Leamington and Ashton-under-Lyne that an illustrated edition of Shakespeare published in 1885 and the second volume of the first edition of *Pendennis* possess no commercial value. And so forth and so on—a complete waste of ink, paper, stamps, time, temper, and nerves. Feeling like nothing on earth, I dress, hie me a cab and drive to Westminster to dine with good Mrs Belloc-Lowndes, who gives me an excellent meal with champagne, after which I fall asleep! Apologise and leave early, that best of hostesses and kindest of friends realising that I am ill. And don't close an eye all night. About five o'clock I am convinced, as of old, that I am suffering from a combination of D.T.'s and G.P.I. Think of making my will, but make some tea instead. Round about six fall into a stupor so deep that the charwoman belabouring the south entry fails to wake me. Better this morning, and thoroughly ashamed of myself for failing to recognise my old friend Dyspepsia.

June 2 Spent the day writing an
Wednesday.

OPEN LETTER TO SIR ALEXANDER KORDA

DEAR SIR ALEXANDER,

First let me say how glad we are to see you back in this country again. We have missed your imagination, your drive, and your personality. But my purpose in writing you is not to pay compliments however well deserved, but to make a suggestion. It is always said that criticism should be constructive. Very well, then, let me construct.

"The future," says Paula Tanqueray, "is only the past again, entered through another gate." Since the war must end one day I suggest that the film industry take a lesson from the last war *now*. That lesson is that the moment hostilities cease, the public will regard war-films as so much poison. They did last time; and they will again this. My suggestion is that one of the big film-producers—yourself for choice—should have a go at Pinero's masterpiece, *The Second Mrs Tanqueray*, which was produced at the St James's Theatre exactly fifty years ago. It is possible that you do not remember the play in detail. Let me refresh your memory.

Aubrey Tanqueray was an English gentleman of wealth and position. In other words, a prig. His first wife was a lady "all marble arms and black velvet." There was a daughter, Ellean, who was sent to a convent in Brussels to be educated. And then the first Mrs Tanqueray died, and Tanqueray made the acquaintance of the exotic and alluring Paula Jarman. But Paula was Mrs Jarman by courtesy only, just as she had previously been Mrs Dartry, Mrs Ethurst, and Mrs Ardale. To cut a long story short—and the point about Pinero's stories is that they never seem long when he is telling them—Aubrey married Mrs Jarman and took her to live at Willowmere, a dead-and-alive hole in the heart of Surrey. Now Paula was mistress of the direct statement. Here, in half a dozen lines, is her impression of life on the Hog's Back:

"And so we shall go on here, year in and year out, until the sap is run out of our lives, and we're stale and dry and withered from sheer, solitary respectability. Upon my word, I wonder we didn't see that we should have been far happier if we'd gone in for the devil-may-care, café-living sort of life in town! After all, *I* have a set and you might have joined it. It's true I did want, dearly, dearly, to be a married woman, but where's the pride in being a married woman among women who are—married!"

Worse still, the married women—who include Mrs Cortelyon, Aubrey's neighbour—have 'rumbled' Paula, and decline to have anything to do with her. Comes Ellean, "hither all dewy from a convent fetched," and, as Montague says of the type, "as breathless and monosyllabic with aghast innocence as if she had run all the way." Ellean had intended to become a nun, and would have done so had not Mrs Cortelyon taken her to Paris, where she met handsome Captain Ardale who had been awarded a V.C. for quelling a mutiny in India.

At this point you are wondering, my dear Sir Alexander, where your picture is to come from. Meaning, where the snag is. The snag is this. Paula, in her pre-Jarman days, had 'kept house' with Ardale! Now in real life, on hearing that her former lover had fallen for her stepdaughter, Paula would just have decamped and turned up at Juan-les-Pins as, say, Mrs D'Urberville. But the theatre being necessarily more romantic than real life, the stage Paula reflects:

"Even now I notice that the lines of my face are getting deeper; so are the hollows about my eyes. Yes, my face is covered with little shadows that usen't to be there. Oh, I know I'm 'going off.' I hate paint and dye and those messes, but by and by I shall drift the way of the others; I shan't be able to help myself." After which, in an access of revulsion, she shoots herself.

And now I hear you ask, "How do you suggest that I cast this drama?" And I reply, "Paula, Marlene Dietrich; Ellean, Vivien Leigh; Aubrey, Cedric Hardwicke." (This is ideal casting, of course, and provided the stable arrangements fit.) I can see you holding up your hands in horror. A heroine who comes to an unhappy end—you faint. Vivien Leigh playing second fiddle—you swoon. I now come to that part of my suggestion which is pure genius: *Vivien does not play second fiddle.*

But first a word about Marlene. She is at the point in her career when she must be looking for rôles suited to her age. (As arclights are more powerful than footlights, so they are crueller.) Paula is exactly right for her. And now brace yourself for the great news. *The heroine of your picture is not Paula. It is Ellean!!!!*

And the happy ending? How are you to manage this? The simplest thing in the world. *There are two Captain*

Ardales. Paula's Ardale was called Hugh and had never been within smelling distance of a V.C. Ellean's young man is called Geoffrey. Which means that St George's, Hanover Square, can be told to get ready. All the same, Paula begins to have twinges. She cannot forget Ellean's face when the Dartry, Ethurst, Ardale, and Jarman cats were let out of their bags. Not suicide, perhaps, but certainly retreat is indicated. And where does Paula retreat to ? Why, to the very convent where Ellean was brought up ! !

Whoever makes the scenario will have a sitter. He will give us, first of all, Ellean as a little girl being shown off to her dragonsome mother's visitors in that chilly drawing-room in Kensington. Pigtail, antimacassars, and all that. Next, Ellean, in her convent " in shady cloister mew'd, Chanting faint hymns to the cold, fruitless moon." Then rapid cut to Jarman's yacht. (" I wonder what Algiers looks like this morning from the sea ! Oh, Cayley, do you remember those jolly times on board Peter Jarman's yacht when we lay off . . . ? ") Then cut to the first Mrs Tanqueray's funeral. Family vault at Kensal Green. Then Vienna, whither Aubrey has gone to recover from his bereavement. Cayley Drummle, an old friend coming over to cheer him up, takes him to supper at the Hotel Bristol where he meets Paula, who invites him to drive with her in the Prater. A veritable camera orgy. Kensington, Brussels, Algiers, Vienna. And, of course, Mrs Cortelyon's trip to Paris with Ellean. What more can a director want ?

A delightful period film, my dear Sir Alexander. A period in whose gorgeous clothes Marlene could flaunt it to the top of her bent, and Vivien execute her languorous sway like a tulip in Kew Gardens. A period full of seemly magnificence. The one thing I do implore you is to get your set-designer to acquire some notion of the scope of English life in the late nineteenth century. To remember that the Hog's Back is not the Beverly Hills, that Willowmere is a small English village and not an off-shoot of Hollywood, and that " Highercoombe " is an English country house and not a film star's palace. " Tell Watts to balance the cart for three," sets the note to perfection. Observe that Paula says " cart." I know it is difficult for a film director to realise that when the Tanquerays drove into the village they used what the English call a dog-cart, and not a coach-and-four ! But let your director make the attempt. And now, my dear Sir Alexander, what about it ?

Your sincere admirer,

James Agate

L'esprit de l'escalier. The letter to Korda posted, I take up Damon Runyon's *More Than Somewhat* and turn to *Broadway Financier*, which begins with Irma Teak and how she "knocks off a Russian duke back in 1911 when Russian dukes are considered very useful by dolls." A few lines lower down I read "But finally Irma Teak goes blind, which is a tough break for her as she can no longer see how jealous she is making other dolls with her diamonds and sables and one thing and another, so what good are they to her, after all ?" Which, of course, is Paula's "Where's the pride in being a married woman among women who are—married !" all over again. Why didn't I suggest a new ending to the Tanqueray film ? Why not make Paula go blind ?

June 4 *Friday.* Is nobody ever going to write material worthy of that great comedian, Bud Flanagan ? Here is a beautiful actor going to semi-waste because no more than half his talent is called into play. To-night in *Hi-de-Hi*, the new nonsense at the Palace, "Monsewer" Eddie Gray was allowed to run off with the show. With his top hat, spectacles, moustache, and what the French call *petit air sainte nitouche* he looked more like Neil Cream than ever. I thought the rest of the show mediocre, and Florence Desmond's imitation of Marie Lloyd less like than I had thought possible. A great deal of nonsense had been talked to me beforehand about Gwen Catley. The only British coloratura singer in the last fifty years ! The only prima donna worth sending to America ! ! I expected to see some luscious, opulently built creature with a rafter-ringing voice ; what I saw and heard was a tiny creature and a tiny voice. But then that is your B.B.C. singer all over. No microphone and where are they ? And how badly the poor girl was produced ! First a shocking hash-up of *Tales from the Vienna Woods*, after which, in the Hyde Park scene, they trundled her on in a bath-chair—an ordeal which Melba and Tetrazzini put together couldn't have survived. In the second part there was some attempt to give the young woman her status as grand-opera singer. This took the form of a full-dress presentation of "Caro Nome" complete with stairs, balustrades, and balconies. But by this time it was too late. I am angry when this sort of thing happens. Having got a charming little artist with a charming little voice, why not give her some charming little songs to sing—Mozart, Schubert, and so forth? Why pull her about the stage tweeting nonsense?

June 5 *Saturday.* It is now established that Leslie Howard was on the Lisbon plane brought down by the Germans this week. Because Leslie, in private life, was an entirely delightful person, most, if not all, of his obituarists have fallen into the trap of regarding him as a considerable actor. Do I have to go over the old ground for the hundredth time? Yes, I suppose so. Irving was always Irving, with this important proviso; that there were at least twenty Irvings, and all of them different. Thus, Lesurques in *The Lyons Mail* was always Irving, but so was Dubosc, who in no way resembled Lesurques except in the matter of physical likeness. Similarly with Hamlet and Jingle, Macbeth and Dr Primrose. "Leave Irving out of it," you say impatiently. "What about Gerald du Maurier? Was he not always himself?" Yes. But himself in the way that what he put on the stage was an urgent, heightened, *theatrical* presentation of Geraldism, whereas what Leslie Howard sought to give was a subdued, abstract, non-theatrical precipitate of Howardism. Perhaps because of his physical limitations Leslie chose to be the super-quietist. I find that in my first notice of him, dated August 1926, when he played the part of a gigolo in a play by Lord Lathom entitled *The Way You Look At It*, I wrote that Howard "achieved the very considerable feat of making the audience like the actor while loathing the character"! Throughout his entire career he played to be liked. Presently came *Her Cardboard Lover* (1928) with the same gigolo all over again. More likeable than ever in *Berkeley Square*, he did no more than skim the surface of this play's passion. Then in 1933 he appeared as Shakespeare in *This Side Idolatry*. Turning up what I wrote, I find that he "possessed Shakespeare's mask and could look the beatific sheep to perfection, but that in the way of acting all he could do was to thump his chest gently once and say that that was where Hamlet's tragedy took place." I ended: "If this Shakespeare wrote *Antony and Cleopatra*, then one must believe that a mouse can give birth to a mountain." His Hamlet I did not see; but I remember that at one time he contemplated making a film version of the play. I still have the account of an interview given by him at the time. Asked why he cut the scene on the ramparts, he replied, "I think it's a good idea to start *Hamlet* off on a rather brilliant and noisy note, instead of in the quiet undertone of the sentries' conversation, so we begin with the second scene, inside the castle." He told the interviewer of his intention to discard "Come, bird, come!", Hamlet's swearing of his friends to secrecy, the "fellow in the cellarage" passage, "Well said, old mole!", "There are more things in heaven and earth," the intimation about the antic disposition, the "Rest, rest, perturbèd spirit!" He ended the interview by announcing his intention to alternate *Hamlet* with a film by James Hilton about a shy little Presbyterian minister. But then, all Leslie's characters were shy little ministers, and he played them all to perfection. And he was always the English gentleman, the slow-of-uptake and thoughtful-of-answer sort, the kind you see in tubes and buses any morning in war-time. As a film actor he exuded more charm than anybody I have ever seen; one sensed that the books he and his pipe were always shyly peeping over were whimsies by A. A. Milne. Is this a harsh judgment? I believe it to be a true one. Leslie gave me a great deal of pleasure; but it was the pleasure that comes not from the riot of acting but from the delighted sense of privileged contact with a sympathetic personality and a sensitive mind. And an English mind. Everything about Leslie was English—his manner, look, talk, pipe, slacks, and golf-jacket. He was of Hungarian extraction!

Have just heard that my old friend Alfred Chenhalls was on the plane. In spite of the fact that if he mislaid pipe or spectacles he would scream like a rogue elephant and was, or pretended to be, a mass of nerves, everybody knew him to be the kindest of souls. He was the *gayest* man I ever met.

June 6 *Sunday.* From an article on Duse in to-day's *Times*: "The few in whose ears still rings that gaily mischievous call to the waiter, 'Fabrizio!' may remember also a glowing tribute to Mirandolina by 'A. B. W.'" With to-day's article I complete twenty years' service with the *Sunday Times*. And I am wondering how many calls or cries heard during that period still ring in my ears. Precious few, I fear. But one or two come to mind. Wolfit's long agonised scream: "A horse! A horse! My kingdom for a horse!"—

any of Marie Tempest's squawks—Edith Evans's scandalised " A HAND-bag ! "—this is all. Yet I have an exact and vivid recollection of the inflections of sentences uttered thirty, forty, even fifty years ago—inflections which still come into mind and are as fresh to-day as when I heard them. Let me recount a few. Lots and lots of Irving and Bernhardt. But not only these. I can still hear the hoarse croak of Réjane in Bataille's *La Vierge Folle* saying to the Duke whose daughter her husband has seduced, " Vous parlez comme si la défloraison de votre fille était une défaite nationale." Janet Achurch as Nora, and the sudden drop in her voice in her " Let me pass, please " to Dr Rank. Her stirring " That's a good bid, Eugene " in *Candida*. And I can still see her sitting bolt upright on that Egyptian throne saying

> Give me my robe, put on my crown ; I have
> Immortal longings in me.

Benson in that orchestral voice of his, a bit weak in the strings perhaps, but with what lovely wood-wind ! And what astonishing brass, with cymbals when you least expected them ! How right was my brother Harry when he said that Benson never walked on to the stage ; that he always came *clanking* on ! I can still see the noble and classic gesture with which Forbes-Robertson accompanied his exquisite delivery of Hamlet's " Give me that man That is not passion's slave." And still recollect Edward Terry saying in *Sweet Lavender*, " Blame, blame, blame ; but praise—oh dear, no ! " And the rudeness of Mrs Pat as Paula Tanqueray saying to her neighbour, Mrs Cortelyon, " I fancy I *have* observed a roof." Or John Hare as the Gay Lord Quex, sneering, " ' Félix Poubelle, Carte d'or.' It will appear, I am afraid, that you had been preparing for the entertainment of some amorous footman." And Irene Vanbrugh's " I'll make short work of you, my lord." Or George Alexander in *His House in Order* saying suavely, " You should treat my lady to Paris oftener, Sir Daniel " : and in the same play, Irene's devastating " I go to no park to-morrow ! " One could go on and on. Hawtrey's drawl and Miss Compton saying in her deep voice, " Have a bit on Flickamaroo ! " I could add a hundred others, all equally delightful and all dating from before the last war. Is virtue no longer in the players of to-day ? Or has it gone out of me ? The last seven words are sheer mock modesty. To real talent I am as responsive as ever.

After Leo had gone to-night—we worked all day as a kind of celebration—I found on my desk the following :

VINGT ANS APRÈS

The Savoy Grill, 1963. *A very old gentleman stumps in leaning heavily on an enormous stick. Several waiters hurry towards him.*

HEAD WAITER. I am sorry, Mr Agate, but Sir John Gielgud and Dame Vivien Leigh couldn't wait. They said you arranged to meet them at one o'clock, and it is now three.

THE OLD GENT (*testily*). Don't talk so much . . . take my hat. Take my stick. Here, damn you, be careful with that stick—it belonged to Hazlitt. Find me a chair. A mahogany chair—not oak—I loathe oak chairs. Bring me two double Scotches, a single Scotch, and then two doubles.

WAITER. Are your guests arriving now, sir ?

THE OLD GENT. Guests ? Are you mad ? These drinks are for me, DOLT ! [*Takes out a manuscript and begins to read it—a lady approaches.*]

LADY. Dear James . . .

JAMES. Who are you ?

LADY. We haven't met since you received the O.M. I am——

JAMES. I know who you are—you are the woman who mumbled herself off the stage.

LADY. I married.

JAMES (*interrupting*). Never mind your marriage. *Revenons à la réalité*. What do you suppose *this* is, Valerie ?

LADY. Not Valerie, James.

JAMES. What the hell does it matter what your name is ? Look you here, child. This is my new life of Sarah. [*The Waiter brings some soup.*] Listen, Xenia, I'll read you the bit where Sarah first—— [*The manuscript falls into the soup.*

LADY. Oh, James !

JAMES (*with a touch of the old gusto*). Now I'm in a fine pickle. I can't drink the soup because my script has fallen into it. And I can't read my script because it has fallen into the soup ! Oh, my dear . . . dear Adrienne—

Partons, dans un baiser, pour un monde inconnu.
Éveillons au hasard les échos de la vie,
Parlons-nous de bonheur, de gloire and de folie,
Et que ce soit un rêve . . .

[*He falls asleep.*

June 7 *Monday.* In the Haymarket this afternoon I met a young woman, chinless, with projecting false teeth, a dab of putty for a nose, eyes peering through pebble glasses a quarter of an inch thick, bleached hair, and a ravishing hat which, of course, accentuated the poor girl's lamentable looks. And at once the old problem presented itself. Should her friends encourage her to dress idiotically, or tell her that if she wore a hat nobody would look at twice she wouldn't run the risk of being looked at once ? I can understand the magnificently ugly woman braving it out, but not the grotesque sort. Or, don't women know when they're grotesque ? And should one tell them ? The old story of Ibsen's Dr Relling and his famous theory : " If you take away make-believe from the average man you take away his happiness as well." What is this but Bacon's " A mixture of a lie doth ever add pleasure. Doth any man doubt, that if there were taken out of men's minds vain opinions, flattering hopes, false valuations, imaginations as one would, and the like, but it would leave the minds of a number of men poor shrunken things, full of melancholy and indisposition, and unpleasing to themselves ? " But whether Ibsen or Bacon, this question is always cropping up in one form or another. Every day, by every post, from all parts of the country, plays, novels, stories, essays, poems come pouring in, all without scrap of merit, and always their authors wanting to know whether they should go on writing or not. Up to now I have based my answers on Horatio's

> If there be any good thing to be done,
> That may to thee do ease, and grace to me,
> Speak to me.

In other words, I have told the poor wretches that their stuff is worthless, but to go on turning it out if it gives them relief. What are the alternatives ? If I tell them to stop writing they may turn into drunkards and wife-beaters. If I tell them to go on I am adding to the flood of pernicious nonsense. On the whole I think that a reasonable drunkard and moderate wife-beater does less harm than a worthless and incompetent writer. It takes a lot of drink to kill a man, and most wives would be the better for an occasional thrashing.

Michael Redgrave has never got over *Thunder Rock*. This afternoon he turned Lafont, the lover in *La Parisienne*, into another of his solemn lighthouses. But Becque's play is a comedy, Lafont is an ass, and whoever plays him must show that his jealousy is ridiculous. A grand part for Alfred Lunt. Michael gives him no fun at all, wrapping him in a mantle of what Mr Polly called "Exultant, Urgent Loogoobuosity." No Frenchman would have appeared in Clotilde's drawing-room with a frock-coat buttoned up like a soutane and a muffler to hang himself by. This is pure Rakitin. Michael should either acquire a sense of comedy or stick to gloom-dispensing *à la russe*. The mixture of the two is fatal.

June 8. *Tuesday.* A few days ago I received a letter from a gentleman with a foreign name saying he had been a constant reader of my *S.T.* articles for years, and had never been able to make head or tail of them. Would I lunch at the Ritz and explain them? I accepted, and found a remarkable little man, plump and dapper, who started by telling me that he was seventy-two, the father of six sons in the Forces and six daughters in convents, that he was extremely rich, had never borrowed money, was possessed of sexual powers which would astonish me, and was utterly weary of life, the span of which, however, he not merely desired, but claimed to be able to lengthen. He then told me that he was a scientist. "Look at the two of us," he said. "Compare your veins with mine." And he held out a hand as podgy and creaseless as a baby's. "Do you not think it dreadful," he continued, "that in some five years' time, perhaps less, you will be carried out in a box and either burnt, or buried in a hole in the earth? And in a little while you will be as completely forgotten as Gladstone or Mounet-Sully. Now, my dear sir, you can, if you desire it, live to be three hundred years old, and I alone know the secret." Which turned out to be that one mustn't wash one's face in warm water. Finally this eccentric, straight from the pages of Smollett, drove me to the Savage Club, and as the taxi was turning round, put his head out of the window and said, "If you will visit me at my house on the Cornish cliffs I will show you a postcard from Ibsen."

June 9 *Wednesday.* I was asked to-night why I won't have truck with intellectuals after business hours. But of course I won't. 1. I am not an intellectual. Two minutes' talk with Aldous Huxley, William Glock, or any of the *New Statesman* crowd would expose me utterly. 2. I am too tired after my day's work to man the intellectual palisade. 3. When my work is finished I want to eat, drink, smoke, and relax. 4. I don't know very much, but what I do know I know better than anybody, and I don't want to argue about it. I know what I think about an actor or an actress, and am not interested in what anybody else thinks. My mind is not a bed to be made and re-made.

I had hardly written the last word when the postman brought the latest number of *Modern Reading*. I open at random and find this in an essay by John Cowper Powys:

> An elderly idealist is bound to feel a bit nervous and inclined to step gingerly, like a clergyman entering a bar, as he makes his first advances among the frequenters of the Terraqueous Tavern of Finn Mac Cool; but coming to Joyce's Freudian, Pantagruelian, Shandyean, Macaronic *English-Irish*, straight from a struggle with the *Welsh-English* of what might be called "The Six Hundred Years' War," since it ranges round the question as to whether the perpetually reincarnating Taliesin might, in the ordinary sense of the word, be regarded as having "lived" in the Sixth or in the Twelfth Centuries, I am compelled to make that special and curious plunge required of anyone who passes from an atmosphere of "Brythonic-Iberian Esotericism" into an atmosphere of Goidelic-Nordic Burlesque.

Is it thinkable that after a day of hard work I want to spend the evening racking my brains over stuff like this?

June 10 *Thursday.* A letter:

> *Warre House*
> *Eton College*
> *Windsor*
> *June* 7, 1943
>
> DEAR MR AGATE,
>
> This is I am afraid something of an impertinence, but I hope that the fact of *Ego*, Vols 1–4 (and soon 5) being my favourite bedside reading will prevent your classing me with the stranger who asked you "if your name was Agate," as he liked to be sure of such things. But as *Ego* will probably be

edited, as time goes on, as much as Boswell, I venture to point out 3 errors in *Ego* 2.

Page 150. In Rupert Brooke's line " A pulse in the eternal mind, no less . . . " the words " no less " go with the verb at the beginning of the next line, and do not qualify " mind." There is no comma after them. A pedagogue's correction, but I know you like to be accurate !

Page 184. Albert Trott's hit over the pavilion. I am afraid the only comment on Mr Cobb's statement is the same as Dr Johnson's when told that a Mr Pot called *Irene* the finest tragedy of modern times : " If Pot says so, Pot lies." The hit was off the bowling of M. A. Noble in the match M.C.C. *v.* Australians July 31, 1899. Wisden says nothing about it, but it is recorded in *Cricket*, August 1899.

Page 321. " The King's life is moving peacefully *to* (not ' towards ') its close." I could swear to this. Surely the beauty of the sentence would be severely damaged by *ds* coming in the word immediately before " its."

Please do not dream of answering or acknowledging this; you are far too busy a man. And every moment of your spare time should be, and, I hope, is, devoted to the compilation of *Ego* 6.

Yours sincerely,

GEORGE W. LYTTELTON

June 11 *Friday.* Is Simonov's *The Russians* a muddled play ? Yes. Badly constructed ? Yes. All over the place ? Yes. Is it, in turns, drama of incident, psychological study of a people in time of unbearable stress, pure film-fodder ? Yes. Is the story of a marooned band of guerrillas an exemplification of the fog of war, the fog of war in Russia, the fog of a Russian play about war ? Undeniably, yes. Has it something of the poetry of heroism ? Is there a love-story of some nobility tucked away in it ? Is it the product of an adult mind ? Is it conceived in terms of the stage and not of the lecture platform ? Is it well laid out for actors ? Is it exciting ? Is it, in fine, worth while ? Enormously so. Superb performances by Michael Golden and Freda Jackson.

June 12 *Saturday.* Lunch with Korda, a witty, cultivated man who has all Cochran's artistry but rather more power of keeping it in check. He tells me that in every film he makes he has constantly in front of him the notion that some cowboy has ridden fifty miles in order to go to a cinema. I say I think that even the popular film should be five per cent. over the heads of the audience. Korda says, "You're quite right. When I get a member of the public coming to me and saying 'I liked it immensely, but of course it will be over most people's heads,' I know I've got a winner." We talk about good French pictures like *La Fin du Jour*, and Korda says, "I'm not worried about good little films. They aren't my job, and one way or another they will always get made." We discuss Orson Welles, and Korda says, "He would be a very great film director if the intellectuals would let him alone. They did their best to ruin Charlie Chaplin by pretending that when he dropped the ice down the duchess's corsage he was symbolising proletarian revenge."

To Lord's afterwards to see the Civil Defence Services beat the Army and the clock. This was due to some magnificent cricket by Gimblett and James Parks, who put on 200 runs in 100 minutes. Gimblett's score of 124 included three 6's, one a gigantic hook off Nichols which carried 120 yards, into the crowd.

June 13 *Sunday.* I hear that Kligerman has gone back to his old job at the "Q" Theatre. Which means good-bye for the time being to his proposed career as a virtuoso. I am afraid it's largely my fault for turning down an offer from Ibbs and Tillett, who wanted him to go to Cardiff or Swansea or some such place for a fee of ten guineas, out of which he must pay railway fare and hotel bill. I stuck out for fifteen and got no answer. I was wrong. The proper thing to do was to jump at the offer and pay the expenses out of my own pocket. Alexis has never reproached me, but I am still kicking myself.

June 14 *Monday.* To-day, it appears, Leo completes his second year as my secretary, amanuensis, typist, and general factotum. Of his efficiency in some of these occupations perhaps the less said the better. But I find a deal of truth in a note which he left on my desk last night, and from which I quote the following:

> Having no head for figures, I sought the help of a friendly accountant, who, after I had told him that my two years in your employ represented some 616 days of eight hours each,

not including Sundays, arrived at a total of 4928 hours spent with thee, dear heart! About "strings of pearls" I say nothing. What I should like to boast to the world is that you, the most irritable, impatient, intolerant of men, should have survived nearly *five thousand* hours of my company, all within a couple of years! I told this to H., and he said, "James deserves the Victoria Cross!" No one said anything about what *my* deserts might be, but I waive this, as a poor employee has only a few holding notes while the employer is lording it over the entire score.

Some silly people have thought your picture of me in the *Egos* malicious. They are wrong, you have done me more than justice. You omitted to tell of my worst faults and habits; of my maddening garrulity, my tactlessness, my absurd and quite irrational alternations of ecstasy and despair, my mutterings and gurglings and talkings to myself. And the habits! On the incessant sneezings and coughings you have remarked. But how about the spittings on the floor, the belchings and the dribblings, the dubious linen, frayed clothes, and those greasy old hats? I shall laugh as long as I live over that day when you rashly took me to the Savoy to lunch with Sir Something Somebody and his smart friends, and when we got there eyed the suit I was wearing and with quite unwonted tact slipped a pound-note into my hand and suggested that I shouldn't like the people or the food and would be happier lunching elsewhere. Which, cheerfully, I did.

I am glad we have stuck it together even thus long. Wonderful, when one thinks how instinctively I fly from my friends and am attracted only to my enemies!

LEO

June 15 *Tuesday.* Who is this William Saroyan that he should dare to take such a title as *The Human Comedy* for the inept balderdash I sat through at the Empire this morning? The story centres in Mickey Rooney, who, while attending High School, is hired as night messenger boy at the town telegraph office. This because he must support a widowed mother and a baby brother at home, and a sister at college. Now I don't believe that even American telegraph boys earn all that money. And why put all the burden on Mickey's shoulders—except, of course, to make the picture? Why didn't the daughter give up college and take a job of typing? Why didn't Mum quit sitting around twanging the harp and take a job as office cleaner? Fay

Photo Tunbridge-Sedgwick

Leo Pavia

Photo Tunbridge-Sedgwick

The Balcony Room

Bainter, sweeping the strings instead of floors, and through them delivering homilies to the five-year-old couched at her feet and in imminent danger of having his nose amputated by the pedals—here was stupendous bathos unparalleled in all my film experience.

In the afternoon to the Leicester Square to see the even more preposterous *Forever and a Day.* All about a house inhabited by five generations. The kind of film in which the director chokes himself with period, and even so doesn't get it right. A young woman having been abducted, her guardian and his attorney come to retrieve her. Do they arrive in a barouche ? No. They come in a tandem-drawn gig with the box seat occupied by the two gentlemen and the groom perched in the dickey. *Where did they propose to put the girl if she had consented to come back ?*

June 16 *Wednesday.* Noel Coward and Gladys Calthrop fulfilled a promise to lunch made six months ago. They called for me, and I showed them round the flat, which they liked very much. Gladys fell in love with the balcony room and vowed she would use it in her next set of designs, while Noel said he should write a new and sparkling comedy round it. I had intended to introduce Leo to them, but the old 'un had a sudden access of coyness or temper or something, locked himself in the bathroom, and refused to emerge till we had departed. Michael Shepley joined us at the Ivy and everything was very gay. Discussing an intellectual actor who can't act, Michael says, " The worst thing about him is the way he whinnies." I say, " I think you mean ' neighs.' Only mares whinny." Whereupon Noel claps his hands and cries, " Splendid ! You've given me the title for my new comedy—*Only Mares Whinny* ! "

Cochran's *Seventy Years of Song* went off without a hitch except that in the excitement the band left out " The Lily of Laguna." The most popular item was Vi Loraine and George Robey singing " If You Were the Only Girl in the World," with another great welcome for Ivor Novello in " Keep the Home Fires Burning." Ivor, who was fifty last January, didn't look a day over thirty-five ; his charm is as amazing as ever. I shall always say that there are more brains and more sheer acting capacity in this young man than anyone has ever supposed. An oversight to leave out " Take Me back to Dear Old Blighty," musically speaking the best of our soldier songs. And I should like to have heard the sentimental " There's a Long, Long Trail a-Winding." Parry's " Jerusalem " was a first-class mistake. But then I have lived at Swiss Cottage and know what comes of building Jerusalem in green and pleasant Hampstead !

June 17 *Thursday.* Luncheon to Lord Kemsley and W. W. Hadley, respectively proprietor and editor of the *Sunday Times,* to mark my twenty years of service. Lady Kemsley graced the occasion, and the party, again at the Ivy, was if possible gayer than yesterday's ! After lunch I showed them round the flat, which seemed to amuse them. This time Leo remained on view and received my guests very graciously.

To *The Lisbon Story* at the Hippodrome. Only the British would think the occupation of Paris by the Nazis to be a fitting subject for a musical play. High spot of the evening two Polish dancers locking themselves together and gyrating endlessly like twin legs of mutton revolving on a spit.

June 19 *Saturday.* For twenty years I have been taking tickets in the Savage Club Derby Sweep. Eight tickets a year and never drawn a horse. This year I decided to stay out, but yielded five minutes before the entries closed, taking the last four tickets. The last drew the winner, Straight Deal ! The first prize was £75, and as I also backed the horse for £2 each way the result was a nice little bonus of some £116, and no concern of dear Stanley ! Invited George Mathew to supper and champagne at the Café Royal, but forgot the champagne ! Probably the numbing effect of the first Prom. Bax's London Pageant, which led off, is just Elgar without his good tunes but a lot of clever-clever scoring to make up. Wood in goodish form after his illness. His beat still has vigour—he was never the sort of conductor whose arm swims about like a goldfish in a bowl—and he set about Beethoven's Fifth Symphony as though he and we weren't sick of it. Left at the interval.

Fatras. War or no war, I think the advertisement in the front page of to-day's *Times* beginning " Lady over military age " is ridiculous.

June 20 *Sunday.* It occurs to me that during the twenty years in which I have served on the *Sunday Times*, my sixteen on the *Tatler*, twelve on the *Express*, eleven on *Country Life*, and nine on *John o' London's Weekly*, I must have received some 40,000 letters of which at least 35,000 have been answered, endearingly or waspishly, by Jock and Leo. *I hereby solemnly disavow all letters not signed by me personally.* If those written in my name, but not by me, are epistolary masterpieces—which I doubt not—so much the better for the recipients. But I claim no credit for them. *Palmam*, etc.

June 21 *Monday.* " We take this to be, on the whole, the worst similitude in the world," said Macaulay. What would he have said of this jewel in the *Times*' racing correspondent's account of Saturday's Derby ?

> Coming down into the Dip, ten or it may be a dozen of the field were in line abreast across the course, as grand a sight as fifteen or more destroyers sweeping up the Mediterranean with the great battleships behind.

As *grand* a sight ?

The Musée Sarah Bernhardt acquired a new treasure to-day, a total stranger having written to tell me that an enchanting marble female head sculpted by Sarah was going for next to nothing in a little shop off Baker Street. Went round at once and got it for five pounds. Very pretty indeed, but not, I imagine, what the modern art critic calls " purposive "—only Sarah would have thought of giving wings to a young lady in evening dress. I note that she has reproduced her own exquisite nose with the little ridge in the middle.

June 22 *Tuesday.* George Richards writes :

> Last night on the wireless Priestley talked about the people in one street with not enough to eat living next to a row of people with too much, whereas of course anyone who has ever shared a working-class *ménage* knows that really poor people never stop eating or pouring out cups of tea from the time they get out of bed till the time they go back to it. The English middle classes also glut themselves, but that is chiefly as an antidote to boredom, and as their range of poisons is

slightly wider and less monotonous it is somewhat longer before their countenances begin to develop that typical resemblance to thick yellow wall-paper.

Fatras. Our Critics. " If *Ghosts* were a new play one would condemn it for its theme. The spectacle of a father's sins recurring in his son, and gradually turning the promising young man into an idiot, is not inspiring. But Ibsen is a skilful dramatist, and is presented as a vehicle for stage art rather than for the messages in his plays."

From " Talk of the Day," in the " Evening News."

June 23 *Wednesday.* That pretty girl and nice woman, Veronica Rose, having given me a bottle of whiskey, I asked a few people in last night to drink it. Read them some modern poetry, choosing the last stanza of one of George Barker's *Sacred Elegies*, published in the new number of *Horizon* :

> Incubus, Anæsthetist with glory in a bag,
> Foreman with a sweatbox and a whip. Asphyxiator
> Of the ecstatic. Sergeant with a grudge
> Against the lost lovers in the park of creation.
> Fiend behind the fiend behind the fiend behind the
> Friend. Mastodon with mastery, monster with an ache
> At the tooth of the ego, the dead drunk judge :
> Wheresoever Thou art our agony will find Thee
> Enthroned on the darkest altar of our heartbreak
> Perfect. Beast, brute, bastard. O dog my God !

Michael Shepley broke the silence by saying, " Gosh, that's beautiful. I must hang it over my bed ! " This reminded me of something, and leaving them to the whiskey I hunted till I found it. It turned out to be a passage in *The Theatrical World for* 1893 in which Archer writes, " ' It is the ambition of my life,' a poet-dramatist once said to me, ' to write a really *obscure* poem.' " Being scrupulously conscientious, I telephoned Cyril Connolly, who edits *Horizon*, to ask whether ' friend ' in the sixth line should be ' fiend.' He said, " I don't know. It is ' friend ' in the typescript which came to me from America. Nine-tenths of the poem is beyond me, but it has beautiful lines which make me feel that Barker is a poet. I printed it for this reason, and also because I understand he is hard-up." A significant criticism of modern poetry that it doesn't matter whether you print the word the poet meant or its opposite !

June 24 *Thursday.* Give the devil his due! I confess I never thought that Jack Priestley had the gift of being able to laugh at himself. Imagine my surprise on finding the author of *They Came to a City* writing in his new novel:

> Bert Ogmore's visions of a Soviet Britain, confused but bright, owed much to Russian films and the excellent photographs in the U.S.S.R. propaganda publications, and something to his fond memory of Party outings; they were filled with healthy, merry workers in shorts and open-necked shirts, with vague People's theatres and opera-houses, with mysterious but attractive towering new white cities drenched in a sunlight that would presumably replace our familiar sullen weather once the last bourgeois Government had gone.

June 25 *Friday.* Further letter from George Lyttelton, this time about the misprints in *Ego* 5. I have sent him this:

MY DEAR GEORGE LYTTELTON,

Let us drop the "Mr." Particularly as I have just torn up a letter to you beginning "Imbécile!" Congreve's "morning bride" on page 170 of *Ego* 5 is *not* a misprint. It is an exquisite joke based on Millamant's "*Adieu*—my morning thoughts, agreeable wakings, indolent slumbers, all ye *douceurs*, ye *sommeils du matin, adieu.*—I can't do't, 'tis more than impossible—positively, Mirabell, I'll lie abed in a morning as long as I please." If this misfires with you, how can I be certain that some three hundred years hence some cretinous editor—forgive me—will not put back the "u" into "morning" and so be-crêpe the dazzling creature?

I thank you for reminding me of Sam Weller's "Ain't nobody to be whopped for takin' this 'ere liberty?" I should certainly like to "whop" whoever in line 16, page 41, left out the circumflex accent on the word '*sûr*,' and in line 22, page 271, makes me read in bed till 4 P.M. instead of A.M.

Do you ever come to London? If so, will you lunch with me? It would be delicious to hear more of what you call "scrannel pæans." The Ivy is the place where I propose to "shove away the worthy bidden guest," who, I hope, will depart swollen with more than wind. My Milton is a little shaky, but I still deserve full marks for my Ruskin.

Yours very sincerely,
JAMES AGATE

P.S. At 3.38 this morning I became, after years of resistance, a convert to the Baconian theory. Alas, poor Will!

Arnold Bennett complained that, in later life, he found himself reading everything with the proof-reader's eye. This has begun to afflict me. Having finished the letter to Lyttelton, I take up Sacheverell Sitwell's *Liszt*, and on page 48 find the name of the young French poet who courted Madame d'Agoult given as "Ronchard" and, ten lines later, as "Rouchard." And what does Sitwell mean by saying of Liszt, attending a performance of *Tristan* on the last Sunday but one of his life, that "He sat through the opera in the private box of the Wagner family, at the back of the theatre, in darkness, invisible to the audience. After the death of Isolda he could bear no more"? There were only eight more bars to bear!

June 26 *Saturday.* Reflections after twenty years of service with the *Sunday Times*:

The War. Pinero's Lady Ridgeley told Derek's governess that in time of sorrow it was not to Chopin and the pianoforte that she turned for healing and consolation. In war-time we English are all Lady Ridgeleys; it is not from the great dramatists that we draw inspiration and courage. Congreve? Gielgud would fill the theatre whether he played John Worthing, Macbeth, Valentine, Box, Cox, or Mrs Bouncer.

Playwrights. Shaw wrote his best play within this period. And then, as Synge nearly said: No man at all can be writing masterpieces for ever, and we must be satisfied. Sean O'Casey flamed in the Dublin sky with two blazing masterpieces after which his genius has seemed for the moment to burn itself out. Noel Coward appeared as the successor to Wilde and Maugham. Priestley, with *Dangerous Corner* and *Eden End,* looked like becoming a dramatist of the first rank, and then, alas, fell into the slough of metaphysics and sociology.

Acting. Three considerable performers. Gielgud, the legitimate successor to Forbes-Robertson. Charles Laughton, a born actor who drifted to the screen. Edith Evans, our nearest approach to a great actress. What of our younger players? What indeed! This is largely the fault of the films, where nicely parted hair or a pretty face will make a young man or woman into a star overnight, provided they have no knowledge of acting.

The Cinema. Has the cinema seduced a certain number of theatre-goers ? Yes. Because while the best films cannot compare with the best flesh-and-blood acting, an evening at the "pictures" is as a rule less boring than one spent in a theatre. The film-goer is certain of being able to hear as well as see, and his seat is cheaper and more comfortable.

The General Level. A popular cant phrase is that while we have no great actors to-day the general level has improved during the last fifty years. This is complete and utter nonsense. The cast for Wilde's *A Woman of No Importance* produced at the Haymarket on April 19, 1893, contained the following: Beerbohm Tree, Fred Terry, Holman Clarke, Henry Kemble, Mrs Tree, Julia Neilson, Rose Leclercq, Mrs Bernard-Beere. Is it suggested that we can show modern galaxies of this brilliance ? The decay of acting is entirely given away by the invention of:

The Producer. This is a person engaged by the management to conceal the fact that the players cannot act. No actor-manager of the old school would have brooked a producer saying, "No, no, Sir Alfred. Turn your face away, please. This will show your infirmity of purpose." All any actor who can really play Macbeth wants in the way of a producer is a stage-manager to see that the ghost of Banquo bobs up at the right moment.

The Lighter Stage. The last twenty years have witnessed the arrival of the performer without a voice. For this the microphone is responsible.

The Future. Whither the theatre ? Nowhither. Or rather, no calculable whither. I am not worried about good little plays, which, as Korda says about good little films, will always happen. In the book, *Impressions de Théâtre*, written by Jules Lemaître in the 'nineties, this occurs:

> Obviously it is absurd to suppose that in a democracy of thirty-six millions the majority should possess artistic sense ; Paris is not Athens, and our age bears no resemblance to that of Pericles. To demand that it should would be childish. The more art is vulgarised by the mob, the greater will be its cultivation by the non-mob. The more art turns on the one hand to pounds, shillings, and pence, the closer on the other will it draw towards the Holy Grail. The firmer democracy takes hold, the more copious will be the flow of works of art inaccessible to the mob in their pride and mystery.

What is the post-war application? Presumably in a Beveridge-ruled world the mob will have more opportunity to exercise its theatrical taste. Since mob-taste must always be execrable, then, if Lemaître is right, we can look forward for a short time to an influx of better plays as the last dying kick of a departing aristocracy. This leads to the question of:

Decentralisation. In plain, brutal English this means repertory at Kettering and Yeovil, with a drama about the village pump and everybody in the village playing the lead in turn. The trouble is the old one—the scarcity of actors worth seeing. It may be, of course, that third-rate actors—and when every town has its repertory this must mean tenth-rate actors—are better than none. Perhaps I agree. After all, village cricket is better than no cricket at all. But that is no reason why a Neville Cardus should criticise it. And I refuse to believe that London readers care tuppence about Slowcombe-on-the-Crawl's production of Vaclav Brszk's *Zinc.*

June 27 *Sunday.* Vignette in Holborn. Two old men are sitting reading. One has his eyes bent on this:

> Vois sur ces canaux
> Dormir ces vaisseaux
> Dont l'humeur est vagabonde;
> C'est pour assouvir
> Ton moindre désir
> Qu'ils viennent du bout du monde.
> —Les soleils couchants
> Revêtent les champs,
> Les canaux, la ville entière,
> D'hyacinthe et d'or;
> Le monde s'endort
> Dans une chaude lumière.

The other is smiling over this loveliness:

> Upon her head a plaited hive of straw,
> Which fortified her visage from the sun,
> Whereon the thought might think sometime it saw
> The carcass of a beauty spent and done:
> Time had not scythed all that youth begun,
> Nor youth all quit; but, spite of heaven's fell rage,
> Some beauty peep'd through lattice of sear'd age.

The telephone rings, and a Scotch voice says, "If you turn on the wireless, Jamie, you'll hear some beautiful singing." J. A. puts down his *Lover's Complaint* and does as he is bid. It is

Maggie Teyte singing Duparc's *Phydilé* and Berlioz's *Spectre de la Rose.* At the conclusion of the second J. A. turns off the wireless and resumes his Shakespeare. L. P. takes up his Baudelaire again.

June 28 *Monday.* I have it in my bones that to-night's revival of *The Master Builder* at the Westminster is going to give me a lot of trouble. What do I really make of the most difficult of Ibsen's plays, counting *When We Dead Awaken* as not for competition ? Roughly I take it to be about an old man and a young woman. Now what sort of old man and young woman ? Well, Halvard Solness is not very old—fifty perhaps—but he is exhausted in body and mind, a miserable combination of coward, sensualist, idealist, and ferocious egoist. Realising that he can fulfil his architectural mission by pulling down the family mansion and building something better, he does not dare to do this because his wife likes the old place. He prays to the Fates to arrange a fire. They oblige, his two little boys lose their lives, and he makes his fortune. And then what? The Fates turn into Furies. Solness builds churches ; but over his shoulder stares that face from which he dare not run away, the gloom-stricken visage of the children's mother. To bolster up his architectural skill he gathers young assistants round him and absorbs their brains. Solness is that unhappy thing, a sensualist with qualms. Also he has a bad memory. He forgets having tousled and mousled a little girl called Hilda, the step-daughter of Ellida Wangel. Alas, Solness has never seen Ibsen's *Lady from the Sea,* or he would know better than to take risks with any of the fishy brood. And here comes Hilda to demand that Solness shall fulfil that promise he made her in a drunken frolic ten years ago—the promise to build her a kingdom and install her in it as his Princess. She makes it obvious that she has come to stay, whether Mrs Solness likes it or not. Hilda is probably the most irritating young woman in Ibsen's gallery—a bouncing, vigorous, self-opinionated harpy as much over-vitalised as Hedda Gabler was under-vitalised, but cursed with the same notion of running some man's life for her own excitement and glory. Solness has just completed a house with a magnificent tower plus weathercock, and nothing will suit Hilda but that he shall climb the tower and hang a wreath round the vane. Solness has never had any head for heights. He protests that the feat is impossible at his age. So they bargain. He will do it if Hilda will give herself to him. On the spiritual plane, of course. She agrees. He climbs the steeple and everybody is adjured to keep quiet. But Hilda isn't going to be deprived of her triumph. She yodels and jubilates, and waves a shawl to attract his attention. Solness falls and is killed instantaneously. And Hilda, realising that she won't have to keep her part of the bargain—Shaw pointed out long ago that she cares as much for Solness as a Cornish fisherman cares for a conger eel—shrieks with wild intensity that she hears harps in the air.

Is Hilda mad ? Ibsen didn't think so. Had the old man—meaning Ibsen, not Solness—gone gaga ? I know of nobody saner than the author of the two plays which immediately followed—*Little Eyolf* and *John Gabriel Borkman.* What I am faced with is finding a reasonable explanation *before Sunday.* Sit up till 3 A.M. making what I realise is only a first draft. Am relying on to-morrow's performance to give me something to catch hold of.

June 29 *Tuesday.* Begin the day by tearing up all I wrote last night about *The Master Builder.* Produce fresh provisional article. See the play and am more flummoxed than ever.

As everybody is fire-watching and since I cannot get anybody to stay with me I put up at Norman Newman's, where I spend half the night arguing with Dennis Arundell about his production of *Ghosts,* which I haven't seen but suspect to be all wrong. Now, Dennis is a man of great culture, highly sensitive and inclined to be shy and reserved. This did not prevent me from being rude to that gentle soul, who maintained that acting to-day is as good as it ever was ! I asked whether he had seen Sarah, Duse, Réjane, Coquelin, Guitry, Irving, Forbes-Robertson, Mrs Kendal, Achurch—the usual lot. No, he hadn't seen any of them. " In that case," I said—perhaps shouted—" shut up about acting. Even a highbrow should know that you can't compare B with A unless you know something about A." Yes, I admit I was rude. But I shall always be rude on this subject, wilfully, conscientiously rude.

June 30 *Wednesday*. Home shortly after 10 A.M. and clear the decks for action in the matter of the *Master Builder* article. In other words, I again sweep everything I have written into the waste-paper basket, and start afresh. Lunch at the Dorchester with Basil Cameron, who makes me drink the best part of a bottle of Chambertin. Back to Grape Street, where for the next three hours my drenched nature lies in swinish sleep. Wake feeling extremely ill, drink coffee, then go to the Comedy Theatre to see *The Fur Coat*, a piece by the late Archie Macdonell which he wrote for a tall actress, and which turned out to be altogether too tall for me. A pity to have put it on. Archie had great intelligence, but was curiously uncritical of his own work. I remember the *Observer* printing a poem by him whose scansion would have been poor for a twelve-year-old. Apart from my dislike of not being able to endure Archie's play —he was kind to me during those months at Oxford in 1940— there was the boredom of having to sit through three hours of something one knew all about after ten minutes. One could sense the play's quality, and plays don't alter. The acting ? But I have seen Henry Kendall and Jeanne de Casalis in twenty plays, and no modern actor or actress alters. Rush home and work till four with the aid of a bottle of whiskey. When I put my pen down I think I am drunk ; in fact, I know I am. Very drunk, i' faith ; the forty-foot passage bobs up and down like the deck of a destroyer ! " No man," observed Dick Phenyl in Pinero's *Sweet Lavender*, " is quite so sober as the individual who is occasionally otherwise. All his acuteness is concentrated upon his brief lucid intervals, and in those intervals his acuteness is devilish." With me the case is the contrary one. I don't often get drunk, though in my rare bouts of intoxication I attain a lucidity I do not command at other times. Perhaps because I only get what I call drunk really late at night when I am alone, working, and putting everything I know into my work. What an old Lancashire woman at my father's mill used to call, " All ten fingers and toes going."

Here is a bit of what I finally produce :

What, in our modern vulgar parlance, is biting Solness ? The prospect of death ? Other men have died from time to time and worms have eaten them. His decreasing powers ? That, too, is in nature. His parleyings with God, the result of which has been the depriving him of, first, his joy in building churches, and second, his satisfaction in erecting homes for human beings ? The burden of sin ? But Solness believes he is in thrall to a troll, which enthralment negatives responsibility. The fear of madness ? But there is no evidence that he is " dreadfully attended." His sinister gift of hypnotism ? He has not misused it. His illicit traffic with " helpers and servers ? " The fact that he was morally responsible for the burning down of the house whereby his wife lost her two children ? But that was twelve years ago, and Ibsen knows better than anybody that in twelve years one gets over anything from pitch-and-toss to infanticide. And then Solness doesn't care a fig for moral responsibility—he has a boyish wish to resemble the Vikings who sailed to foreign lands, plundered and burned, killed men and carried off women. Why can't he have a robust conscience like them ? And now, perhaps, we are getting nearer ? " La débauche veut des âmes fortes," wrote Balzac. Is Solness's unhappiness due to his recognition that he is a super-egoist without the courage of his egoism ? Professor Herford suggested that in this play Ibsen " was seeking to place one more crown, under the eyes of expectant Europe, upon the towering fabric of his finished work." If so, then are Solness's churches Ibsen's poetic dramas ? Are the homes for human beings his purely domestic pieces ? Are the castles in the air the three or four plays he felt he still had it in him to write ? Endless and fascinating speculation ! Agreed that we must allow, as usual, for the old man's love of perversity. One of Ibsen's kinks was to make things more difficult than they need be. Why not allow the fire to break out in Solness's hopefully neglected flue ? Why insist that it started in a different part of the house ? Because he knew it would tease. Of one thing we are in no sort of doubt. This is that every line of this great poem proclaims dramatic genius of the highest order. The duet in the second act is the greatest colloquy in drama since Hamlet had that pow-wow with his mother. Mr Wolfit, who is a master of make-up, had contrived something suggesting in turns an amiable gorilla, a seaside phrenologist, and the late lamented Dr Pritchard. Quickly overcoming this handicap, he proceeded to make out a brilliantly argued, immensely cogent case for Solness. " Look, whether he has not tears in's eyes," one found oneself murmuring. And he got as good as he gave, Miss Rosalind Iden putting up a great fight as the Nietzschean Hilda, a being, in Archer's words, " radiantly, unscrupulously, immorally sane." What ! Have we got to the point where a dour matter-of-fact Scot like Archer can call young women encouraging old men to break their necks sane? Yes, we have. And I suggest that a play which can bring about this feat must be getting on for a masterpiece.

Not too bad after three-quarters of a bottle of whiskey.

July 1 *Thursday.* My lucidity in drink is the real thing and not merely an excuse. Before I brush my teeth I go through what I wrote last night and find it set down in my neatest script, meticulously punctuated, and doesn't want a word altering. Give orders for it to be typed *instanter*, and rush it down to the *S.T.* before I can see it again.

In my mail I find this letter from George Lyttelton:

June 30

My dear James Agate,

Many thanks for your kind and forgiving letter. I think you must have a very beautiful nature! Your letter *should* have begun with "Imbécile," and if the prefix had been 'cretinous' I should not have uttered a word of complaint. A tragic fact is that as I lay in bed after the day on which I had written to you, it *did* occur to me that "m.b." was not a misprint at all, and I determined to look up the play on the next day, and then forgot. I have not read it for a good many years. But I make no excuse. I take shelter behind the massive form of the great Doctor, who confused a horse's knee with his pastern.

Talking of the Doctor, I was reminded last night of his telling Boswell that his Scottish accent was "not offensive." This was when I was listening to your ex-secretary's broadcast on films. What a charming voice he has! I believe he could reconcile one to any accent, even the Australian.

I should immensely enjoy lunching with you one of these days. I cannot get away till the holidays come, but may I suggest a date then? I should particularly like to know by what steps you have become a Baconian; perhaps we shall hear all about it in *Ego* 6. Pearsall Smith will have to enlarge his note about ". . . that view of the authorship of S.'s plays which is so firmly held by one of His Majesty's judges, by officers in the Navy and the Army, and the manager of more than one large drapery establishment, and is corroborated by the authority of Mark Twain, Mrs Henry Pott, Prince Bismarck, John Bright, the late Mr Crump, K.C., and several thoughtful baronets."

But I don't really believe it. At 3.38 A.M. anything is possible. I once composed a poem at that hour.

Yours very sincerely,
GEORGE LYTTELTON

Here is my reply:

MY DEAR GEORGE LYTTELTON,

That's settled, then. You ring me up the moment the holidays start.

No, I shall not give my reasons for joining Pearsall Smith's "great lunatic asylum, that dark domain of ghosts and pedants, of blatherskites, monomaniacs, fanatics, and fools." One would have to review the entire literature of the subject, which Heaven forfend! I may say that hardly any of the arguments put forward by the Baconians have had weight with me. In ninety-nine cases out of a hundred the evidence isn't strong enough to convict a man of stealing a pair of boots!

In the meantime, do you know a little book of which the title-page is as follows:

A
DISSERTATION
on reading the
CLASSICS
and forming a
JUST STYLE
Written in the Year 1709
and addressed to the
RIGHT HONOURABLE
JOHN LORD ROOS
the present
MARQUIS OF GRANBY
BY
HENRY FELTON, D.D.
Rector of Whitwell in Derbyshire

The Second Edition, with large Additions

LONDON:
Printed for
JONAH BOWLER,
at the Rose in Ludgate Street
1715

Somebody has sent it to me, and I find it enchanting. "I hope Your Lordship will not think I have recommended any

Thing to You below your Quality : Your Fortunes place You far above the Necessity of Learning, but nothing can set You above the Ornament of it : And I am the more bold to press it upon Your Lordship, because these Accomplishments appear with greater Advantages, and do really sit more handsomely on Persons of Quality, than any other." (I wonder whether it is possible that this learned divine knew Mascarille's, " Les gens de qualité savent tout sans avoir jamais rien appris.") There is a delightful Preface : " But, perhaps, I had a Mind to be the first Modern that ever composed a Piece of this Nature without the Pomp of Quotations ; and since I did not see the Necessity of it, I was willing to avoid all Ostentations of Learning." And the end is charming : " The Additions must answer for themselves, for I don't care to enlarge this Preface any more."

I have given myself the pleasure of copying out a bit of the best which you may possibly like to read to your pupils. Happy thought—I shall be delighted to lend you the little book when we meet.

Yours very sincerely,

JAMES AGATE

July 2 *Friday.* The Paris German-controlled wireless says that to-morrow, July 3, the date fixed for the Invasion of Europe, is " off." Reason ? " The British never start anything at the week-end." *Deus quos vult perdere, dementat prius.* Never mind about Waterloo. Have they forgotten that Neville Chamberlain declared war on them on a Sunday ? Or that the invasion of North Africa happened at the week-end ? Their own poet Schiller provides the best answer : *Mit der Dummheit kämpfen Götter selbst vergebens.*

At the Café Royal to-night W. J. Turner and Sheila Shannon said that they both very much wanted me to write a volume for their series *Britain in Pictures*, published by Collins. They proposed Great British Actors and Actresses. I am immensely flattered and at once ask how much. Fifty pounds down and no royalties. I ask how many words. They say 14,000. Being fairly quick at mental arithmetic, I realise that, the average line containing seven words, this means 2000 lines. Now 2000 into £50 means 6*d.* a line. But hold on a bit. I don't get 6*d.* a line, or anything like it. If my arithmetic holds I get, after deducting tax, typing, etc., 1·714285 pence a line. So I say, " Let's talk about something else." They agree, and what we talk about is nothing but my conversion to the Baconian theory. Here I am violently opposed by Turner, and vitriolically by Sheila, so that I begin to waver. I agree that, arguing from style, the author of the essays must have had great difficulty in being the author of the plays. I just can't see Bacon writing about a cook and her eels: "She knapped 'em o' the coxcombs with a stick, and cried, *Down, wantons, down!*" And I have to admit that from the philosophic angle it is almost impossible to believe that Antony's spendthrift

> Let Rome in Tiber melt, and the wide arch
> Of the rang'd empire fall! Here is my space.
> Kingdoms are clay: our dungy earth alike
> Feeds beast as man: the nobleness of life
> Is to do thus;

was written by the "ca' canny" author of:

> A man's own observation, what he finds good of, and what he finds hurt of, is the best physic to preserve health. But it is a safer conclusion to say, *This agreeth not well with me, therefore I will not continue it, than this, I find no offence of this, therefore I may use it.* For strength of nature in youth passeth over many excesses, which are owing a man till his age. Discern the coming on of years, and think not to do the same things still; for age will not be defied.

So I compromise, and declare myself at most a non-Shakespearian, which is the half-way house to a Baconian.

Decide that I must apprise George Lyttelton of all this before I go to bed. But before I can do this I go to the Club, where I meet Frank Cellier, who tells me that when he came to London after ten years in the provinces he was seventeen months out of a job. And then, one afternoon when he was whitewashing the hen-house, he got four days' notice to replace Aubrey Smith in Tree's production of *Pygmalion.* After lots of whiskey I drive him home to Chelsea. And then to Grape Street, where I broach my last bottle, write to Lyttelton, and jot down the day's doings. To bed at four, *etwas besozzled.* In one of my earlier volumes of *Ego* I took for motto the saying of Napoleon's Marshal Hoche: "Donnez-moi un remède pour la fatigue, mais que ce remède ne soit pas le repos." Find me a way of abstaining from whiskey except not drinking it! As an interim measure have made a vow not to touch the stuff till 6 P.M. In accordance with this, drank at lunch to-day a pint and a half of beer and a small glass

Photo Guttenberg

Live-stock Men of Mark, No. 35
Mr James Agate

Photo Tunbridge-Sedgwick

Donald Wolfit as Richard III

of brandy. Snoozed for two hours all the same. Can it be that I shall have to be teetotal in the daytime ? Glum prospect. But I remember Aimée Tessandier saying to me at Arles during the last war, " A mon âge je n'ai pas le droit de jouer au-dessous de mes forces." Have always sworn to give up any vice that impinged upon my work, and up to the present have kept that vow. And now I begin to have the uncomfortable feeling that when I sprawl in my chair—my custom always of the afternoon—I begin to look like one of Rowlandson's more unpleasant cartoons. But surely the man who is an inveterate burner of the candle at both ends is entitled to blow it out between lunch and tea ? And then again I have the impression that my Diary was never livelier. This may be self-deception, against which I have taken steps. I have appointed Jock, George Mathew, and Brother Mycroft to act as a Committee who are to tell me when I *radote*, or drivel, or whatever the English word is. I am sworn, when this fiat goes forth, not to contest it but to put Finis to *Ego*, and henceforth hold my peace.

July 3 *Saturday.* To Dulwich to respond for the guests at the luncheon given by the Estates Governors of Alleyn's College of God's Gift, generally known as Dulwich College. The Master, G. H. Gilkes, made a fine and dignified speech—all about restoring the prestige of the old grammar schools so that a man, instead of coming back to his native city as an old Etonian or Wykehamist, will maintain himself as a Liverpudlian or Bristolian, and help to conduct the affairs of that native city in that spirit. Yes, but fancy being a Bacupite or a Rawtenstallian ! Fancy going through life talking like the tacklers in my old mill at Nelson, or any Lancashire member of the House, about a " con-cession " to Germany as though it were the opposite of a " pro-cession " to Hyde Park. A man may talk like a Scotsman, an Irishman, or a Welshman ; he must not have the local accent of Glasgow, Belfast, or Cardiff. Fancy never hearing English as the sons of gentlemen speak it, which, with some knowledge of cricket, was the only thing I got out of Giggleswick. This consciousness of speech may not matter after the war when there will be no more gentlemen. It was an odd genus, and great fun ; I regret its passing.

But to return to Dulwich. Realising that I was expected to

entertain, and the Board of Education being represented, I let myself go on the theme of Pope's

> Some are bewildered in the maze of schools,
> And some made coxcombs nature meant but fools.

except that I altered the first " some " to " all," and the second " some " to " most." Outlined my theory of education, which is briefly this. All boys to attend Council Schools until they are fourteen, at which age the masters will select by some process other than examination a certain number of proficient pupils. These will then be sent to Eton, Harrow, Winchester, Dulwich, and so forth, where, when the boys reach eighteen, the winnowing process will be repeated, the most promising to go on to the Universities. All education to be at the expense of the State, and nobody allowed to buy admission to public schools and universities. Women to receive instruction in the domestic arts only. Talked about the menace of internal-combustion engines and how, with the coming of the aeroplane, every fool in New York can be at Liverpool in half a day and every fool in Liverpool at New York. A bold theft (Ruskin) detected, I think, only by Gilkes. Told them what I thought of the dramatic critics who, rating plays on the Baedeker system, will print some such list as

* * * * * *Hi-de-Hi*
* * * * *La-di-Da-di-Da*
* * * *The Man Who Came to Dinner*
* * *A Month in the Country*
* *Love for Love*
The Master Builder

Told them about Basil Cameron at rehearsal refusing to go on with the Shebalin Symphony, and saying to the orchestra, " Gentlemen, this doesn't make sense ! " Asked why editors of literary reviews and highbrow magazines did not apply the same test to modern poetry. And a lot more persiflage as airy as feasible, but always coming back to the point of the uneducability of all women and the mass of males. In support of this quoted a conversation I heard in a bus one day this week :

YOUNG MAN (*combing hair with pocket-comb*). If I 'adn't seen 'im gettin' inter a fust-clawss kerridge I shouldn't never 'ave fawt 'e didn't 'ave nuffink.

YOUNG WOMAN (*powdering face*). Never mind 'im, Sid. You wasn't goin' ter take me ter the pictures Setterday, was yer ?

Argue that the fact that we have failed to educate this generation is every reason why we should not waste more money on the next. The reason water runs off a duck's back is not that you don't pour enough on!

I suppose there is a sense in which all of us are to some degree uneducated. Coming back by bus, I travelled with two little boys carrying jam-jars containing "tiddlers." I asked how often they changed the water. The elder, who was about eight years old, said with infinite contempt, "Don't jer know that changin' the water makes 'em die?" I queried this, and a grave-looking man behind me said, "I should 'ave thought everybody knew *that*!"

July 4 Sunday. News from Basle or Stockholm or Spitzbergen or somewhere pretends that Hitler has retired to Berchtesgaden with a nervous breakdown, the fifth within six months.

> O, that the slave had forty thousand lives!
> One is too poor, too weak for my revenge.

In what Max calls "the meantime, the great pale platitude of the meantime," the *Master Builder* article reads all right, I think. The *Observer* is in cracking form to-day. William Glock leads off with a piece of nonsense I should like to inscribe in gold ink on purple vellum:

> Innumerable performances of Tschaikowsky's piano concerto fail to yield the elementary lesson that such music should be abandoned.

While Alan Pryce-Jones says of something called *Caught*, "This is Mr Green's best book. He has always filled his own place in English letters; shown himself the equivalent of, say, Jouhandeau—an odd, haunted, ambiguous writer." Mr Green's syntax "is blurred—often unnecessarily so." But surely this should make your modernist think all the more highly of it. Silver ink on puce vellum.

Better, here is A. L. Rowse seeing in Shakespeare's Octavius Cæsar the counterpart of Cecil defeating Essex and the forerunner of Richelieu and Robespierre. But where did Stratford's young butcher pick up that political science which Bacon had at his finger-tips?

To the Ambassadors' Theatre in the afternoon to hear Leading Aircraftman Denis Matthews play the Emperor Concerto crisply, grandly, authoritatively, and Beethovenishly. An old man's head on a young man's shoulders. He was recalled again and again, the L.S.O., who know what's what, leading the applause. I went round to congratulate him, in which I found myself forestalled by Myra Hess. She was lovely to him, and I did my best to discard the bear, and beam instead of growl. I gathered that the boy is modest; in short, I saw no flaw anywhere. Let's hope he sticks to pianism and has no truck with transcribing Byrd for the glockenspiel. He is, I believe, twenty-four. Odd that our potential next great pianist should look like a composite portrait of Mickey Rooney and Eleonora Duse! After the interval, and still immensely moved, to my seat for Sibelius No. 2. Slept throughout and, I am afraid, snored. This worries me. But if I will sit up till 4 A.M. reading, and marvelling at, *Sketches by Boz*, what can I expect? But also how put down a book containing such miracles, at twenty-two years of age if you please, as "Mr and Mrs Butler are at present rusticating in a small village at Ball's Pond, pleasantly situated in the immediate vicinity of a brickfield"?

July 5 Monday. Foolish of me to get into a paddy over our mewlers and pukers. Some good poetry is still being written, and here is a moving thing sent me this morning. The author is a Mr William Booth, who writes to me from the Manor House, Drayton Bassett. There is, alas, no market for this kind of poem, too intelligible for the highbrow reviews and too rare fort he popular Press. This being so, I quote a few stanzas here:

THE HOME-COMING

We shall come home again
and the grey cliffs
radiant with sunshine,
and the white gulls
will welcome us.

We shall come home again
maybe in April
when the high clouds
are casting their shadows
over the Downlands
golden with buttercups;

and the wild birds
will sing to us
from the green hedgerows,
and the pale primrose
will hail our homecoming.

After the weary years,
after the waiting,
—waiting and watching—
watching the blue smoke
curling and trailing,
dreaming and waiting
endless the waiting—
after the longing,
maddened with dreaming,
we shall come home.

Shall we stand moodily
at the street corners,
strangers in village streets,
home towns and playgrounds
that once knew our footsteps ?

Shall we be pale ghosts
haunting your peace feasts
and spoiling your revels,
or will a great People
remembering greatly,
proudly and gratefully
welcome us home ?

The guns will be silent
and silent the bugles
and the green grasses
will cover the war scars.

Forgotten the war news,
forgotten the sirens,
forgotten the long years,
but we shall remember
—and the grey cliffs
and the white gulls,
they will remember us
when we come home.

July 6 *Tuesday.* That pleasant fellow and clever photographer Russell Sedgwick came to-day and took some pictures of the new flat. The one which I am going to like best shows me drinking tea on the roof with the housekeeper, Mrs Titford, her sons Peter (next to me) and Steve. As the parapet is less than a foot high, and as the waitress at the Crown appeared to be waving a tea-cloth at me *à la* Hilda Wangel, I stayed up there for as short a time as possible. None of your Master Builder nonsense for me ! On the ground floor I do not think I am at all like Solness. *I am not jealous of the younger generation.* When, this evening, I opened my *Punch* and read Jock's notice of *Tobias and the Angel* in Regent's Park beginning " The evening is heavy with the perfume of the late June roses. Brightness falls from the air, and a late finch twitters in the garden-croft (if Nashe, Henley, Keats, and the Weather Clerk are all agreeable) " my first thought was how rarely, in our modern criticism, do intelligence, charm, poetry, and fun interlace and intertwine as they do with my old pupil, now a master in his own right.

July 8 *Thursday.* Letter from Pamela Brown, who has left the cast of *Claudia* through illness kept at arm's length for months :

Wingfield Hospital
Headington
Oxford
3rd July, 1943

Dear Mr Agate,

I write to you because I always write to you when I am taking any kind of step, not that this is exactly a " step " but I felt I'd like to write all the same.

I have gone on playing Claudia until I really ceased to be able to walk, let alone run up and down stairs and pretend I was nineteen. I should be doing it still, I expect, but God sent me a temperature of 101½ for no reason at all and the matter was out of my hands. Sir Arthur Hurst, who is a wise and wonderful man, got me in here, where they have everything there is to cure legs that refuse to work. I won't bore you with details, but I am to have gold injections to cure the bug, and every sort of device to stop the legs from stiffening up. It may be a longish job—a matter of months rather than weeks, but I am not coming out until I am better.

So remember, if all the plays you have to see suddenly seem boring—and the theatre despair—that Sunday morning is made a better thing for me because I can read your *Sunday Times* article. Or am I too bold ? Yes, I am.

Love from
Pamela

In reply to which I wrote :

Flat 1
Queen Alexandra Mansions
*Grape St., W.C.*2
July 8*th*, 1943

MY DEAR HEDDA (no, *not* Claudia),

Do you remember Mr Nicodemus Dumps ? He comes in *Sketches by Boz*, the story called *The Bloomsbury Christening*. Dumps is the godfather of Master Frederick Charles William Kitterbell, and here is part of the speech he makes at the " sit-down supper " after the ceremony : " I hope and trust, ladies and gentlemen, that the infant whose christening we have this evening met to celebrate may not be removed from the arms of his parents by premature decay : that his young and now *apparently* healthy form may not be wasted by lingering disease. You, I am sure, will concur with me in wishing that he may live to be a comfort and a blessing to his parents. But should he not be what we could wish—should he forget in after-times the duty which he owes to them—should they unhappily experience that distracting truth, ' how sharper than a serpent's tooth it is to have a thankless child. . . .' " In other words, I do not think that you can look forward to a time when your state of health will permit you to be whirled about the stage in the manner of Juanita and the Ganjou Brothers.

Dear Pam, let's face it, you may never return to the stage. Having squared up to this tragedy—for that it would be—let's look around and see if we can espy any comfort. I think we can. I'm not going to tell you that victories are not always won on battlefields. You are an artist, and any consolation to be found for you must be such as befits an artist. Very well, then, I am not discouraged.

I foresaw all this at Oxford. I said to myself, " Here is a great little player who may, or who may not, have the health to grow into a great big one." I then bethought me of my favourite passage in all literature. It occurs at the end of Théophile Gautier's *Mademoiselle de Maupin* : " Combien sont morts qui, moins heureux que vous, n'ont pas même donné un seul baiser à leur chimère ! " I determined that you should have your heart's desire and greatly play a great part. This you did. Nothing can take from you the knowledge that, judged by the highest standards, you were as grand a Hedda Gabler as an actress of your age could hope to be. I am not lying to please you. I stake my critical reputation, such as it is, on the beauty and understanding of your performance. You followed this up by glamourising tosh—a great triumph, since the mark of the second-rate actress is that she is no good in anything except the masterpieces. If you return to the stage, be sure that if I am alive I shall be there to welcome you. If you do not return, may I be a perpetual guest in the theatre of your mind ? Attend first nights with me in spirit. Let me write you from time to time what I really think of that wan blossom, Miss X, and that splendacious orchid, Miss Y.

Now cheer up. The summer's flower is to the summer sweet, though to itself it only live and die. But it wasn't summer—it was February, if I remember aright. And your Hedda lived triumphantly.[1]

Ever your sympathetic
JAMES AGATE

July 10
Saturday.
Donald Wolfit sends me an amusing photograph of himself as Richard III, his best part. Somebody asked me to-day what was the greatest thrill I have known. My first Hallé concert ? My first glimpse of Sarah ? My first article in the *Manchester Guardian*, the *Saturday Review*, the *Sunday Times* ? The publication of my first book ? Presenting the prizes on speech-day at my old school ? I had to say, none of these. The proudest moment of my life was when, in 1913, I saw my photograph in the *Live-stock Journal*, inscribed :

LIVE-STOCK MEN OF MARK. No. 35

MR JAMES AGATE

July 11
Sunday.
While away the morning making a list of my Ten Best Short Stories. English language only. They are:

1. Kipling's *The Brushwood Boy.*

"'Ha ! Ha !' said the duck, laughing."

2. Osbert Sitwell's *Low Tide.*

" She often sits up quite late expecting Frederica to return, till the light in her eyes equals the flame of cheek and hair. I saw her last at low tide, one winter morning, dressed in a white-flannel costume (a new departure for her) and very much made-up. She must really be old by now."

[1] It gives me the greatest pleasure to record that Pamela has made a magnificent recovery, and as this book goes to press is rehearsing Ophelia in the forthcoming production of *Hamlet*, with Robert Helpmann.

3. Henry James's *An International Episode.*

How two American ladies, sisters, came on a visit to England, and how the Duchess of Bayswater thought the younger and unmarried one was trying to ' hook ' her son, Lord Lambeth.

4. Richard Middleton's *On the Brighton Road.*

About a young tramp who dies of pneumonia but still walks the Brighton road.

5. Arnold Bennett's *A Letter Home.*

Appeared originally in the *Yellow Book* for July 1895, when A. B. was still calling himself Enoch Arnold Bennett. A companion piece to No. 4.

6. Stacy Aumonier's *Miss Bracegirdle.*

About the English maiden lady who in a Paris hotel hides under a strange man's bed.

7. Saki's *Sredni Vashtar.*

About ten-year-old Conradin and how he gets his own back on his dragonsome guardian.

8. Ernest Hemingway's *The Capital of the World.*

The story of a little Spanish waiter rehearsing a bull-fight with another waiter who bound carving-knives to the legs of a chair to represent the horns of the bull.

9. Rebecca West's *The Salt of the Earth.*

About one of those pestiferously well-meaning women it is a pleasure as well as a duty to poison.

10. Damon Runyon's *The Brain Goes Home.*

" There is no denying Bobby Baker is a very smart little doll, and in the four or five years she is one of The Brain's dolls, she gets more dough out of him than all the others put together, because she is always telling him how much she loves him, and saying she cannot do without him, while Doris Clare and Cynthia Harris sometimes forget to mention this more than once or twice a month."

As I was in the middle of this Leo came in in a vile temper. " Why this sudden passion for short stories ? " he grumbled. " I loathe short stories." To which I retorted, " What the hell do you know about short stories ? You couldn't write one if you stood on your head ! " Whereupon he departed slamming the door. And re-appeared exactly twenty minutes later with some typed sheets saying, " Is *this* any good ? And I have *not* stood on my head ! " I read, and discover that *this* is pure Strindberg.

MARRIAGE

They sat facing each other at the breakfast-table as they did every morning at nine o'clock—ten on Sundays. He reading his *Daily Mail*, she playing with a piece of toast. Then she yawned.

"Why are you yawning?"

"Why do you ask silly questions?"

"At any rate it is a civil question. You might give a civil reply."

"Might I?"

"What's the matter with you this morning, Alice?"

"Why particularly this morning?"

"Are you ill?"

"No, I'm not ill."

"Then why so silent and morose?"

"Do you really want to know?"

"Of course I want to know."

"I AM BORED."

"Why?"

"Why am I bored? Because you bore me always, always."

"Is this a recent development?"

"No. You started boring me on our honeymoon. You can't help it, you *are* a bore. You bore every one. You were born a bore."

"And you, my dear? Are *you* amusing? Do you think I enjoy *your* company? I am glad to get away from you. You haven't an idea in your head. And if you had, you are too silly to be able to express it. You are a bore, if you like. Crashing! Devastating!"

"Henry, why do we go on like this, day after day? We don't like each other. I don't think we ever liked each other. We never ought to have married. We ought to have separated long ago. After all, I have a job, I can keep myself. Why do we have to go on boring each other? We shall hate each other soon."

"I often find myself hating you, Alice. And you are getting so plain. So *dowdy*. You were always rather an unattractive woman, but these days you are almost hideous."

"I know, you're telling me nothing fresh. Unhappy women all get ugly. Do you find me repulsive?"

"I'm afraid so. That is why it is such a long time since . . ."

"I know. I'm glad. I always hated *that*. Do you think I haven't always loathed you in that way? There is something about you that has always made me squirm every time you came near me."

" Perhaps it would have been different if we had had a child."

" Strange for *you* to say that. When I could have had a child you didn't want one. Then after my illness, when I couldn't have a child, you suddenly wanted one."

" Shall we always go on like this ? "

" Yes, always. Only worse."

" Can't we alter it ? "

" Only by leaving each other."

" We can't do that. We've been over that ground over and over again. We can't leave each other."

" Then we must just put up with it. Won't you lose your train ? I should hate you to lose your train. I might have to talk to you a little longer."

" I'm going now. I shall be back at the usual time."

" Yes, only death can save me from that."

" If I were you I should run away. I often wanted to."

" Why didn't you ? "

" I should have had to come back."

" Why ? "

" Habit. The thing that makes most married people endure each other, live with each other. I should have come back."

" So should I. You'll miss your train."

" Good-bye, Alice."

" Good-bye, Henry."

July 12 *Monday*. Cheated one of my old time three-in-the-morning nerves-cum-wind attacks last night by reading Damon Runyon's story about a dramatic critic.

This Ambrose Hammer is what is called a dramatic critic by trade, and his job is to write pieces for the paper about the new plays that somebody is always producing on Broadway, and Ambrose's pieces are very interesting, indeed, as he loves to heave the old harpoon into actors if they do not act to suit him, and as it will take a combination of Katherine Cornell, Jimmy Durante, and Lillian Gish to really suit Ambrose, he is generally in there harpooning away very good.

I love " the new plays that somebody is always producing on Broadway." This perfectly hits off the extraordinary casualness of the profession. This story, *What, No Butler ?*, also contains the remark I like best in the whole of Runyon. Mr Justin Veezee is in the Club Soudan only a few hours ago watching the Arabian acrobatic dancer turn flip-flops, " although personally,"

Ambrose says, "I do not think she is any more Arabian than Miss Ethel Barrymore."

Montague writes approvingly of the author who "Treats you as no blind horse, but a man who has some wit of his own and can take a thing in." D. R. has the same tact; if the reader doesn't get a point, that's his loss. "I am surprised you fall for etchings," Ambrose says, speaking very severely, indeed, to Miss Cleghorn (the Arabian dancer). "It is one of the oldest build-ups of a doll in the world," he says. Five pages later Ambrose is saying to the narrator in strict confidence, "The last time I see Miss Cleghorn up to to-night is the night I invite her to my own apartment to look at etchings, and they are better etchings than Mr Justin Veezee shows her, at that." If my memory is correct the works of art with which Lavedan's Marquis de Priola used to entice ladies to visit him were called "almanacks." Etchings or almanacks, they have always been whatever is the French for "build-ups."

July 13 *Tuesday.* There being no first nights this week and the *Sunday Times* column staring blankly at me, I square up this morning to the task of deciding who wrote Shakespeare's plays. Just as I am in the middle of this a knock comes to the door and a dirty-nosed Guido Reni cherub presents me with a note. He turns out to be a messenger from the *Radio Times* asking for 750 words on *Peer Gynt*, the occasion being the forthcoming Grieg jamboree. In something under half an hour I produce the following:

> There were three playwrights in Ibsen. The third was the familiar Ibsen who wrote about the purse-proud, snobbish, down-at-heel, dowdy inhabitants of dull, convention-ridden Norway—vital, significant plays smelling of yesterday's cold mutton. The first Ibsen wrote historical dramas in prose. The middle Ibsen wrote poetic dramas, the second and last of which is *Peer Gynt*.
>
> To this play Edvard Grieg wrote some very pleasant, tuneful, and entirely harmless incidental music. How much of the play shall we be hearing on the air? Not more, I imagine, than just enough to hang Grieg's incidental music on. I may be wrong. Anyhow, this is the place to say that all the important parts of Ibsen's drama are the later ones, and just those for which Grieg did not provide any music. Doubtless

the composer was under the thumb of the dramatist, and I guess that Edvard only provided what Henrik wanted. In other words Ibsen probably said to himself: "Give 'em the jam, and perhaps they'll stay for the powder."

Now let's go back a bit and see what *Peer Gynt* is about. First we must realise that Ibsen's mind was made up of three things: obstinacy, logic, and consistency. Obstinacy. In comparison with his obstinacy granite is a melting jelly. His most famous play, *A Doll's House* (1879), suggests that a wife may be right to leave her husband. Logic. At this there is an outcry whereupon Ibsen sits down to write *Ghosts* (1881), which shows the horrible results accruing when a wife insists on sticking to her husband. Consistency. *Peer Gynt* shows that fifteen years before this Ibsen was pursuing the same game. The previous year's poetic drama, *Brand* (1866), showed how an unselfish man can cause more suffering by his unselfishness than a sinner by his selfishness. A hullabaloo resulting, Ibsen creates in Peer Gynt an egoist who thinks to get through the world by setting up as his criterion of conduct the satisfaction of his own will. Glamourising himself he became a liar, a cheat, and a snob, and finally goes mad. "I present you in Brand with a howling prig and in Peer Gynt with a howling cad; buy your stall and take your choice," Ibsen may well have chortled behind his hedgehoggery of whisker.

Quite how the B.B.C. is going to hang this appalling drama on to Solveig's Song and Anitra's Dance is still to be seen. (I beg the reader's pardon—I mean heard.) At any rate let the reader be assured that if he does not hear the Sphinx Scene, the Madhouse Scene, the Funeral Scene with the priest's magnificent speech, the all-important Onion-Scene and the long colloquy between Peer and the Button-Moulder—a figure symbolising possibly Death—he has not heard Ibsen's play, whatever inessentials may have filtered through. Is the Button-Moulder a bit of a button-holer? Yes, but he is an essential part of Ibsen's play. Is the Boyg rather less than the broth of a Boyg? Yes, but he, too, is part of Ibsen's play. In short, it's a masterpiece.

The first half is as mother's milk—none can be so poor of imagination as not to behold his own boyhood in this shaggy young Norwegian. Ase's death is one of the most grandly inspired things in all romantic drama. The boy astride his chair, driving his mother hell-for-leather to the gates of Heaven, and all to the honour of his wild, poetic, impossibly romantic self—this is a conception not above, nor below, but beside Shakespeare. Up to Ase's death there is nothing which the most intrepid producer can cut, except, perhaps, about half of everything everybody has to say, and all the queer political allusions. No bulk excisions are possible. But two hours have passed, and less than two remain for all those diffuse yet reinforcing experiences of Peer's later life. Forty years of greed, vanity, egoism, braggadocio, heartlessness, sentimentality, courage, cowardice—each quality a facet of Gyntism, a way of " being oneself "—if Ibsen couldn't get this into two hours it is certain his abbreviators can't.

I am not sure that any producer, however skilful, can prevent the audience from interpreting Solveig's last consolatory appearance as the conventional melodramatic apotheosis of Redemption by Love. This is Peer's view of the situation which Ibsen is at such pains to deny. Demolition ought to come in with the Button-Moulder's cackling threat that they will meet again at the last cross-road, " and *then* we'll see whether . . ." His voice trails away. What is to be seen at the last cross-road is whether a good woman's love can redeem a weak man's paltriness.

The production of *Peer Gynt* is a devil of a job in the theatre. What the radio will make of it we have still to learn.

The fact that I dug most of this out of old articles is nobody's business. After the interruption I find I have lost my bearings in the Shakespeare-Bacon controversy and have to start all over again.

July 15 *Thursday.* My frisk in the *S.T.* on the Shakespeare-Bacon affair takes shape as follows :

This is to announce that I have half joined what Mr Logan Pearsall Smith, the author of the wittiest, sensiblest, and most lovely of all books on Shakespeare, calls the " herds of Baconian believers, as they plunge squeaking down the Gadarene slope of their delusion."

What does it matter ? Nothing at all, unless dramatic critics are to be become dramacologists, which is the equivalent of Mr Newman's " musicologists." Does it matter to any lover of the *sound* of *Tristan* whether or not Wagner's father was a Jew ? No, but exact knowledge of Wagner's parentage might explain why, in the third bar of the Prelude, he wrote D sharp instead of D natural. Similarly we might reason that Antony's " The nobleness of life is to do thus " must be Shakespeare, since the author of *Regiment of Health* must have held that " age will not be defied."

Have I read all the evidence ? No. Life is too short to read the multitude of books on the subject. Besides, I have half-joined the Baconians *in spite of* the evidence rather than because of it. Nine-tenths of it is mere "piffle before the wind;" the last tenth is overwhelming. It is complete nonsense to suggest that because Shakespeare wrote "O gross and miserable ignorance!" he cannot have neglected his daughter Judith's education, or that "Beauty lives with kindness" proves that he could not have left his widow shabbily provided. All this is too much like the clergyman composing his sermon on the text of "Suffer little children" and opening his window to threaten the urchins playing beneath that if they don't go away he will wring their unwashed little necks.

Ciphers and Cryptograms. But how miserably inadequate and ineffective are these! I made a bet with myself recently that within half an hour I would invent a cipher more convincing than those generally adduced, and with no more cheating than the Baconian Theory allows. In twenty-five minutes I produced the following. The initial letters of the First Sonnet are: F.T.B.H.B.F.M.T.T.A.W.A.P.T. Now take, in their published order, those of Bacon's Essays which begin with these letters. They are Friendship, Truth, Boldness, Health, Beauty, Fortune, Marriage and Single Life, Travel, True Greatness, Adversity, Vain-Glory ("Put it down a we, my Lord, put it down a we"), Atheism, Parents, and Things (Vicissitude of). Where does this lead us? As I read it, Bacon is saying to the author of the Sonnets, his young collaborator—only collaboration can reconcile the fluidity of the poet with the aridity of the essayist—"Fair youth, in return for my Friendship consider that in the matter of Truth a mixture of a lie doth ever add pleasure. The right use of Bold persons is that they never command in chief but under the direction of others. Political Health doth not permit me to be known as a dabbler in roguish and vagabond Beauty or to take concern for the Fortunes of players. The stage is more beholding to love than the life of man, and had you not contracted Marriage with Mistress Anne Hathaway I must have found another prop. In the matter of Travel consider whether we twain are not a mutual pair—you to whom travel is still a part of education, and I, the picked man of countries, to whom it is a part of experience. Know too that the True Greatness of an authour consists in his writings and not in the fame thereby gained, and least when that fame brings on the sourer uses of Adversity. Why then should I trouble about Vain-Glory? I desire not to be the idol of parasites or the slave of my own vaunts. The Almighty is not less the Almighty because of Atheists, and Bacon will not be less Bacon because you, Shagsper, will be deemed the Parent and onlie begetter of his dramas. My brain, young sir, shall prove the female to your soul. And that, my imp of fame, is how Things stand between us." Can I produce another cryptogram? Ay, and twenty such.

Too little research. And how weakly these Baconians pursue their quarry! One writer makes great play with the fact that in 1588 at St Albans Grammar School, of which Bacon's father was a governor, there was a master called Holocomes, implying that Bacon drew Shakespeare's Holofernes from him. But why not compare Holofernes's "I abhor such fanatical phantasimes, such insociable and point-devise companions, such rackers of orthography" with a passage in Bacon's own letter to Burleigh: "If I could purge it [knowledge] of two sorts of rovers, whereas the one with frivolous disputations, confutations, and verbosities, the other with blind experiments and auricular traditions and impostures, hath committed so many spoils, I hope I should bring in industrious observations, grounded conclusions, and profitable inventions, and discoveries"? The date of this latter is 1589, the very year of the writing of *Love's Labour's Lost*, presuming managers took the usual couple of years to decide about producing a play.

To sum up, I think I am anti-Shakespeare, but not pro-Bacon. In betting parlance, I regard the odds in the Great Tudor Handicap as Collaboration a hot favourite at 2-1 on, Bacon 11-8 against, Shakespeare 7-2 against, and 100-1 any other.

July 16 *Friday.* Panic-stricken at discovering in the Café to-night that in the frenzy of typing and re-typing, a line in my Shakespeare cryptogram has got dropped. The gods being charitable, I procure a car, collect the copy, and rush home to make the necessary corrections, which the driver returns to the office about one in the morning.

July 18 *Sunday.* Ivor Brown ends his article in the *Observer* to-day: "What is wrong now is not a vulgar choice of play, (ancient and modern classics are booming in London), but the reluctance of the many to see these plays unless they are festooned with star-names in the cast. True, the stars have usually earned their stardom, but we shall never have any innovation and vitality in the drama if nobody will attend the unstarred article." My experience over fifty years is that the unstarred article is the article not worth starring. Where, pray, are the actors to come from ? I put the number of players in London worth watching at 300. If every town and village in England is to have its complement, then some 30,000 will be required. And they won't and can't be there. When I was a young man I was content to sit on a stool in a dingy Manchester warehouse writing out tickets and gumming them on to samples of flannelette day after day and week after week, knowing that when I had saved enough money I should have my jaunt to London or Paris and see Mrs Patrick Campbell or Réjane. The essence of a capital is that provincials will put up with their drab existence in order to enjoy, once every three months or so, a delirious week-end of theatres, restaurants, and what-not, such as only a capital can provide. For the provincial who has talent London should still be a battlefield. " A nous deux maintenant ! " exclaimed Rastignac, shaking his fist at Paris. I cannot see that " A nous deux, Barrow-in-Furness ! " can ever be the same thing. Or that Beardsley's

> réclame and recall,
> Paris and St Petersburg, Vienna and St James's Hall

can be translated into

> réclame and recall,
> Poplar and St Margaret's, Llandudno and the parish hall.

July 19 *Monday.* Horrified to read in an article by Hamilton Fyfe in *John o' London's Weekly* :

> If my Fielding were not all in one vast volume I should be tempted to throw away *Tom Jones,* which has long seemed to me the boringly boisterous chronicle of a stupid young man's sexual adventures.

Though I am not a Proustian, Heaven forbid that I should describe the *Recherche* as " the boringly brainsickly chronicle of a super-sensitive young man's homosexual researches " !

July 20 *Tuesday.* Letter from Cambridge :

> With reference to your article in this week's *Sunday Times* : Do you think it likely that in three hundred years the plays of Emlyn Williams will be attributed to Sir Stafford Cripps, on the ground that nobody brought up in a pub in a North Wales mining village could have written them ?

My reply:

No. Because the critic of three hundred years hence will realise that there is not a word in any of Emlyn's plays which could not have been written by a young Welsh miner of lively imagination and warm sympathies. He will make the point that such knowledge of the polite usages of the day as evinced in, say, *Night Must Fall* is just as much or as little as could be gathered by any young Welshman coming to this country to take a job as houseboy. Indeed, the only doubt that the critic of A.D. 2243 will have is whether Emlyn the playwright can have been identical with Emlyn the stage-player. This in view of the ignorance of stage ways exposed in *The Light of Heart*, in which an impresario of the acumen of C. B. Cochran is alleged to engage to star as King Lear at a leading theatre—a notorious dipsomaniac!

July 21 *Wednesday.* Desmond MacCarthy hit the nail on the head when he wrote on Sunday last in *A Letter to the Common Reader*: "But when we [the highbrows] want to relax over a book we can't get distraction or entertainment from the tosh you read. The habit of attending to the written word is too strong, and of thinking what's what as we go along." This goes for me at the cinema. I would rather spend two hours scrubbing floors or peeling potatoes than sit through the average sentimental film. The answer, of course, is that I am not a scrubber of floors or a peeler of potatoes, and that the people who are normally engaged in these humdrum occupations find that romantic which I find merely common. Well, I don't think romantic commonness is good for cinema-goers, and if I had any share in making the new world I should first of all establish a Censorship of Taste. How, then, would I propose that the lower classes fill in that time which my censorship would empty, since the taste of the masses is insusceptible of improvement? I would restore the old English sports and amusements, bear-baiting and cock-fighting, wrestling, boxing with naked fists, and open-air dancing. I would increase the strength of beer while lessening its price, and would let every man drink as much as he could decently carry. I would establish municipal dance halls and jazz parlours in which tap-dancing and swing would be non-stop and compulsory. These, being vulgarities of the body, do not soil the mind. I would consider restoring public executions, so much less demoralising than the average film. They may be revolting, but at least the revolt is against horror and affrightment; there is nothing cheap and sentimental about a hanging. The age which indulged in these pastimes produced Spenser, Marlowe, Ben Jonson, and Shakespeare. The age of the mushy novel, the cinema, and the wireless has produced the bosom clasper, the film star, and the crooner. Bah!

July 22 *Thursday.* A letter:

Cotswold
Freeman's Lane
Staines, Middlesex
20.7.'43

DEAR MR AGATE,

The Proustian who replied, in answer to your query, that you must give up your whole life to reading Proust, was talking nonsense, and unoriginal nonsense at that. He probably had in mind Joyce's reported answer to Max Eastman, when the latter suggested that *Finnegan's Wake* made too heavy a demand upon the reader and that the author should provide a key: "The demand that I make of my reader is that he should devote his whole life to reading my works." The story is told by Edmund Willson.

In any case, Proust is not a life's labour but a life's love. He makes no demands of the reader save that the reader shall descend with him into a sort of heavenly Hell—and even then he doesn't care much whether the answer is Yes or No, because he is having such a lovely time himself. The only pre-requisite the English reader needs for enjoyment of the book is a certain knowledge of the structure of French society over the period of action: That duchesses are smarter than princesses, that to the *ancienne noblesse* the Iénas, the Borodinos, and the rest of the Empire aristocracy are what my grandfather would have called "cag-mag."

Knowing Proust is like having the map of an enchanted island and a boat to take you there. The monstrously tragic comedian Charlus, the frightful bitch Oriane, who is a dream of delight for all that, little Marcel himself with his glossy dark eyelashes, the only man in the girls' Paul Jones, have nothing in common with literary blood and sweat and tears.

When I die I rather hope to go to Heaven and become a Guermantes. Meanwhile I did enjoy *Ego* 5 and look forward to being annoyed and cheered by 6.

Yours sincerely,
PAMELA HANSFORD JOHNSON

July 23 *Friday.* I ought to have foreseen the avalanche of letters that would descend on me as the result of last Sunday's frisk in the Shakespeare-Bacon affair. Fortunately I realise that the writers don't expect an answer, that they are merely cleansing the stuff'd bosom of that perilous stuff which weighs upon the heart. What my correspondents haven't realised is that the controversy doesn't really interest me except as a detective puzzle. I am not curious about the private lives of great writers, or even about the way they worked. How many hours Flaubert wasted lying on the sofa, smoking cigarettes and pretending to be gestating the *mot juste*, how many cups of coffee Balzac drank, how much opium Coleridge consumed, how many of his housemaids Dickens romped with—these things seem to me not to matter. Further, I hold that life is not long enough to admit of more than one thing of each kind. In the matter of sagas mine is the *Comédie Humaine*, which leaves me no time for the Rougon-Macquart brood, the Forsytes, the Herrieses, and the Rakonitzes. My mystery is the Dreyfus case, and I still lie sleepless o' nights wondering exactly what part du Paty de Clam played in that nefarious business. Or I wake up to find him standing at the foot of the bed dressed as a Veiled Lady and handing me a Secret Document. Let my last word be that since all argument is for Bacon and all belief for Shakespeare, to combine the two can't do much harm.

July 24 *Saturday.* I am disposed to write to-day about golf. Why? Because it is a fine Saturday, and if it were peace-time and I were eight or ten years younger I should now be getting into the car and running down to Thorpe Bay to challenge, at the odds of four bisques, my old foe Fred Winsor, from whom I heard this morning. A letter from Mars would not have seemed stranger. Winsor writes:

> Since joining the service (R.A.F.) two and a half years ago and running the pro's job at Ruislip I seem to have had all my time occupied, even so I feel very guilty in not having written to you before. I sincerely hope you are in the best of health, and that although times are difficult you still manage to have a game of golf. I play quite a lot at Moor Park for the R.A.F. which I will admit is very fortunate for me. I often think of the blood-matches we used to have—Thorpe Hall, Orsett, and Burnham-on-Crouch, and I wish we could arrange

to have a game this season. Perhaps you would let me know if this is possible and if so the most convenient course for you. Hoping you do not mind me writing to you, and also it will not be long before we get back to those clever bisques of yours. . . .

" Clever bisques." What a world that brings up, a world I thought I had forgotten. Let me face it ; I shan't play golf again. Unless, of course, they lay out a special course with a moving belt like an escalator running along the fairway. I might manage six holes on a flat course, but what would be the good of that ? Yet I mustn't complain. I have had my good times, and I was a goodish golfer. Who but a goodish player would have got down to a handicap of two without ever mastering, indeed always muffing, the key-shot of the game ? Despite hours, days, and weeks of coaching and practice, I never mastered the mashie. I remember hearing Tommy Renouf tell Edgar Baerlein, who was plus 3, that his mashie shot was a glorified jab. Mine wasn't even glorified. It was nothing. My driving was longish and fairly accurate. (Shall I ever forget four superb tee-shots at the four last holes at Deal ?) My spoon-shots were dreams of Hiltonesque efficiency. (I remember a bobby dazzler at Newcastle, County Down). My iron-play was like Drake's conquest of the Pacific. (Was there not a cleek shot in the teeth of a gale at Walton Heath which settled the match and took us out of the rain ?) My niblick ? Not Hagen ever got more successfully out of cattle-trodden ground. Why, then, were my mashie shots hopeless ? But I must stop drooling. That way melancholy lies.

July 25 *Sunday.* Can't help comparing Enid Bagnold's thriller, *Lottie Dundass*, with Abel Hermant's wry little masterpiece, *La Fameuse Comédienne*. Consider the four principal characters in the French play. Honoré Bourgevin, proprietor of the cabaret called " La Levrette en Paletot," fat, lazy, unable to lift his feet and, when he stands up, obviously dreaming about sitting down again. Madame Bourgevin, the traditional *dame de comptoir* and anywhere between the ages of forty and seventy. Aurélie, fourteen, snub-nosed, tender-eyed, common. Lucien, " jeune, grand, mince, joli, équivoque." Everybody who has had his elbows on the zinc recognises Bourgevin. Every modern French painter has painted Mme Bourgevin. All Montmartre knows Aurélie. And Lucien is at the beck and call of every Paris *miché*. Pure Paris, and Montmartre-Paris at that, all richly comic personages waiting for your best French actors. Now consider the heterogeneous collection at the Vaudeville. The father—in the asylum—has to be a ham actor and the son of a great actor, in order to explain his daughter's talent and her mental instability. The mother is St John Ervine's Jane Clegg all over again. Lottie is a character out of a tragic novelette instead of any stage-struck little tart. And Leppie, the honest plumber who courts her, comes straight out of any domestic drama by J. B. Priestley. A mixture of Hull and Bradford and Brixton and Brighton, with none of that French precision which makes you know not only the town but the street the characters live in. Contrast Sybil Thorndike's admonition to Leppie, " Come, lad, it won't do for thee to wed my lass "—I don't pretend that these are the exact words—with Lucien's opening remark to Aurélie : " Ça me fait drôle de te voir en blanc. Pourquoi que tu t'es f . . . en blanc et ta mère en soie ? " Am I committing the oldest of all mistakes, that of liking something less than I should because it isn't something else ? Yes. And this time I have no qualms about it. Sybil's performance has quite bowled over Ivor, who writes in to-day's *Observer* :

> " We shall have to move house again." These are simple words, but aching with shame and weariness of a " flitting " enforced. As a Home County " Mum " Dame Sybil far outranges the tragic potentialities of a barbaric Medea.

I despair of getting Ivor to see that maundering in monotone—and Sybil does it very well—is as much easier than the true delivery of Medea's great speech beginning " O my sons, my sons, you have indeed a city, and a house " as the first movement of the Moonlight Sonata is easier than the last. What a pity Ivor doesn't play the piano ! What a still greater pity he didn't have another look at his Euripides !

July 26 *Monday.* " Reckoning fish as nothing." Mussolini's resignation brings to mind the great Elliston's pronunciamento, recorded by Lamb. " I never eat but one thing at dinner, reckoning fish as nothing." The object of the Allies in this war is to make a meal of Germany, reckoning Italy as nothing.

July 27 Letter from a schoolmaster in Cumberland :
Tuesday.

As a schoolmaster I contend that our cramped educational system gives no scope for the wayward brilliant. It fosters the bookworm and nurses the intellectual. But of the irresponsible young hopeful whose scintillating wit flashes but rarely, it takes no cognizance. I enclose one of these flashes by a boy of 9, a youngster who has little use for the routine of the classroom, one who *may* be classified as "slightly retarded" under modern educational standards. Without preliminaries, he produced this work for a Nature Magazine, a feature published regularly in this school and exchanged with a rural school in Westmorland. I should be interested to know

(*a*) your opinions of his work,
(*b*) what suggestions you would make to foster and develop this boy's ability.

From time to time he has produced work of a similar standard entirely unaided.

Enclosed is the following poem :

OUR WONDERFUL WORLD

"Blue, all blue, it's a wonderful world!"
Sang the skylark soaring high—
"It's green, all green, and the fairest seen!"
Said the field-mouse in reply.
"Oh, away with your blues and away with your greens,
That I haven't eyes to see;
The earth is my hole—that I love," said the mole,
"And it's black, all black to me."

NOBLE BIRKETT (*age* 9)

My reply :

I think the thing to do is to let the boy alone. There may be a budding poet here or there may not. In any case I shouldn't attempt to force the child. I am afraid my general views on education are unorthodox. In my opinion the forcing of book-learning on young people indiscriminately is a mistake. The essence of schoolmastering is to find out what a child is fit for. If a boy is interested in aeroplanes teach him mathematics. If in forestry, show him how to plant an acorn and fell a tree. If in music, then give him piano lessons. If in poetry, then leave Palgrave's *Golden Treasury* lying about. But as a rule I should reduce book-learning to a minimum and teach all boys shorthand, typing, and the simpler trades. The girls I should teach to sew, cook, and sweep floors. If there are any budding Abraham Lincolns and Anna Sewards among them they will educate themselves.

Letter from India :

Talukdari Girassia College
Wadhwan Camp
Kathiawar
India
12*th April* 1943

DEAR MR AGATE,

A query !

Picture of your study facing page 97 of *Ego* 5—Is the lower picture, centre of the wall, a photograph of your horse Ego or of the " Divine Sarah " reclining on a couch ?

I should like to tell you how very much I have enjoyed your *Ego* series. I possess the last 4 volumes, which I hope to get you to autograph for me when the world returns to normal and I am free of this distasteful sub-continent for good. I was brought up in Dublin in the Abbey Theatre atmosphere (I knew Sean O'Casey in the days of his tentative early efforts !). With six years in the service of the Siamese Government and eight years as Principal of a College for potentates' offspring (the atmosphere akin to Akbar's days) I've been cut off from civilisation to a great extent and have doubly relished your volumes.

Peace and *Ego* 6 are two things to which I look forward eagerly !

Sincerely,
C. R. MANDY

July 28 *Wednesday.* A. V. Alexander, at lunch at the Club to-day, lectured me on where I had gone wrong in my criticism of Esther McCracken's *Living Room* and insisted on its superiority over Shaw's *Widowers' Houses.* I listened with a brilliant assumption of patience. When he had finished I said, " Would the First Lord like to hear my views on naval strategy ? " Am bound to say he took it very well.

At the Café Royal to-night met James Bridie, who was pleased to say that I am this country's best essayist and worst critic.

July 29 *Thursday.* To the Arts Theatre for the revival of *The Constant Couple*. Doran talks of the " absurd and unnatural scene between Farquhar's hero and Angelica." Nonsense ! What about Maupassant's delicious *Une Soirée* ? The sergeant Varajou, having a week's leave and being low in funds, decides to spend the time at a dull hole in Brittany where he has a married sister, one Madame Padoie. He is staggered by the desolation of the place, dinner is uneatable, and it is manifestly impossible to pass the evening *tête-à-tête* with his hostess. *Quoi faire ?* He seeks the local café, gets *un peu blotto,* and then :

— Hé, l'employé !
— Voilà, m'sieu.
— Dites, l'employé, ousqu'on rigole ici !
— Vous demandez ousqu'est la maison ?
— Mais oui, parbleu !
— Vous prenez la deuxième rue à gauche et puis la première à droite—C'est au 15.
— Merci, ma vieille. V'là pour toi.
— Merci, m'sieu.

But Varajou forgets to ask whether in leaving the café he should turn right or left. He decides to chance it. Arrived at No. 15 he finds four ladies, one elderly and three young, all *décolletées* and obviously expecting visitors. He breaks the ice. " Eh bien, on ne rigole donc pas. Je paye une bouteille de vin. . . ." At that moment the door opens and his brother-in-law, Padoie, comes in. This is heaven for Varajou, who sees stretching out before him an unending vista of forced loans and blackmail. He throws his arms round his brother-in-law's neck. " Farceur ! farceur . . . Tu fais donc la fête, toi. . . . Et ma sœur ! . . . Tu la lâches, dis ! . . ." And then over Padoie's shoulder he sees two more visitors, *en habit, décorés.* He is not where he thinks he is, but at a party given by a high civic dignitary ! The story ends with Padoie bellowing, " Ah ! Ah ! Canaille ! canaille ! canaille ! canaille ! "

In the play to-night Sir Harry Wildair is Varajou, and Lady Darling and her daughter Angelica are the ladies in Maupassant's story. Consider the opening of Act 2, Scene 2. Enter Wildair with a letter. " Well, if this paper-kite flies sure, I'm secure of my game. Humph ! the prettiest bordel I have seen ; a very stately genteel one—(*Footmen cross the stage*) Heydey ! equipage too !—'Sdeath, I'm afraid I've mistaken the house ! " Then Lady Darling enters, whereupon Sir Harry has his " No, this must be the bawd by her bulk." And so on. The more respectable half of the plot is concerned with the belated coming together of Colonel Standard and Lady Lurewell. Of the Colonel, our old friend Archer says that " he is a bluff honest soldier, not a saint, but still less a blackguard. . . . Gives clear evidence of an innate decency of feeling denied to other playwrights of the time. . . . The character is not very vividly drawn." What Archer is trying to say is that the Colonel is a heavy bore. By the way, whenever he could forget that he was a Scot and a puritan the critic of the *World* was capable of great perception ; he was the first to make out a case for Farquhar as a better *dramatist* than Congreve, Wycherley, or Vanbrugh. He points out that when Congreve strayed into the country he took his London cast with him and made a house-party of them, whereas Farquhar made a play out of the people he found at Shrewsbury and Lichfield. Alec Clunes very good to-night.

Aug. 1 *Sunday.* Greatly shocked to hear of the sudden death yesterday of Owen Nares. He was on an E.N.S.A. tour, had reached Brecon, and had just signed the visitors' book at Mrs Siddons's birthplace, the Shoulder of Mutton Inn, when he collapsed. The B.B.C. asking me for a few words, I sent them this :

Owen Nares was a much better actor than most people supposed. As a young man he was handicapped by excessive good looks, a lisp, and a babyish air which consorted ill with his wicket-keeper's hands and the stature of a heavy-weight boxer. Playgoers did not at the beginning take him seriously. They did not realise that this downy-faced, velvet-mannered young man had a steely will and an entirely incorruptible artistic sense. He determined to be a good actor, and unlike most of to-day's aspirants he conceived the extraordinary notion of learning his job thoroughly, from the start. He began by studying under Rosina Filippi and playing small parts in plays by Ibsen and Pinero. He was a natural player and though success dogged him it could not spoil him. He even overcame the handicap of being a matinée idol, and this was perhaps his greatest feat. His best performances were in *Old Heidelberg*, *Milestones*, and *Romance*. Owen Nares steered a sensible course between the ultra-popular and the super-highbrow. He was a player and did not pretend to be anything more. He gave the spectator what he had paid his money for—acting. Behind the scenes he was looked upon with respect and affection. In a word he was a player on the stage and a gentleman off it. His charm was extraordinary, and in losing him the stage parts with some of its magnetism.

In the hurry I forgot to say that Owen was one of the wittiest after-dinner speakers I have ever heard. One did not look to him for wit; when he rose to speak he was ablaze with it.

Aug. 2 *Monday.* The first letter I opened to-day was from Owen. He must have written it on the morning of the day he died. It was to tell me how much the troops were liking *The Petrified Forest.*

Aug. 3 *Tuesday.* With Leo to Cheltenham for a Brains Trust in connection with that town's "Holidays at Home" week. Empty carriages as far as Reading, where a lady and two children got in. The children more lovely than amours on a ceiling. But their behaviour! For three hours they climbed all over me, alternately petted and pummelled me while their mother looked on rapturously. "I don't pretend they're manageable," she said. "I was unmanageable at their age. Besides, their father likes them like that." "What is their father?" "A colonel." "And where is the Colonel?" "In India." And with that she settled herself to sleep. While all this was happening Leo sat unmoved in his corner reading Goethe's *Faust,* and it occurred to me that a painter, to do justice to the scene, would have to be a combination of Raphael and Goerg! We found the Brains Trust winding up a hectic day which had included a Chepstow and Wye Valley ramble, a talk at the Art Gallery on "The Geology of Gloucestershire," a mixed doubles American handicap tennis tournament, a bathing ramble, a cricket match, a baby show, donkeys, and Prof. Bofeys' Punch and Judy show. Exactly like a day in the city Jack Priestley's characters came to.

Aug. 4 *Wednesday.* Leo, going through my mail, discovers a letter which, he alleges, is from Hampstead, though I seem to recognise the typing.

45 Nibelung Road
Swiss Cottage, N.W.6

HONOURED MR AGATE!

You excuse bad englisch. I take already lessons, but I am here only since six months and I speak so much german with my friends I cannot make advances in englisch. The purpose of this letter is then to ask you to read my Tragedy *Heinrich von Hohenstaufen* in Five acts. It is, my friends say, a very fine play. It is in the art of Grillparzer. My brother-in-law Dr Israel Bauchpresser now translates it into the englisch. Here my proposal. First I come to you and read to you the play in german, then my brother-in-law reads to you the play in englisch. I beg that no other would be present. Then you pray the directors of the theatres to produce this child of my phantasie. I make perhaps much money, then I give you a good Honorar. You do this, yes ?

Your admiration-full

ERNA KATZENGEBISS

Aug. 5 *Thursday.* Deliver an address at the " Into Battle Exhibition " at Dorland Hall. Sweltering heat, a cubicle the size of the Black Hole of Calcutta into which some hundred and fifty people are crammed, microphone to the crowd overhead which can be heard tramping about and obviously paying no attention. Twenty minutes in my wittiest and most eloquent vein. No laughter, and no applause. Fiasco !

Aug. 7 *Saturday.* Telephone call in the early hours of this morning to ask me to judge to-day at Sutton Coldfield Horse Show !!!!!! I didn't know that such things were. But I learned on arrival that they are. Scores of horse shows. Strictly amateur affairs, more or less confined to small tradesmen taking to showing as a means of getting rid of some of their new riches. No professional horses, but great fun all the same. All the old excitement. In the big class was a four-year-old bay gelding, the exact height, colour, and markings of Ego. And, incredibly, the same exquisite quality. Placed him first, in front of a common pony going great guns. Add that this beautiful mover was shown by Albert Throup, and how could I not think of the old days ? Inquired after Ego, and was told that the new owner " wouldn't let the wind blow on him if he could prevent it." Pure Hamlet.

Aug. 8 *Sunday.* Found this letter awaiting me :

DEAR JAMIE,

Congratulations upon entering the English Dictionary (*vide* enclosed review from the *Spectator*). I have my doubts, as you know, about the lastingness of the millions of words you have added to English literature. But to have added one word to the English language is something.

Ever,
JOCK

The sentence in the *Spectator* occurs in a review of O. B. Clarence's autobiography, *No Complaints*. "This unassuming autobiography will doubtless please amateurs of first nights and of anecdotes which could safely be printed in *Punch*. Plainly, O. B. Clarence is a good actor and a self-effacing man—but one rather misses the flamboyant agatism which characterises most writers on this subject."

Have countered as follows:

DEAR JOCK,

Hoots ava! or whatever your uncouth language understands as friendly objurgation. Didn't our adored Miss Mitford say of Wordsworth that he demanded to be admired *en masse*—all, every page, every line, every word, every comma? I am less exacting; there are several commas that I concede posterity may fail to remember. You notice that I avoid the absolute "forget."

More seriously, here is something I have long wanted to write to you about. Leonard Russell, the best-meaning fellow in the world, alluded to me at the Dorland Hall affair as "the best dramatic critic since Hazlitt." This makes me blush. Dear Jock, as you love me, never let it be said in your presence without instant contradiction that this was the notion I entertained of myself. I have always had a complete contempt for the man who thinks his horse must be the best in the show because it is *his horse*. I know exactly where we all stand. Judging the dramatic critics as a harness class I should put them in this order:

Hazlitt
G. H. Lewes
G. B. S.
William Archer
C. E. Montague
A. B. Walkley

Coming to our own day, I should put Desmond MacCarthy first, except that there isn't enough quantity to go with the quality. A show-horse has to keep it up—brilliant flashes won't do. Max? No, he is a trifler and has willed it so; the most exquisite trifling in the world, but still trifling. I was genuinely shocked by that passage in the Rede Lecture in which he said about Strachey's *Elizabeth and Essex*: "A very robustious, slapdash writer might convince me that he was in close touch with the souls of those beings whose actions and motives are to me as mysterious as those of wild animals in an impenetrable jungle. You rightly infer that I am *not* a sixteenth-century man. And I make so bold as to say 'Neither was Lytton Strachey.'" What sort of a critic of Shakespeare can a man be to whom everything Elizabethan is an impenetrable jungle? If penetration be not the essence of criticism, what is? You realise that in *Around Theatres* Max writes about seven Shakespeare plays and no more? And don't think I am not a great admirer of your god. Isn't the first of my newspaper-cutting books stiff with extracts from Max? You know that it is. (By the way, I am not satisfied that the *Spectator* will have more luck with its "To agatise" than Max had with his "To bouch." You remember the passage. "BOUCH, *v.i.* To advertise oneself with great industry, but without discretion; to advertise oneself in such a way as to make people tired of one or sorry for one. [*Deriv.*: Bourchier, an English actor.] BOUCHER, *s.* One who bouches." My cutting-book tells me that the date of this is August 11, 1906.) No, Max is not an Elizabethan, and further I would guess that Cowper and Crabbe are his poets, not Milton. Now I am nothing if not logical. I do not demand that anybody should be an Elizabethan unless he sets up, or is set up, as a dramatic critic. I never tire of quoting Lewes's "The greatest artist is he who is greatest in the highest reaches of his art." What can a critic to whom Shakespeare's verse is a jungle make of Lady Macbeth's "Nor heaven peep through the blanket of the dark"? No. Max is worshipful in such phrases as "that agile and mellifluous quodlibetarian, Dr Joad"—only those who have brains-trusted with C. E. M. J.—that last fatal initial, the little more and what worlds away!—can judge of the felicity of this. To finish about Max, I place him in the Charles Lamb category, just as Desmond in the theatre properly links up with Arthur Symons, Maurice Baring, and other too-occasional writers, but never with G. B. S. or C. E. M. To get back to the main thread. I am satisfied if it be thought that I keep my nose level with Cookman and Ivor, conceding that Charles Morgan was too critical for the rough-and-tumble of the theatre, and St John Ervine insufficiently so. But what is that flurry of critics on the horizon coming up hand over fist? Nothing but J. C. Trewin, the new critic of *Time and Tide*, and that daarlin' man, Alan Dent.

Don't be thinking, now, there's anything "derogatory," as Fluther Good would say, about bringing up the rear. The race is a long one, and you've got twenty-eight years—the difference in our ages—in which to catch up. Or look at it another way. It is thirty-six years since I joined the *Manchester Guardian*; you have written for that paper for a meagre eight! And now let me tell you why I am not really afraid of you, though I pretend to be. Because in Parker's *Who's Who* you give your recreations as "serendipity and cribbage." Which almost tempts me to coin another word, viz., DENTIFY, *v.i.* To like little things because they are little. To miniaturise. To shrink from notoriety. *Deriv:* Dent, an English critic. DENTIFICER, *s.* One who dentifies. In any case, who can tell which of us will live, as they call it? Who would have backed Louisa M. Allcott against Mrs Henry Wood or Miss Braddon? Who, except the author of *Preludes and Studies*, remembers what was the Shadow of Ashlydyat or Lady Audley's Secret? Whereas Mrs March's Meg, Jo, Beth, and Amy are as much alive to-day as Mrs Bennet's Jane, Elizabeth, Mary, Lydia, and Kitty. But I grow too long.

Your auld, daft, haverin'

JAMIE

Aug. 10 *Tuesday.* If I were to write: "Wilkes was witty, ugly, and had a way with him, therefore, given half an hour's start, he would back himself for a lady's favours against the handsomest man in England," I should expect any schoolboy to point out that Wilkes succeeded because of his wit and his way and in spite of his ugliness, and to tell me that I had committed whatever in logic is the term for muddle-headedness. Yet here is somebody in the *Evening Standard* writing about *Love for Love* on its transfer to the Haymarket, "This brilliant bawdy masterpiece deals exuberantly with the pleasure and intrigue of illicit love. The governors of C.E.M.A., *therefore* [italics mine], decided that the Treasury now recognises this kind of thing as one of the cultural studies of mankind." I protest. The governors of C.E.M.A. recognise Congreve's play because of its brilliant and masterly qualities and in spite of its bawdiness. I should like to take this cloudy fellow by the scruff of his neck and shove his nose into Hazlitt's

The room opened into an old-fashioned garden, embellished with beds of larkspur and a leaden Mercury; it was wainscoted, and there was a grave-looking, dark-coloured portrait of Charles II hanging up over the tiled chimney-piece. I had *Love for Love* in my pocket, and began to read; coffee was brought in in a silver coffee-pot; the cream, the bread and butter, everything was excellent, and the flavour of Congreve's style prevailed over all. I relished this divine comedy better even than when I used to see it played by Miss Mellon, as Miss Prue; Bob Palmer, as Tattle; and Bannister, as honest Ben.

Hazlitt was as good a moralist as most. Yet his word for Congreve's play is "divine."

Aug. 11 *Wednesday.* Does the *camera obscura* still exist? It was, as I remember, a little shanty which at seaside resorts would show you the crowds on the pier and sands, the cricket match in progress near by, and the switchbacks in the joy park. It gave you an epitome of the town's turmoil, and similarly I take it that *War and Peace* at the Phoenix to-night is an epitome of the hurly-burly of Tolstoy's great novel. The whole thing was immensely exciting, and succeeded in giving the impression that it had been chipped off a masterpiece. The setting consisted of *montagnes russes* of an acclivity which our pleasure-beaches have never envisaged. There was more than jesting in Morris Harvey's complaint that what this production calls for is not actors but steeplejacks who can speak lines.

Aug. 12 *Thursday.* I am not going to count Peter Ustinov's *Blow Your Own Trumpet*, at the Playhouse to-night, as a wasted evening. Half a dozen *ratés* are in the habit of meeting at a cheap Italian café. They are a conductor who has never conducted, a second-hand dealer who aimed at being a fashionable fiddler, a psycho-analyst whose only patient is himself, the keeper of the café who wanted to be Pope, an English diplomat *manqué*, and a spy who was no good as a painter and can't even spy. The café is an asylum where all these architects of failure—how well I know them!—chatter about the malignity of Fate which has kept them down. What about their children? These are petrol-minded, and, tinkering with their motor-bikes, decline to give up the low thing they can do in favour of the high thing their fathers couldn't. And the moral of the play is: Better a dirt-track at Wembley than a Castle in Spain. Ibsen would have agreed, Browning not.

By courtesy of the "Daily Express"

At the Café Royal
Sallon

Photo W. A. Rouch

Good-bye, Ego!

Is this a good play? No. Did it entrance me? Yes. Ustinov possesses every quality of the first-class playwright except one. He cannot think of a story. Power of characterisation, lifelike dialogue, feeling for the stage, wit, fun, with a glozing of philosophy—all these, yes. But they are not enough. What this clever young man should do is to resist London, have his plays produced at Hull or Plymouth or Manchester, and so learn his job away from any public that matters.

Aug. 13 *Friday.* In addition to my ordinary work this week I have (*a*) corrected the proofs of the new version of *Responsibility*, (*b*) made a synopsis for Cape of *Red Letter Nights*, the proposed companion volume to *Brief Chronicles*, and (*c*) assembled D. B. Wyndham Lewis's book *Standing By*, which I am re-naming *Take It To Bed*. This has meant going through three years of the *Tatler*, and turning out what I hope is a good foreword. I wrote it three times. Also took the chair at a lecture to Free Hungarians on the Hungarian Drama! How long I can keep up this amount of work I don't know. I find myself falling asleep at all sorts of times and in all sorts of places. And surely there must be something wrong when I find myself looking for telephone numbers in Webster's Dictionary, and for the finer shades of meaning in the Telephone Directory.

Aug. 14 *Saturday.* Cape phones that he will take *Red Letter Nights* for publication some time in 1944. Also that he has sold out the whole edition—3500 copies—of *Brief Chronicles*. A book of reprints, and reprints of dramatic criticism, and dramatic criticism about Shakespeare—here were three reasons why the book shouldn't sell. And now it quadruples what I expected, my previous best in this line being 800 or so.

Fatras. From a woman's paper:

> Miss P—— T—— was out having a cocktail the other day. She was wearing a beautifully ample leopard-skin coat, and has considerable eyelashes and charm, as well as being a most talented sculptress. In the daytime she bicycles, and has a tin hat, the only disadvantage of which is its top-heaviness. She says that to wear it when bicycling is to be predisposed to topple head-first over the handlebars.

Aug. 15 William Glock in the *Observer* is at it again:
Sunday.

> Tom Harrisson returned to the attack last week, saying that appreciation of Tschaikowsky is a stage towards higher things. I don't think so. With their feverish tunes, their persuasive orchestration, their blatant crescendi of excitement, his symphonies and concertos are the very antithesis of the profound equilibrium one finds in Mozart.

There we go again. Why, in God's name, can't we be allowed *both*? What rule of æsthetic bids us admire "The pity of it, Iago!" and reject "I will chop her into messes"?

To the Cambridge Theatre this afternoon to hear Alec Whittaker exquisitely phrase a Handel concerto for oboe and strings. Alec is too modest. Instead of making a soloist's entrance he clambered through the orchestra like a Wagner herdsman. Clifford Curzon in the Grieg, of which, Nature exercising its sway, I heard only the first ten bars and the last. Woke up in time for Tschaikowsky's *Francesca da Rimini*—one of the rowdiest and emptiest display pieces in all music. It is worse than Liszt's bosh on the same subject. Or so it seemed this afternoon. Do I remember some quiet stuff in the middle? Alec tells me there is a nice bit for him. But I didn't hear it. Perhaps I dropped off again.

Walking, after the concert, in the churchyard of St Giles-in-the-Fields, I came across a tomb, the inscription on which seemed to me to say the last thing on earthly renown. On one side

THE MEMORY OF
RICHARD PENDRELL
THE PRESERVER OF THE LIFE OF
KING CHARLES THE SECOND

On the other this verse:

> Hold, passenger, heres shrouded in this herse,
> Unparalleld Pendrell thro' the universe,
> Like when the Eastern star from Heav'n gave light,
> To three lost Kings, so he in such dark night,
> To Britain's monarch, lost by adverse war,
> On earth appear'd a second Eastern star,
> A pole, a stem in her rebellious main,
> A pilot to her royal sovereign came.
> Now to triumph in Heaven's eternal sphere,
> He is advanced for his just steerage here,
> Whilst Albion's chronicles with matchless fame
> Embalm the glory of great Pendrell's name.

Dryden? Doggerel? That is not the point. The point is that until this mention I don't suppose anybody has given a thought to Pendrell for a hundred years, except the editor of the *Dictionary of National Biography*, who spells his name Penderel.

Aug. 16 *Monday.* An exchange:

T. S. "*Mercury*"
Hamble
Southampton
Aug. 14, '43

DEAR AGATE,

In passing . . . I've just read you on *Peer Gynt* in the Radio paper. . . .

1. What a bloody good writer you are;
2. and devilishly clever.

As I'm an amateur in everything except cricket, the above is unlikely to harm you.

Yours truly,
C. B. FRY

Queen Alexandra Mansions
Grape Street
*W.C.*2
Aug. 16, '43

DEAR C. B. FRY,

You shouldn't write letters like that. They rouse a bug that I try to stifle. Milton was wrong about fame; he should have written "*first* infirmity of noble mind."

Now you have got lasting glory, and I don't begin to grasp it. It's there, but just out of reach. Whereas you did it when you projected your body through so and so many feet, and they came and stuck a wooden peg in the ground, and the Provost of Oriel, or somebody, shouted, "Jumping Jehosophat, he's broken it!" Meaning the record.

Immortality is won easily or not at all. You got yours in a couple of seconds. Whereas I have been chasing the damn thing all my life!! To be exact, since June 2, 1932.

Ever,
JAMES AGATE

Aug. 17 *Tuesday.* I am continually making the point that amateur critics are more devastating than the professionals.

At a luncheon party to-day I heard two women discussing historical films. One said, "My dear, they have a certain social value. Until I saw Anna Neagle and Anton Walbrook in the film about Queen Victoria I had no idea that the Prince Consort married beneath him ! "

Aug. 18 *Wednesday.* The *plat du jour* at the Café Royal to-night being sturgeon, I was reminded of the best curtain-line I ever heard. This was after the last war, at the end of some French farce in which Max Dearly, as a colonel in charge of Russian opera, had as personal attendant a *moujik* rather larger than W. G. Grace and bearded even more formidably. The *moujik* was mute until the play's last minute, when a ravishing girl appeared, whereupon he burst into a roar of laughter. " Qu'est-ce que tu as à rire, espèce d'idiot ? " said Max. " Je pensais," replied the big fellow, " que si j'étais esturgeon et si mademoiselle était esturgeonne, il y aurait ÉNORMÉMENT de caviar cette saison ! "

Aug. 19 *Thursday.* Have decided to stop tolerating fools gladly. Some ass from Berkhamsted taking me to task for writing " When Greek *meets* Greek " instead of *joins*, I have replied :

DEAR SIR,
When I wrote about Greeks *meeting* one another I was not quoting your friend Mr Nathaniel Lee but referring to the line in the form in which it is generally used in England. Similarly I should be tempted to write " O that mine *enemy* had written a book," knowing perfectly well that Job's word is *adversary*. I should always write that I had escaped *by* the skin of my teeth, well knowing that the prophet escaped *with* the skin of his. The man who insists on quoting at the foot of the letter is a pernickety coxcomb and a pedantic ass.

Yours faithfully,
JAMES AGATE

Aug. 20 *Friday.* " Non," said Old Man Sarcey, " qui n'a pas vu Talbot dans Théramène n'a rien vu." Similarly I say that whoever has not seen Aubrey Smith shed tears in Technicolor ain't seen nuthin'. And the camels ! And the English soldiery ! And the poor black devils pulling the boats up the Nile ! *The Four Feathers*, revived to-night at the Empire, was always an excellent picture, and is still tops in the schoolboy class. Some one has gone over the old film with a child's box of paints, and now I suppose there is nothing more the cinema can do about it.

Aug. 23 *Monday.* Every country is fated at some time during its history to make a hero of somebody your English fourteen-year-old would call "an awful ass." The hero may be an actual man, or a character in a novel, or even an attitude of mind. A hundred years ago the French were drenching themselves with the romantic poetry of Alfred de Musset; willowy young men walking about Paris wept like anything. Sixty years earlier Germany had the epidemic, and had it worse. Young men dressed in blue coats and yellow breeches shot themselves without provocation but with Goethe's *Werther* in their hands. To-day they dress up in black shirts and with *Mein Kampf* in their hands shoot everybody who hasn't provoked them. And then, with a pang, one remembers the author of *Manfred* and *Childe Harold*, of whom it might be said that whereas Byron was the last person to be called an ass, Byronism is the first word in asininity. Always, of course, in the schoolboy sense. Byron shrouding himself in dudgeon, flaunting his profile, rushing off to Greece because he has made England too hot to hold him and is tired of Italy—here is some one whom Kipling's Stalky would have seized on as "a Flopshus Cad, an Outrageous Stinker and a Jelly-bellied Flag-flapper." To-night's new film at the Tatler picture-house, *Masquerade*, is all about a Russian Prince who is steeped in Pushkin, soused in Goethe, and saturated in Byron. The principal rôle is brilliantly filled by a fine actor who, however, pulls as many faces as if he were playing all three parts of Schiller's *Wallenstein* at once. As for the young actress who partners him, I can only say that she takes all our Kensington chits, puts them to bed, tucks them in, and then starts the business of acting as foreigners understand it.

Aug. 24 *Tuesday.* Why do radio stars with voices large enough to fill the theatre at which they are hazarding personal appearance insist on using the entirely unnecessary and wholly detestable "mike"? The answer is that I have got my premises wrong. The mike is detestable and *necessary*. Sarah Bernhardt's famous *voix d'or* either enchanted the listener or lashed him to fury. We all remember Shaw's complaint about those stale love-scenes and " that *voix céleste* stop which Madame Bernhardt, like a sentimental New England villager, keeps always pulled out." Here it is Shaw who went wrong, and in the matter of " always." Sarah was sparing of the golden voice when she was in good form, lavish of it only when she was out of form or lazy. I have a gramophone record of that twenty-nine-line speech in the second act of *Phèdre*. Beginning with :

> Oui, prince, je languis, je brûle pour Thésée,

Sarah pulls out the *voix céleste* stop for eight lines, and pushes it in again as soon as she has said :

> Il avait votre port, vos yeux, votre langage.

After which there is no hint of it until, twelve lines later, she gets to :

> C'est moi, prince, c'est moi,

when she uses it as far as :

> Que de soins m'eût coûtés cette tête charmante.

After which the full organ is turned on, and the speech is rushed to its frenzied, not golden, conclusion. Sarah, then, confined this ' stop ' to one emotion and one only, that of the strangled dove. For Sarah as tigress, snake, martyr, empress, coquette, or preparing to unpeople Byzantium with a hat-pin, there was an entire register to choose from. And for the critic to exercise his art on.

But your crooner's note is single, thematic material being confined to " memoree of yew." Whence it follows that the sentimental stop must be kept pulled out all the time, ceaselessly, relentlessly. Always the golden voice and never less than the golden voice, known as " crooner's throb," to which, it seems, the microphone is essential. No mike, no throb. George Black told me to-night that the reason radio stars draw large houses is because their " fans " want to see what they look like in public while continuing to sound as they do at home. He said, " If the crooners without the mike out-Caruso'd Caruso their fans would still be disappointed." I have a notion that I shall make my *Sunday Times* article out of this and call it *Crooner's Quest*. The rest of the show at the Palladium very nearly atoned for that rasping, metallic infliction.

Aug. 25 *Wednesday.* Two letters. The first, to a would-be poet, was rushed off before breakfast; the second, to a seaman-gunner, was the result of whiskey-imbibing at three o'clock in the morning after a decent amount at the Café Royal.

Queen Alexandra Mansions
*Grape Street, W.C.*2
August 25, 1943

SIR,

Making a skilful slit in the enormous package with which you recently overwhelmed me, I extracted your letter, gingerly, in the manner of an engineer dealing with a mine. If you will get a clergyman, or a magistrate, or a couple of doctors to certify that you are a poet, I promise to read any ten lines you care to send, provided there are no *longueurs*. But without this I will not read—no, nor even dip into—effusions longer than the *Iliad* and the *Odyssey* combined.

Yours faithfully,
JAMES AGATE

Now for the second letter:

Queen Alexandra Mansions
*Grape Street, W.C.*2
August 25, 1943

DEAR SEAMAN GUNNER,

No, your stuff just isn't good enough, Why must you write *Russian* stories? What would you say of a Leningrad stoker who concocted stories about life in Guildford? Your yarn doesn't ring true, *because it can't.*

I have now to tell you that the urge to write, and the belief that you can write, bear no relation to the capacity. When I see a beautiful building I feel that I, too, could be a great architect. Yet I know nothing about strains and stresses, and cannot lay one brick on another. But don't give up. If I discern no positive merits, yet I don't detect any glaring faults. Your stuff is unindividualistic—and mediocre. You might have written it about an old woman in Godalming and then turned it into Russian.

Write about what you know. Tell us how dodging aircraft affects sailors and what they feel like in action. One of your fellows told me the other day that the chaps near him prayed out loud! Tell us any bloody thing—so long as it's *true.* Study Smollett, Marryat, Conrad. Above all, realise two things. Either you must feel and express something that no other man—sailor or not—has ever felt before. Or you must express in your own, distinguishable way something which all sailors, or all men, have felt but never expressed as you can and do. There is no other justification whatever for print, whether in the form of poetry, drama, fiction, or autobiography.

If you like, keep in touch, and I will send you a goodish story I wrote twenty-four years ago, during the last war, and which is about to be reprinted. I wrote it in France, surrounded by French people whom I knew intimately—I more or less speak the lingo. Nevertheless my novel is all about life in a cotton-mill on the borders of Lancashire and Cheshire, a life which I knew. Even in my nonage I had more literary sense than to write yarns about " furrin parts." All those accomplished novels—mostly by maiden ladies in garden cities —about life in France, Germany, Belgium, Holland, Russia and presently, I feel, Norway, leave me stone cold.

Don't start arguing with me about your work. If you think I don't know, ask somebody who you think does. I have annotated one page of your MS. pointing out the clichés, the worn-out phrases which, having passed through so many hands, have ceased to mean anything. You mustn't be interchangeable with any other author. And don't write " Serge and Boris, in expectation of the enemy, peered *attentively* along the barrels of their rifles." How would you have them peer ? Sleepily ?

" Nay, I have done, you get no more of me." I don't know why you have got so much, except that (1) it is 3 A.M., (2) this is the hour at which I become mellow, (3) my pen is running smoothly, almost of itself, (4) your stuff, though " ordinary," does not show a common mind, (5) I will tear myself in pieces to encourage the promise of talent while tearing to pieces those who lack it and always will lack it, and (6) at bottom I am a soft-hearted old fool. But do not imagine that I am always in this maudlin vein. I am not.

Yours sincerely,
JAMES AGATE

Aug. 26 *Thursday.* Gave the toast at the dinner to-night to Sir Pelham Warner at Lord's Tavern. Had prepared it very carefully, and it went down well, I think. " Plum " made one of the most graceful speeches I have ever listened to, with lots of old-world erudition and an astonishing divagation into the story of Cetewayo and the great Chaka. Only a master-speaker could have gone on without a break to the catch with which Hendren won the championship for Middlesex in the year of "Plum's" retirement. There was a delightful passage in which he spoke of the sounds and odours which make up the symphony of Lord's—"the clink of the roller, the sweet scent of new-mown grass, and the gritty smell of hot asphalt." There was another passage in which he talked about the Last Innings which he has yet to play. He charged them, if that happens in the summer, even if they put the flag at half-mast, not to stop the game. Indeed, he begged that in his honour an extra half-hour shall be played. "Plum" spoke for forty-five minutes, perhaps ten too many. But if a man can't be garrulous on an occasion like this—"shunning, postponing severance" as Whitman says—when can he be garrulous?

Aug. 27 Friday. The notices of *Brief Chronicles* are fine. Raymond Mortimer talks of "the richest gusto, the most wanton prejudice, and the prettiest wit." *Punch* is pleased because I send the reader back to Shakespeare's text. Ivor Brown notes the book's "immensely vivacious form." Best of all is the *Times Lit. Supp.* I enormously like the passage:

> Nothing in this book is more remarkable than the fundamental agreement between this habitual dramatic reporter and the very latest academic opinion—with Mr C. S. Lewis on *Hamlet* for its most recent exponent—that the quiddity of Shakespeare's drama lies not in story, not in character, nor in any sort of 'message,' but first and last in poetry. Mr Agate has a passion for poetry, and an ear for it worthy of his passion.

At last somebody has seen that beneath this critic's horse-coping exterior there lies a love of something which exceeds ponies, golf, music, the obsession of Sarah, cigars, whiskey, and even vice itself. I feel for Shakespeare's poetry what Ernest Newman feels for Beethoven's music during the last six years. But with this difference. Ernest writes:

> I do *not* want pseudo-explanations of the inward change in Beethoven in easy terms of his outer life, his miseries, his isolation from the world of other men by reason of his deafness, his troubles with his nephew, and all that kind of thing. I want a new study of the mighty mind in its last marvellous phase that will make clear to me, strictly in terms of the music itself, the chemical changes, as it were, that had gone on at the very core of the mind.

This is where we differ. I am chary of " chemical changes " in great men. And why stop at chemical changes ? Why not want to know about original chemical composition ? What if Ernest were to discover that the unearthly felicity of Beethoven's last quartets was a by-product of syphilis ? That Schubert's stream of melody was pure alcohol, Chopin's romanticism tuberculosis, Hugo Wolf's lyricism dementia ? No. Chemical criticism is, God save us, a thing of naught. We were all amused when Ernest abandoned musical criticism and became a musicologist. But a chemicologist is beyond a joke. I do not want to discover that we owe Ibsen's *When We Dead Awaken* to G. P. I., or that what sent Shakespeare back to Stratford with a hop, skip, and a jump was locomotor-ataxy.

Aug. 29 *Sunday.* Epitaph for King Boris of Bulgaria, who asked for assassination and got it :

> He made a very handsome corpse, and became his coffin prodigiously.
>
> *Goldsmith's " The Good-natured Man."*

Aug. 31 *Tuesday.* Entertain at the Ivy George Lyttelton, a nice, large affable creature in the early sixties. We talk about *Ego*, and I tell him how nothing—which includes nerves, fatigue, worries, and what is supposed to be my work—has been allowed to interrupt it. I tell him something of the manner of its writing, how it is part written by hand, part dictated ; typed, corrected, re-typed and re-corrected ; how I sit up till four in the morning over it ; how, since the war, one copy has been "evacuated" to my brother at York, and another deposited at the typist's. How some of the pages are re-written five or six times. How every alteration down to semicolons (but not commas) is sent on to Brother Harry. How, every three months, there is a small revision, and every six months, a grand one. How the sheddings are so great that what ultimately appears is less than half of what I originally wrote. At this point Lyttelton asks why I don't write a supplementary volume containing all the things I have so obviously avoided. I say : " Meaning conduct, religion, sex, and all that ? " He says : " Yes. You could deposit it with the British Museum with instructions that it shan't be printed for a hundred years." I say : " My dear fellow, have you seen

Edward D. Johnson's *Don Adriana's Letter* ?" He says he hasn't. I go on: "This shows how in the course of the Letter's twenty-five lines Bacon inserts the words 'See the Design,' and then in a faultlessly symmetrical pattern insinuates no fewer than seventeen statements as to who wrote *Love's Labour's Lost.* I have been as liberal as Bacon with my pointers. We then go on to discuss religion, the colour bar, and A. E. Housman, and lunch ends with G. L. inviting me to go down to Eton and talk to his boys.

When I get home I take up David Masson's study of De Quincey and read once more the pathetic story of his love for the little Oxford Street drab. Am struck by a passage of immediate, personal concernancy. "He had not told the *whole* truth about his London vagrancy, he said, because that was impossible, but he had told nothing but the truth." Later I glance at the *Illustrated London News* and read how somebody has discovered two new planets, the nearer of which is associated with the double star 6I Cygni, 75 million million miles away! And I reflect that if G. L. were present I could give him my views on all the things we talked about. Briefly these are: That sometime, somewhere, somehow, two people who have wished to be united in this world shall be united in the next independent of age, station, colour or any other bar. As I wrote in *Responsibility*, the most bizarre conceptions assail me in the matter of what I should consider a satisfactory Heaven. I want a Heaven in which Jack shall have Jill, and Darby, Joan; in which poets shall find their Evelyn Hopes and their Shropshire lads; a Heaven in which Narcissus will not tire of his body's perfection, and Leda shall dally with her Swan, and Sappho burn no longer. I conceive an ingenious metaphysical limbo where one has one's desires though they may run contrary to the other person's, where all love is requited though the requiter may know nothing about it. Here Madame Potiphar shall enjoy her Joseph without the knowledge of that simpleton, Lady Booby ensnare her footman without diminution of his virtue, Lady Wishfort have her fill of unwilling gallants, and the rich socialite smooth out the crinkles in some bored jazz-drummer's hair. Myself? I want to meet again my first grand passion, with whom, more than fifty years ago in a Derbyshire lane, I exchanged fewer than a dozen words. To go back to where we started. I hold that if those two specks, De Quincey and Little Ann of Oxford Street, are not reunited, then, despite its 75 million millions, the Scheme of Things shrinks to a Joke in Singularly Poor Taste.

Sept. 1 *Wednesday.* George Richards in exceptionally good form this morning. I extract

Conversation

A. I have just been to a party at which the famous Czech soprano, Mme Brtchka, gave a recital.

B. Do you mean the one who tried to escape and was nearly shot by the Gestapo ?

A. No, I mean the one the Gestapo threatened to shoot if she *didn't* escape !

Holiday in 1943

8 A.M. Arrive Poole station and take third-class monthly return to Ludlow (Shrops.) hoping to find accommodation in lavatory if not in the corridor.

8.01 A.M. Train arrives and proves to be almost empty. Pass most vivid and interesting journey, the only other occupant of the carriage being a nun with a bun.

3.50 P.M. Arr. Ludlow. Introduce myself to the station-master and present him with a small donation to the Superannuated Signalmen's Benevolent Fund on discovering that he has the unique distinction of *not* having set Housman's "In Summer Time on Bredon" to music. Take a walk round the castle, then, looking at my watch, remember suddenly that this is the night the B.B.C. are broadcasting a Rare Event Which I Mustn't Miss. Return to station just in time to catch homeward-bound express.

9.20 P.M. Arrive home and, palpitating, tune in just in time to hear opening bars of Tschaikowsky's B flat minor concerto ! !

Golden Rule

I rarely let a day pass without committing to paper some Moral Precept or Help Toward the Good Life. Here is today's : The Golden Rule in life is to take no notice of what other people say or what the Good, the Holy, the Learned and the Respectable teach. Cultivate instead an ear for the small voice and, when you are certain there is not a smaller one still, obey it.

Literary Cat

When I showed your ailurophobic article in the *Express* to my superhuman, super-sagacious Siamese cat Boniface (alias Whymper) he merely commented: "A dramatic critic, yes. I like to read a dramatic critic occasionally."

[An allusion to Sir Daniel Ridgeley's remark in Pinero's *His House in Order*: "A cat, yes. I like to watch a cat occasionally."—J. A.]

Sept. 2 *Thursday.* A bottle of whiskey and a wet towel have failed to produce anything about *Uncle Vanya*, which I saw with Leo to-night at the Westminster, as good as the stuff I wrote in the old *Saturday Review* twenty-two years ago.

Tchehov's *Uncle Vanya* is an embroidery upon the theme of apprenticeship to sorrow: "L'homme est un apprenti, la douleur est son maître." It is a theme which no age or country escapes. Musset may sing it after one fashion, Shakespeare after another. Yet it has been known to cause the practical mind to suffer impatience when it comprehends that Tchehov's sorrowful apprentices are *fainéants*. Vanya, the sentimentalist, unpacks his heart with words, nags at the fate he will not unbend his idealistic soul to conquer. Astrov, the man of action, gives his life to drunkenness and the cultivation of trees. Serebryakov, the invalid, is pure humbug. His wife Elena, in love with Astrov, lacks the courage of adultery; she is in no sense moral. Sonia, his daughter, loving Astrov, is a sick lily. We watch these people curiously, but without comprehension and almost without pity. They are, oh, so exasperatingly Russian! "At last," says Stevenson of the death of Bragelonne, "the little Viscount has done something. C'est, ma foi! bien heureux." But these Tchehovians do nothing. C'est, ma foi! bien malheureux. They do not even commit suicide, and when they shoot to kill, they miss. They make up that most hopeless of corporations, the spineless introspective. They do not indulge in that last Western consolation: "No dog so wretched but it wags its tail sometimes." We English have few wounds which a ride to hounds will not heal. Your Russian, we are always told, is a great huntsman. But these characters of Tchehov do not hunt; they are hunted. The ideal pursues them, flays them with a whip.

What does one think of the play after twenty-two years? Is the first act a little too Tchehovianly steeped, so that it plays like a burlesque of the master ? But the second is still the entire and perfect chrysolite. Consider that " curtain." It is round about four in the morning. Elena feels like playing the piano, and sends Sonia to ask whether Serebryakov, sleepless with gout, minds. Sonia comes back and says, " No, we mustn't." I know no other playwright, except, of course, Ibsen, who would not have lowered his curtain on Elena sitting down to a whacking concert grand and ladling out the 1899 equivalent of the Warsaw Concerto. The play's total gesture ? Total, yet tripartite. First, the love of forests and the birds and beasts which inhabit them, an echo from *The Seagull.* Second, the immense hope in the future, to be insisted on later in *The Three Sisters*. Third, present boredom. And why not, in a countryside whose population would seem to be seven to the square mile ? What a pity the young man who played Astrov to-night made himself up to look like a combination of one of Ouida's baronets and the juvenile lead in a burlesque of Victorian melodrama ! The rest of the cast quite good, rising to excellence with the really moving Sonia of Vivienne Bennett.

Sept. 3 *Friday.* The war enters on its fifth year, and I am sticking to my resolve to say nothing about it. Instead I have received a letter from my old friend Aubrey Fitzgerald enclosing something he calls

OUTRAGEOUS CONDUCT OF A COMMANDING OFFICER

Last night, whilst an E.N.S.A. party was entertaining a certain unit in a Northern Command, an order was received somewhat late after the fall of the curtain that the C.O. would like the company to assemble at the Officers' Mess as soon as possible. Unfortunately, before this command was received, three of the actors, unaware that arrangements had been made for their entertainment, proceeded to the Sergeants' Mess for a humble glass of beer. Suddenly becoming aware that all the company was not present, the pompous colonel inquired as to their whereabouts, and on learning they were being looked after by the Sergeants' Mess, flew into a rage, ordered them back immediately, under escort, and placed the ladies in our travelling coach *under an armed guard,* whilst he assembled the male portion of the company in the anteroom and before all his officers proceeded, in the most abusive language, to lecture them as to their conduct and the deference due to him as commanding officer and to the officers under his command. A request from our manager that he should remove the armed guard from the coach as the ladies were frightened, was refused, and the guard was kept there until such time as we were actually allowed to leave the barracks pursued by incoherent threats that within three days the company would be non-existent, the actors out of work, and E.N.S.A. parties never again allowed to darken the doors of his mess.

Sept. 4 *Saturday.* Some time ago Ibbs and Tillett wanted Kligerman to go down to either Swansea or Cardiff for an inclusive fee of ten guineas, which was to include railway fare and hotel expenses. I stuck out for twelve, and the engagement fell through. And I rather blamed myself for having bungled matters, Moiseiwitsch having told me that young pianists must be satisfied if they can get a footing plus fourpence-halfpenny. To-day Alexis telephones to say that I. and T. have offered him fifteen guineas to play the Grieg Concerto at Burnley. Which looks as if things may come right after all. I have no doubt that they will, provided the young man can be got to see that fireworks are not everything.

Sept. 9 *Thursday.* " What, is it you, you dogs ! I'll have a frisk with you," said Dr Johnson. Came to the conclusion on this, my sixty-sixth birthday, that my life is short of frisks. Having so decided, sat down and wrote this letter to an address in Scotland :

Queen Alexandra Mansions
*W.C.*2
September 9, 1943

DEAR YOUNG LADY,

You are shocked because I have called eight years ago " the other day." I am shocked because apparently you don't know your Isaac Watts:

A thousand ages in Thy sight
Are like an evening gone.

In my sight, eight years is " the other day."

Now don't let this degenerate into a correspondence, as I am busy writing one book, reading the reviews of two others, correcting the proofs of a fourth and fifth, and laying plans for a sixth. This may not sound like truth, but it is so. Would you care for a copy of my forthcoming Monograph for High School Students—*Mythology Made Moral*? By the way, are you the snub-nosed, freckled sort, or the long-nosed projecting-teeth variety? Do you wear spectacles? Do your parents allow you to write to strange men? Will you marry me? I am divorced in France, and would consider finding out how I stand in this country. Think of the day when you will be able to call yourself the Relict of a Proliferous, or do I mean Prolific, Author. I rather think I am both.

Yours sincerely,
James Agate

Sept. 11 *Saturday.* Maxwell Anderson's *The Wingless Victory* at the Phœnix Theatre last night turned out to be fearful nonsense. All about one Princess Oparre, an intense young woman who begins life prancing about Malay battlefields waving a spear with her enemy's head impaled. But she has inklings of a better way of life, confirmed when an American sailor that she found trussed up on an altar gives her a New Testament. They marry, and a few years later the sailor takes her and their two kids to his family in Salem, who just aren't having any truck with savages. But would our own Mrs Pardiggle have permitted her eldest to play marbles with a Tockahoopo Indian, or Mrs Jellyby allowed Peepy to chum up with a couple of Borrioboolan brats? In this matter I give the Salem ladies best. The reason they won't invite the Princess to their tea-parties is because they are afraid that, just as *Moby Dick's* Queequeg would take off his boots only after he had put on a top hat and retired under the bed, so this semi-negress will be up to strange tricks like balancing her tea-cup on her head before attacking the bread and butter. This daft play falls between the two stools of ironic comedy and poetic tragedy. One just doesn't believe in a young woman who, after playing rounders with her enemies' heads, bursts into blank verse:

> Dark oracles of Heav'n, that blaze and burn,
> Swung by an unseen hand, forgive me if I give
> My god no name, for men have many names. . . .

Or in the little Salem maid who, when her old sweetheart fails

Photo Tunbridge-Sedgwick

Sur les Toits de Londres

(*See p.* 213)

Photo R. D. Stone

George Richards

to recognise her, instead of remarking " Sakes alive! Don't say you've forgotten me ? " has the preposterous :

> No spark, no glimpse ? But all those fond farewells. . . .

And all the time Anderson dodges the essential point as sedulously as the cyclist at the Coliseum avoids the pedestal and flower-vase in the middle of the stage. Always Oparre is the perfect lady ; not once does she slip into the natural of " You low-down rat, you can't do this to me ! " And there is not a hint of the first fact to be noted about archipelagic ladies—that the fifteen-year-old " pouting little slut " (Hazlitt's phrase for a charming Irish actress) turns at twenty-five into a blowsy slattern.

Sept. 13 *Monday.* Lady Kemsley's dinner-party at the Dorchester was a brilliant affair. The Spanish Ambassador (the Duke of Alba), Lord Portal, and the Chairman of the Westminster Bank. After screwing myself up to talking International Relations, Supply, and High Finance, I found that we were discussing the old subject : Whether Best-sellers can be Wholly Rubbish. And presently heard myself expounding—I am afraid at some length—how, given a sufficiency of housemaids and shop-girls, to-day's successors to Charles Garvice and Ethel M. Dell need only to think like housemaids and shop-girls to run into as many thousands as their publishers can find paper for. Asked why Miss A. and Miss B. succeed where Miss X. and Miss Y., whose minds run in exactly the same groove, fail, I had to reply that *that* is the one inscrutable thing. Presently the talk widened, and His Excellency said he thought that the world-languages of the future would be English and Spanish, the second because South America was capable of holding another 500 million inhabitants who would naturally speak Spanish. The Duke also said, " The language of diplomacy has always been the language of the Empire holding sway at the time. Your Queen Elizabeth wrote to my ancestor in Spanish." He struck me as possessing great charm and polish, and finally drove me home. A very pleasant evening, with K. talking very well and Lady K. looking her handsomest in a pre-war crêpe-de-chine Schiaparelli decorated with innumerable dwarfs, clowns, satyrs, scaramouches, and polichinelles.

Sept. 19 *Sunday.* Thought it diplomatic, in view of our American visitors, to make serious return to the subject of Maxwell Anderson's play which I tore to pieces last week in the *S.T.* To-day's article takes the form of an open letter to Anderson. Am rather pleased with some of it:

Let me get back to Whitman and the passage in which he makes the point that Tennysonian poetry cannot stomach the "great radical republic's loud ill-pitched voice, fights, errors, eructations, repulsions, dishonesties, audacities," and that American genius must still hold to "the sturdy, universal, democratic character, a feature far above style or polish." Now, Sir, it seems to me that *The Wingless Victory* is not, in the Whitmanesque sense, American, but that your newest play, *The Eve of St Mark*, is. This piece was, as you say, "shown" in London to the U.S. Forces only, on this year's American Independence Day, and I judge by reading only. That the idiom and the way of life exposed here are obscure to me is nothing to the play's detriment. We know nothing of Whitman's "native Michigan or Tennessee repartee." But we are willing and even eager to learn. On the other hand, you cannot teach us anything about Malay princesses of a hundred and fifty years ago prancing about battlefields with their enemy's head on a spear. Was not our own Thomas Southerne writing turgid, romantic nonsense about a native chief called Oroonoko at the very time when Penn was giving his name to Pennsylvania? That is why we are not gammoned when your Princess Oparre breaks into blank verse. The trouble with *The Wingless Victory* is not that it is too American, but that it is not American enough. If you, Sir, one of America's most distinguished dramatists, will consent to take a hint from an English well-wisher, it is that you should reverse the advice given in that great little masterpiece, *The Belle of New York*, so that it runs

And since you can never be like us,
Be as *un*like as you're able to be!

Sept. 20 *Monday.* Prepared the script for a three-minutes' broadcast talk:

I want to call attention to the subtle degradation that is being brought about by a certain type of film. I allude to the desecration of the masterpieces by swinging them.

I saw a picture one day last week in which a lot of representative young Americans, students in a musical college, decided to abandon classical music and go over to the other sort. First they jazzed Schubert's *Ave Maria*, and then they swung Hamlet's " To be or not to be " soliloquy. When they came to the line " To die ; to sleep " they stamped their feet, slewed their behinds, snapped their fingers, and crooned :

To die—to dee—to day—to duh.

Walt Whitman deplored that the poetry of Shakespeare " exhales that principle of caste which we Americans have come on earth to destroy." What about cultural caste ? There is a great poem by Whitman entitled *When lilacs last in the dooryard bloom'd*. How would he have liked it if some cretin had swung his poem so that it ran

When lilacs—leelocks—laylocks—luhlocks.

It is all very well for people to say—and certain of the long-haired, corduroy-trousered, café-haunting brigade do say it—that swinging the classics sends people back to the classics themselves. I don't believe it. In the same performance in which I heard Shakespeare travestied, the screen told me that Tschaikowsky's well-known Piano Concerto in B flat minor, although performed publicly for over seventy years in this country, had never become popular until Mary Astor played it in a film, the name of which I forget. Actually, of course, she only played the opening bars and a few snippets. " Then," said the screen, " as is inevitable with all classics, words were added, and we got the popular song 'Concerto for Two.' " Which rubbish, I am told, sends listeners back to Tschaikowsky's Concerto for One.

Well, I just don't believe that the worse sends people to the better. I do not believe that swinging

Abide—abeed—abayd—abuhd

would send anyone back to the old hymn.

I don't know what you are going to do about this. I don't know whether anybody can do anything, whether indeed there is a remedy, or if there is, how it can be applied. I don't quite see how we can wipe this aspect of the screen mentality off the screen. All I can do is to call attention to that mentality and its latest phase. And anyhow, my three minutes are up.

What I was careful not to tell them was that I did not believe that any German film director would consent to swing Goethe :

Über allen Gipfeln—Gäpfeln—Göpfeln—Güpfeln.

Seventy-five per cent. of listeners would have interpreted this as pro-Nazi propaganda.

Sept. 21 *Tuesday.* George Mathew has more sense in his little finger than most people have in their whole bodies. He said to-night: " What the Beveridge Report amounts to is that whereas in the past society gracefully kept a few Idle Rich, henceforth it must sullenly maintain a great many Idle Poor."

Sept. 22 *Wednesday.* *De gustibus* and so forth is surely the silliest of all pronouncements. You cannot dispute about facts, for these are either ascertained or ascertainable; this sort of discussion is fruitful only when the facts can never be known. Therefore, while I will not argue about the height of the Matterhorn, I am prepared to debate whether somebody did or did not cut the rope in the famous accident of 1865, until the Swiss cows come down the Swiss side of the mountain and the Italian cows down the Italian side. What I feel like debating to-night is: Can a thing be funny in itself, or is it funny only in relation to the contacting mind? Was to-night's new American farce at the Savoy, *My Sister Eileen*, absolutely funny, or only funny because I thought so? I laughed till I cried, literally. Surely one must laugh when Mr Appopolous, the Greek, says, " Look, Eileen. Or may I call you Miss Sherwood? " Provided, of course, that he has any knowledge of that polyglot race which stretches from Greek Street, Soho, to the Golden Horn. Every moment in the farce was visual riot, from the dreadful young gentleman with the comb to the delightful, out-of-work footballer in the top-hat. Sally Gray was worth at least as many peeks as Waldo Winchester took at Dave the Dude's doll, and the farce was so well held together by Coral Browne's poise and charm that one agreed for the plot's sake that the plain sister was worth no peeks at all.

Sept. 23 *Thursday.* From George Richards:

The Dog v. Cat Fight

On going out after rain two days ago what sight do you think filled my gaze? I beheld a member of the contemptible breed of canine fawnsters and mongrel boot-lickers plant itself with an expression of fatuous contentment bang right in the middle of a large rain-puddle and there sit inanely soliciting the admiration of passers-by. Can you by any superhuman stretch of imagination conceive a cat committing such a piece of ineptitude and insanity ?

Each time I awaken my celestial pair of Siamese cats Boniface and Bluebell to inform them that breakfast is served I cannot help reflecting how much more sanitary, wholesome, and savoury their bedding is than my own would be if it were never washed.

Sept. 25 *Saturday.* Taking up Quiller-Couch's *Cambridge Lectures*, read again the penetrative disquisition on *Macbeth*, beginning at " I shall assume that *Macbeth* is an eminently effective play ; that, by consent, it produces a great, and intended, impression on the mind." This magnificent essay has a long quotation from Bradley ending " The failure of nature in Lady Macbeth is marked by her fear of darkness ; ' she has light by her continually.' And in the one phrase of fear that escapes her lips even in sleep, it is of the darkness of the place of torment that she speaks." And I bethink me of the note Steevens appended to Lady Macbeth's " Hell is murky," to which he added a note of exclamation. " She certainly imagines herself here talking to Macbeth, who (she supposes) has just said, ' Hell is murky ' (*i.e.*, hell is a dismal place to go to in consequence of such a deed), and repeats his words in contempt of his cowardice." I cannot believe that even a German critic has exceeded the pedantry of this.

But the play defeated a greater than Steevens. It defeated Dr Johnson, who writes in *The Rambler*, No. 168 :

> Words which convey ideas of dignity in one age, are banished from elegant writing or conversation in another, because they are in time debased by vulgar mouths, and can be no longer heard without the involuntary recollection of unpleasing images. When Macbeth is confirming himself in the horrid purpose of stabbing his king, he breaks out amidst his emotions into a wish natural to a murderer :
>
> Come, thick night !
> And pall thee in the dunnest smoke of hell,
> That my keen knife see not the wound it makes ;
> Nor heaven peep through the blanket of the dark,
> To cry, Hold ! hold !
>
> In this passage is exerted all the force of poetry, that force which calls new powers into being, which embodies sentiment,

> and animates matter; yet, perhaps, scarce any man now peruses it without some disturbance of his attention from the counteraction of the words to the ideas. What can be more dreadful than to implore the presence of night, invested, not in common obscurity, but in the smoke of hell? Yet the efficacy of this invocation is destroyed by the insertion of an epithet now seldom heard but in the stable, and *dun* night may come and go without any other notice than contempt.

And again:

> The sentiment is weakened by the name of an instrument used by butchers and cooks in the meanest employments: we do not immediately conceive that any crime of importance is to be committeed with a *knife*; or who does not, at last, from the long habit of connecting a knife with sordid offices, feel aversion rather than terrour? Macbeth proceeds to wish, in the madness of guilt, that the inspection of heaven may be intercepted, and that he may, in the involutions of infernal darkness, escape the eye of Providence. This is the utmost extravagance of determined wickedness; yet this is so debased by two unfortunate words, that while I endeavour to impress on my reader the energy of the sentiment, I can scarce check my risibility, when the expression forces itself upon my mind; for who, without some relaxation of his gravity, can hear of the avengers of guilt *peeping through a blanket*?

All that can be said of this, perhaps, is that taste changes. To the modern sense the most *poetical* words in this famous passage are "smoke," "knife," and "blanket." Shakespeare knew better than anybody the supreme value of the commonplace word in magniloquent surroundings. Odd, by the way, that Johnson should attribute Lady Macbeth's speech to her lord, and that Professor Raleigh in his Introduction to the *Prefaces* should not comment on this!

Sept. 26 *Sunday.* Spent the day putting together some notes for a Lecture to Young Men I have let myself in for:

> The most misleading pronouncement ever made by a great man is Carlyle's "Genius means transcendent capacity of taking trouble, first of all." Better definition of genius would be "That quality in a man which enables him to do things that other people cannot do, and without taking pains." Thus Mozart had genius when he played the harpsichord at

the age of six. . . . The difference between talent and genius is that talent can be developed, whereas genius never improves. There are things it can do and things it can't. . . . Hear Hazlitt: "He is a man of capacity who possesses considerable intellectual riches: he is a man of genius who finds out a vein of new ore." Produce talent to infinity and it still doesn't become genius. Carlyle's *French Revolution* is a work of infinite talent, whereas *Alice in Wonderland* is a work of genius. On this reckoning Barrie was a genius and Galsworthy not. Sooner or later somebody would have written sociological dramas like *The Silver Box*, *Strife*, and *Justice*; only a genius would have thought of *Peter Pan*. . . . Genius is closely connected with the Latin word *ingenium*, by which the Romans meant the power to attain success, how success must be gone after, how a man must get himself to the front and keep himself there. Contrast two stories. That of the young George Mathew, who, when he was offered promotion, recommended somebody else. And that of how, years ago, on hearing that the film critic to the *Tatler* was on the point of resigning, I proposed to the editor of *Eve*, whose theatre notices I contributed, that it would be amusing if the dramatic and film critics were to exchange duties for one week. How he agreed, and how I wrote the best film article I could. And how, when it was printed, I marched to the *Tatler* office with it, and got the vacant job forthwith. Opportunity is said to knock only once. But be prepared for the fact that it may not knock at all! Quote Bacon's "A man must make his opportunity as oft as find it." . . . Arrive at main point. To possess genius is not enough. Thomas Edison's "Genius is one per cent. inspiration and ninety-nine per cent. perspiration"—vulgar, but true. Think of that master-spirit, Balzac, "plying the pick for dear life, like an entombed miner," or of Flaubert, "sick, irritated, the prey a thousand times a day of cruel pain," but "continuing my labour like a true working man, who, with sleeves turned up, in the sweat of his brow, beats away at his anvil, whether it rain or blow, hail or thunder." . . . The artist's concern for his work not to cease when the work is finished. He owes it to himself, the world, and the work itself to see that it is published, performed, exhibited. No use growing the best peaches or the best pigs if you never bring them to market. A comic song that reaches the boards is of more use to the world than a masterpiece thrust into a drawer and forgotten. Miracles like the retrieval of Schubert's Unfinished Symphony not to be relied on. . . . Artists must not faint or fall by the wayside. They must not let pride stand in their way. Or, like Chatterton, refuse meals pressed on them by landladies and then commit suicide because they cannot face humiliation. The artist must be prepared to crawl, creep, and cringe ; alternatively, to hector, bully, and browbeat. He must stomach the criticism of lesser minds. He must will himself to conquer Time, sleep, hunger, weakness, fatigue. He must drive himself harder than slave-driver ever drove slave, and put up with the neuroses that dog the over-driven brain. . . . He must realise that though he may bring off these feats of self-discipline, their achievement does not make him a great artist. Or even an artist at all. Urge is not talent. . . . Become personal. All of you present here to-night may have the will to create greatly, but you may not possess the talent to rise above tosh. You are taking an enormous gamble. Seventy per cent. of modern plays were better unwritten. Eighty per cent. of modern paintings unpainted. Ninety per cent. of modern music unpublished. Ninety-five per cent. of modern poetry is fit only for the waste-paper basket, with apologies to the other scraps. The risk you young men take is that out of a hundred who steel yourselves to the self-discipline I have outlined, only one or at most two will find that hell rewarded. . . . You may ask whether the game is worth the candle. That is for you to decide. I am not advising you to go mountaineering. I am telling you that if you must tackle Mount Everest this is the way to set about it. . . . Even so, you may fail. The race is not to the swift, nor the battle to the strong. But that is no reason why a man should not run his fastest, or a general refuse reinforcements. That Everest may be won by a careless saunterer who takes it into his head to go for a stroll and gets to the top, is no excuse for not planning as carefully as you may, foreseeing all eventualities, allowing for all kinds of weather, the state of the rock, and every other contingency, likely or unlikely. If you fail you will have nothing to reproach yourself with. If you succeed you will have deserved success. . . .

The foregoing, if I can find some pretty words, will be pure Stevenson. Which is what I mean it to be.

Sept. 27 *Monday.* It was a dire day for the pictures when Hitchcock or somebody discovered that a woman screaming emits the same sound as a train entering a tunnel. Fusion became the rage, what began as woman ended as tunnel, and why she was screaming or who was in the train ceased to matter. It is this kind of thing which makes our highbrow critics hail *King's Row* as a masterpiece. Said one of them yesterday :

" The presentation and development of the characters and their lives are achieved by means native to the cinema. A face half-seen behind a twitching lace curtain and a child calling up the stairs of a voiceless house ; the hypodermic needle lying by the bedroom jug. . . ." This pulls me up short. What sort of a medical student is it who, living in the same house with his grandmother, doesn't know (*a*) that she has cancer, (*b*) that the doctor is giving her morphia ? As a dramatic critic I take no further interest in the measureless ass. As a film critic I must enthuse over a needle.

Sept. 28 *Tuesday.* Heard this story, said to be true. It seems that on the occasion of the Prime Minister's recent visit to America one of our representatives asked the President's Confidential Adviser how he proposed to get over the difficulty which arose on the previous visit. This was the difference between the two statesmen—the President who likes to be in bed by eleven and the P.M. who insists on sitting up till four in the morning. Whereupon Hopkins said : " Don't you worry—I've fixed all that. The President will go to bed every night at eleven. If he sits up having a nightcap with Winston, by twelve o'clock we're back in the British Empire, and by one we get a tentative offer of Dominion status ! "

Sept. 30 *Thursday.* Frisking is fun. On Saturday the *Daily Express* will publish my review of Caryl Brahms's book on Robert Helpmann :

Everybody is going to the ballet. Everybody is thinking and talking ballet. Waiters serve your soup skimmingly. Shopgirls stand on their toes for hours. Postmistresses pirouette. Let us discuss ballet.

I like ballet. It is very pretty. It gives me as an amateur of the human form quite an eyeful of shapely legs and neat ankles. I know nothing more soothing than to sit and watch young ladies pretending to be swans, or swans pretending to be young ladies.

But I deny that ballet can be anything more. I will not believe that a young man twiddling his legs like an egg-whisk is expressing a passion for his stepmother. Or that when his partner executes sixty-four " wheelbarrows " she is suggesting the means by which the old josser, her husband and his father, can be got rid of. Miss Brahms believes all this and a lot more.

> "The rest is silence," said the dying Hamlet. "Nonsense!" says Mr Helpmann, deciding to make a ballet out of the confused images which may occur to a man with a temperature of 106. Thus the Gravedigger becomes Yorick, Ophelia becomes the Queen, Tweedledum turns into Tweedledee, and, I suppose, the Mad Hatter into the March Hare.
>
> Miss Brahms has written a most amusing book, flitting from Ophelia's "kittenish *pas-de-deux*" to "units of the absolute in lengths of coloured tulle." (Art thou there, Beachcomber ?) The brilliant photographs of Mr Russell Sedgwick are, I suggest, too brilliant; they show too plainly how much of his tragic expression the dancer owes to his make-up box. Ophelia's "herb o' grace" picture shows Miss Fonteyn to be in the pink of mental health and, apart from her grease-paints, as little "bats" as Deanna Durbin. I repeat: this book is very, very funny.

Now just as a boxer gives his wrist that little extra turn which drives the punch home, so a few lines later I return to the question of ballet in my review of a super-highbrow compilation called *Transformation*, edited by Stefan Schimanski and Henry Treece. To my great delight I find a passage in this about bayonet-fighting which runs:

> As he is still staggering, you bring the edge of your bayonet slash down on top of his skull; and finally, as he collapses to the ground, you finish him off with a point to the belly. The whole movement is very graceful, very formal, like something in ballet.

My comment is:

> I can just hear the Sergeant-Major bellowing: "Put some guts into it, you blinkin' ballereenas!"

This should annoy the balletomanes quite a lot, which is what I want. If only they were not such idiots! I will go once every three months to see *Scheherazade*. Once every month to hear the Symphonie Fantastique; the composer had a programme in mind which was visual and therefore balletable. Once a fortnight to *Petrouchka* or to the *Baiser de la Fée*. And once a week to *Coq d'Or*. (Ask Sadler's Wells why they never play any of these, and you will be told either that they haven't the orchestra or the dancers, or that the score is lying at the bottom of the Baltic.) What I will not put up with is the implication that when the company joins hands and pulls a supine Helpmann round the stage by means of his hair I am getting a picture of Lust being overtaken by Retribution.

Oct. 3 *Sunday.* Spent most of yesterday and to-day reading the new biography of Hazlitt, *Born under Saturn*, by Catherine Macdonald Maclean. It is unfortunate that the jacket should carry this sentence (in connection with some other book): "Mr Bryant has not his equal in selecting and spot-lighting the telling moment." Unfortunate, because this is just what Miss Maclean cannot do. Nothing less than flood-lighting contents her. Everybody knows how one snowy, foggy January night the actor Kean, having dined (a rare event with him in those early days), set out from his lodging in Cecil Street for Drury Lane Theatre, where, as Shylock, he was to make his first appearance. "I wish I was going to be shot," he said. Now listen to Miss Maclean. I have condensed the passage by two-thirds.

> Courage! little Jupiter *tonans*! To-night you walk through the snow, and as the slush slips over your poor hard shoes, you carry your silken stockings in the pocket of your shabby coat; by the time the spring flowers have come, you shall see your little Charles at play in the shelter of your home—with the yellow leprosy of gold trickling through his baby fingers.

Consider the incident of Hazlitt's dismissal by the egregious Perry, of the *Morning Chronicle*. About this Miss Mitford writes:

> I have just been reading Hazlitt's *View of the English Stage*—a series of critiques originally printed in the different newspapers, particularly the *Chronicle*. . . . I was at Tavistock House at the time, and well remember the doleful visage with which Mr Perry used to contemplate the long column of criticism, and how he used to execrate "the d——d fellow's d——d stuff" for filling up so much of the paper in the very height of the advertisement season. I shall never forget his long face. It was the only time of the day that I ever saw it long or sour. He had not the slightest suspicion that he had a man of genius in his pay—not the most remote perception of the merit of the writing—nor the slightest companionship with the author. He hired him as you hire your footman; and turned him off (with as little or less ceremony than you would use in discharging the aforesaid worthy personage) for a very masterly

but damaging critique on Sir Thomas Lawrence, whom Mr P., as one whom he visited and was being painted by, chose to have praised.

Compare this firm and vigorous stuff with Miss Maclean's:

> He was not dismissed by Perry, but ceased to call at the *Chronicle* office because Perry's manner made it clear to him that he was unwelcome. He had—it is true—many other strings to his bow, and could have filled the columns of the *Chronicle* easily without touching on politics at all, but Perry had little taste in literature, art, or drama. He had no idea of the quality of the work Hazlitt was doing for him—although others were quick to note it—no awareness of the extent to which everything Hazlitt touched turned to literature in his hands.

How Hazlitt, who was a good deal of what Miss Prism called a "womanthrope," would have detested all that sentimentalism which is his latest biographer's alternative to unredeemed flatness! The boy was taken by his father to America at the age of five. Which means that Miss Maclean must treat herself and us to a long fantasia on blue birds, scarlet birds, firebirds, kingbirds, snowbirds, and mocking birds. Some people can never stop talking; this lady can never stop enlarging! She has a dreadful habit of dragging in allusions by the hair of their heads. Coleridge goes to visit Hazlitt's father, a clergyman, at Shrewsbury. How Coleridge preached, stayed the night, and asked young William to visit him in Somerset, saying he would come half-way to meet him, and how next morning the boy set the older man on his way and walked six miles with him—all this is wonderfully described by Hazlitt himself. Here is Miss M. on their parting at that sixth milestone:

> The forces that have brought them together for the momentary intense contact, needful at least to one of them, are already gathering to rive them apart. Is this fantastic? Nay, nay, 'tis true!—*but yet the pity of it, Iago! O Iago, the pity of it, Iago!*

This book runs to 631 large pages containing a quarter of a million words. Which tempts me to say, "O the pity of it, Mr Paper Controller! O the pity of it!"

Fatras. At a recent dinner-party somebody asked Françoise Rosay what she thought of the English theatre. That brilliant and fascinating actress replied, " J'ai vu *Fur Coat* ! " This must be the most damaging thing ever said about the English stage.

Oct. 5 *Tuesday.* Ballet repercussion. This is a round-robin, addressed to the Editor of the *Daily Express* :

> The great man has spoken. Mr Agate has not only read about the ballet ; he has told us what he thinks about it. He finds it extremely soothing to sit and watch young ladies pretending to be swans, or even swans pretending to be young ladies. If we try to imagine the alternative possibility of young ladies watching Mr Agate pretending to be a swan, or even a swan pretending to be Mr Agate, we so readily agree with him. But why should ignorance of the inner significance of ballet prompt such vituperation ? We can well understand the difference between the atmosphere of a shire-horse stable and the ballet stage, but see no reason why the " Swill'd insolence of the loose unletter'd hind " of the former should be adopted, at least without some modification, in speaking of the latter.

This is signed " Rosalinde, Rosemary, Edna, Patricia, Sylvia, Ann, Rita, and Denise, young ladies of the Ballet." Entrancing names, set down in the squiggly characters of those whose talent lies in their toes. I am ravished to think of the *gazouillement* which must have preceded this considerable literary effort. I have replied :

> DEAR ROSALINDE, ROSEMARY, EDNA, PATRICIA, SYLVIA, ANN, RITA, AND DENISE,
>
> Many thanks for your very charming letter, which I shall show to all my friends. It is quite one of the nicest I have ever received, and do please tell me where the quotation comes from. Is it your recollection of Milton, whose *Comus* you dance so delightfully ? I, too, greatly admire Mr Helpmann and Miss Fonteyn. But that is no reason why people should write silly books about them. By the way, you have made one little mistake. My stable holds *hackneys*, not shire horses, and now, alas, only one. But I am happy to think that Lady Viking, as she is called, has the grace of a Fonteyn and a Helpmann combined. I wish I could ask you all to tea. Alas, I have only three cups, one of which is cracked. Almost as badly as
>
> Yours very sincerely,
>
> JAMES AGATE

Oct. 7 *Thursday.* Quite casually Leo produces a Sonata for violin and piano which has lain in his drawer for twenty-six years. Luscious, lyrical stuff, pure 1910, reeking of Richard Strauss and, so far as I can judge, beautifully scored. I use the word to convey the complexity and richness of the texture. A romantic first movement followed by L. P.'s notion of a *marche funèbre*, and ending with a rondo which has all the verve and vim of that other Strauss in his *Fledermaus* period. Inasmuch as listening to it turns one into a Sultan of opérette with Cora Pearl tickling one's feet and Hortense Schneider spraying one with Frangipani, and since there are no *longueurs* and no uglinesses, and since the whole thing has the felicity of being pre-Bartók and pre-Bloch and pre-Berg, and seeing that it requires two virtuoso players who know more about Vienna than being able to point to it on the map—in view of all this the poor thing hasn't a dog's chance of being performed.

Oct. 8 *Friday.* Having, as I thought, successfully ignored Miss Katzengebiss's letter, I now receive this :

45 Nibelung Road
*Swiss Cottage, N.W.*6

DEAR SIR !

From my sister-in-law Frl. Erna Katzengebiss you already since some weeks receive an Offer about her play. Now I ask that you interest yourself in our new Journal INTERNATIONALE which is soon ready to print. We have received Advice that such a journal will be read widely, and we have decided to scatter Copies among the fighting Forces of this Country. Some great celebrities of Europe have already sent articles. So our revered Prof. Sigmund Leitmarin writes on the history of Patagonia, in German ; Dr Chu Li on the antiquities of Chang-chuen-shan, in Chinese ; Erik Bobatzcu in Roumanian of Danube fish ; and Rabbi Cheitz Feitelbaum on the Babylonian Talmud, in Hebrew. Now we should have perhaps an article in Englisch, and I ask from you such a one on some subject upon which you expertise, perhaps on the Theater of Persia in the middle Ages, or the influence of Fichte on contemporary Drama. For this I can offer no Honorar but you will receive from me an Invitation to a collection of famous Refugee artists at Christmas. Only will you be asked to contribute One Pound for expense.

Most respectful Yours,

DR ISRAEL BAUCHPRESSER

Oct. 9 *Saturday.* So many young people in their 'teens and twenties writing to ask how they can get a job as a dramatic critic, I am enlarging on this in the *S.T.* The point is that, speaking broadly, nobody should criticise a play till he is thirty or a player till he is forty. The drama can be in part learned from books, but not acting. I don't expect boys of sixteen to play the violin in public. But if they do they must play it like Menuhin. And if they criticise in public they must do it like young Dents. I shall propose two examination papers, one for beginners, and the other for advanced students.

TEST FOR BUDDING CRITICS

1. Give the names of the four most famous Greek dramatists of antiquity.
2. Which of Shakespeare's characters says: (*a*) "Alas, poor Yorick!" (*b*) "Give me the daggers." (*c*) "I am a man more sinned against than sinning." (*d*) "Sing willow, willow, willow." (*e*) "I am dying, Egypt, dying." (*f*) "All the world's a stage"?
3. Name the four principal Restoration dramatists.
4. In what plays do the following characters occur: Sir Epicure Mammon, Mrs Malaprop, Claude Melnotte, Old Eccles, Christy Mahon, Joxer Daly?
5. Who said: (*a*) "Was this the face that launch'd a thousand ships?" (*b*) "I nauseate walking; 'tis a country diversion." (*c*) "Zounds, madam, you had no taste when you married me!" (*d*) "Ignorance is like a delicate exotic fruit—touch it and the bloom is gone." (*e*) "That's a good bid, Eugene." (*f*) "To die will be an awfully big adventure"?
6. The authors of *The Duchess of Malfi*, *A New Way to Pay Old Debts*, *All for Love*, *Venice Preserved*, *George Barnwell*, *Virginius*, were George Lillo, Sheridan Knowles, Otway, Massinger, Webster, Dryden? Put these in the right order.
7. Who wrote *Le Misanthrope*, *Wallenstein*, *Pelléas et Mélisande*, *The Father*, *The Seagull*, *Anna Christie*?
8. How many women parts are there in: *Hamlet*, *Othello*, *Antony and Cleopatra*, *Twelfth Night*, *As You Like It*, *Measure for Measure*?
9. What essayist and critic, in what connection, was "glad, for a season, to take an airing beyond the diocese of the strict conscience"?

10. " Hedda Gabler was an idealist who turned down rich suitors and married a poor professor whom she really loved. She reformed a dissolute young writer and rescued his manuscript. Blackmailed by a rascally judge, she stabbed herself for her husband's sake." What is wrong here ?

FOR ADVANCED STUDENTS ONLY

1. Name a masterpiece by Plautus, Menander, Terence, Lope de Vega, Calderon, Metastasio.
2. Mention any play by Greene, Peele, Nashe, Chapman, Kyd, Middleton.
3. In which plays do the following characters occur : Sir Pertinax M'Sycophant, Sir Archy M'Sarcasm, Kitely, Stukely, Sir Fopling Flutter, Lord Foppington ?
4. What French tragedies begin with the words, " Oui," " Quoi ! " " Arrêtons un moment ! " ?
5. What is Bradley's " precedent *état d'âme* " theory that Walkley denied ?
6. Mention any rôle created by Mrs Barry, Mrs Bracegirdle, Mrs Oldfield, Mrs Pritchard, Mrs Abington, Mrs Siddons.
7. In what plays do the following appear ? Give author : Lady Jessica Nepean, Lady Mary Lasenby, Lady Alethea Frobisher, Lady Cecily Waynflete, Lady George Grayston, Lady Ridgeley.
8. Mention a play by Gogol, Andreyev, Echegaray, Wedekind, Lenormand, Jean Cocteau.
9. Who said : " Life is simply a *mauvais quart d'heure* made up of exquisite moments." " I assure you, I was within three feet of her when she deliberately Trafalgar Squared me." " A lifetime of happiness : no man alive could bear it : it would be hell on earth." " There are few more impressive sights in the world than a Scotsman on the make." " Women should be beaten regularly, like gongs." " The whole worl's in a state o' chassis ! "
10. Who wrote *Satiromastix*, *Aureng-Zebe*, *Oroonoko*, *Barbarossa*, *Sardanapalus*, *Tom Thumb* ?

ANSWERS

BUDDING CRITICS

1. Æschylus, Sophocles, Euripides, Aristophanes. 2. Hamlet, Lady Macbeth, Lear, Desdemona, Antony, Jaques. 3. Wycherley, Congreve, Vanbrugh, Farquhar. 4. *The Alchemist*, *The Rivals*, *The Lady of Lyons*, *Caste*, *The Playboy of the Western World*, *Juno and the Paycock.*

5. Faustus, Millamant, Sir Peter Teazle, Lady Bracknell, Candida, Peter Pan. 6. Webster, Massinger, Dryden, Otway, Lillo, Knowles. 7. Molière, Schiller, Maeterlinck, Strindberg, Tchehov, O'Neill. 8. Two, Three, Four, Three, Four, Five. 9. Charles Lamb ; Restoration comedy. 10. Everything.

ADVANCED STUDENTS

1. *Menœchmi*, *Thais*, *Heautontimorumenos*, *El Rey Don Pedro en Madrid*, *El Alcade de Zalamea*, *La Clemenza di Tito*. 2. *The Historie of Orlando Furioso*, *The Old Wives' Tale*, *Summer's Last Will and Testament*, *The Gentleman Usher*, *The Spanish Tragedy*, *The Spanish Gipsy*. 3. Macklin's *The Man of the World*, Macklin's *Love à la Mode*, Ben Jonson's *Every Man in his Humour*, Moore's *The Gamester*, Etherege's *The Man of Mode*, Vanbrugh's *The Relapse*. 4. *Andromaque*, *Britannicus*, *Bérénice*, all by Racine. 5. The theory that Hamlet has a life outside the words in which Shakespeare sets him down. 6. Monimia in Otway's *The Orphan*, Millamant, Lady Betty Modish in Cibber's *The Careless Husband*, Mrs Beverley in *The Gamester*, Lady Teazle, Mrs Haller in *The Stranger*. 7. Henry Arthur Jones's *The Liars*, Barrie's *The Admirable Crichton*, Sutro's *The Walls of Jericho*, Shaw's *Captain Brassbound's Conversion*, Maugham's *Our Betters*, Pinero's *His House in Order*. 8. *The Government Inspector*, *The Seven Who Were Hanged*, *Mariana*, *Spring's Awakening*, *Les Ratés*, *Les Parents Terribles*. 9. Mrs Allonby in Wilde's *A Woman of No Importance*, the Duke of St Olphert's in Pinero's *The Notorious Mrs Ebbsmith*, Tanner in Shaw's *Man and Superman*, David Wylie in Barrie's *What Every Woman Knows*, Elyot in Noel Coward's *Private Lives*, Boyle in O'Casey's *Juno and the Paycock*. 10. Dekker, Dryden, Southerne, John Brown, Byron, Fielding.

Oct. 10 *Sunday.* Peter Page is a capital hand at embroidering fantasy while remaining strictly truthful in the domain of fact. As a raconteur he realises that a Lie must always be (*a*) amusing, (*b*) credible, and (*c*) obviously a fabrication. When he tells you about a pre-war holiday spent in Timbuctoo and how it is like, in the actor's jargon, " any number three town," you believe him. (He did, as a matter of fact, once fly there for a week-end.) But when he goes on to tell you how he proceeded to the Solomon Islands and dined with the head-hunters, and how it was indistinguishable from any party at the Savoy Grill—why, then you know he is fibbing and intends you to know this. With the most brilliant tact, and a good deal of wit, Peter sometimes leaves it to his hearers to decide in which dimension he is functioning. It isn't always easy to distinguish, because my old friend, who comes straight out of the *New Arabian Nights*, is the kind of person to whom fantastic things actually happen. At the Club to-day he told us a wonderful story about his initiation into Freemasonry and how his supporters were Willie Clarkson and Kitchener of Khartoum ! This is good enough to be one of Peter's inventions; actually it happens to be true. I think I shall suggest to him that he write his Autobiography in a mixture of both veins, with a key at the end.

Oct. 11 *Monday.* Jock is displeased with my second Examination Paper. He calls it "disingenuous" because he doesn't believe I could answer the questions myself. The point is that I made up the questions sitting at my desk, by heart as it were, and that when they were finished Leo and I found that between us we could answer some 85 per cent. of them.

A note from "Curly," now in Berkshire doing something hush-hush:

> Am recovering from violent attacks on my person by doctors, dentists, chiropodists, and their kind, and am not liking the world, even though, seen from this huge park, it is very beautiful as it sheds its dying life.
>
> In the very heart of the park there is a haunted tree. You cannot mistake the tree; it exudes a warmth. If you stand, very still, beneath its branches, and do not allow the falling chestnuts to perturb you, you will hear voices. Guttural voices, speaking in a foreign tongue. Of course the tree-trunk may be hollow and conceal the headquarters of an enemy espionage outfit. But that would call for action of some sort. I prefer to think the voices are not of this world, so that I can hurry past with a clear conscience!
>
> Heaven knows when I shall see you again. There's not a whisper of leave, even from the latrines, the abode of whispers. I'm fairly miserable. The O.C. doesn't love me any more because I missed the train on the occasion of my last descent upon London. But, strangely, the C.O., who loves me even less, saved me from a Court Martial. And so it wags.

Oct. 12 *Tuesday.* Leo turned up unexpectedly on Sunday to remind me I am due to lecture to-morrow to three hundred London County Council school-teachers, and had I done anything about it? I hadn't. And he sat there patiently while I dictated some five thousand words, which I spent the whole of yesterday revising and re-arranging. When I got in at 11.15 last night I found a beautifully typed MS. There is a story of John Barrymore, when he was playing Hamlet, knocking down his Ophelia because she "looked so bloody pure." Virgin MSS. make me feel the same. When I had finished manhandling the thing it was 4 A.M.

Oct. 13 *Wednesday.* My talk to the school-marms went off fairly well, though Sydney Carroll, who took the chair, complained afterwards that I had not talked enough about the drama. What my old friend meant was that I had failed to declare some modern chit to be the greatest actress this country has produced. Here is a little of what I said in a lecture probably too long:

> There is a picture by Henry Moore in the possession of Sir Kenneth Clark entitled "Crowd of People Looking at a Tied-up Object." This shows a desolate plain with some thirty people all huddled together looking at something three times the size of the Achilles statue. It may indeed be a statue, but since it is covered with a dust-sheet fastened with rope you cannot tell. Now this is the point. I do not know, nor does Sir Kenneth know, what this Object is. The artist doesn't want us to know. What I do know is that the picture gives my eye pleasure; it would be decorative if it were called "Lot's Wife." It may be that for the young men who haunt the Café Royal, modern music and modern verse make the same appeal to the ear and mind that Henry Moore's picture makes to my eye. I am not going to suggest that all of them are humbugs, or even that they are wilfully deceiving themselves. I will concede that they are as single-minded as I am. I do not doubt the sincerity of the solemn ass who, the other evening, said portentously: "Wagner is the Puccini of music!"
>
> But it does seem to me that there is a difference between poetry and the arts of music and painting. I am not and will not be an Imagist. I hold that a poem cannot be judged merely by the liquidity of its vocables or the look of them on paper. A poet deals in words, and the first business of words is to convey meaning. Overtones are not enough. If they were, *Jabberwocky* would be as good a poem as anything by Donne or Browning. I hold with Chesterton when he said of the modern stuff: "It is no more a new school of poetry than sleeping in a ditch is a new form of architecture." This is where I and the young people join issue. In my day artists who failed to make their meaning clear were regarded as having failed in their job. To-day obscurity is hailed as a positive virtue.

This monstrous fashion has spread even to the films. There was a good example in the Orson Welles picture produced a couple of years ago and called *Citizen Kane.* The first shot of this showed something burning, something with the word " Rosebud " written on it. At the pre-view I could not determine what this was ; I imagined that it might be the cover of a child's picture-book. On the following Sunday one of our highest-browed critics admitted to being similarly befogged, but welcomed this befogging since it set forth " the ultimate obscurity in which every life moves." Whereupon I called on the Welles representative in London, and at once the gaff was blown. " It's a mistake," said this gentleman, " and all our fault. In the English version we ought to have made it clear that the thing burning is a sledge—Kane's sledge, in fact, when he was a little boy. It isn't necessary to explain this to an American audience because all American children have sledges to which they give pet names. I remember that my sledge was called ' Firefly.' You may take it from me that there was no intentional obscurity on Mr Welles's part. He just didn't realise that an English audience wouldn't ' get ' it." Triumphantly I reported this. My eminent colleague, who was in no way shattered or even dashed, said : " The fact that we do not recognise ' Rosebud ' as a sledge symbolises how little human beings know of one another." The fact is that *Citizen Kane* was a near-masterpiece helped by the fact that you knew what it was all about. In the critic you have a shining example of the highbrow who insists on regarding obscurity as a virtue.

It was not so in my day. Let us consider a drama by Strindberg called *The Spook Sonata.* In this play there are some queer fish, including a nobleman who is also a colonel, yet in some peculiar way belongs neither to the nobility nor to the army ; a wife who shuts herself up in a cupboard for twenty years and finally emerges with the voice of a parrot ; a cook who, instead of nourishing the family, drains its life-blood and keeps it in a bottle normally used for gravy extract ! Critics rightly hailed this play as a masterpiece because of its extraordinary stagecraft and in spite of its incomprehensibility. To-day's young men, ignoring the stagecraft, will acclaim this work because of its incomprehensibility. Of Ibsen's last play, *When We Dead Awaken,* Montague wrote :

" Is Irene the poetic drama ? Or is it a parable of the bad bargain an artist may make in sacrificing the whole-hearted, headlong fruition of life to the austere business of standing apart to observe and express it ? Or is Irene an embodiment of the perfect love, the authentic passion not to be disobeyed but at risk of atrophy to the soul, and does Rubek embody the spirit of compromise ? Is Squire Ulfheim, that super-virile sportsman, the genius of conquering vitality and sane animalism ? Is Irene's black-robed attendant formal religion, the Church, viewed with some blend or other of sympathy and irony ? And if everybody is something, what on earth is the Inspector at the Baths ? "

And then that great critic came perilously near to hedging. " It is rather a cheap game to run people down because you cannot see what they are at, as boys perceive at school that 'Euclid is all rot' ; safer, perhaps, to assume that an art as potent as Ibsen's has got hold of something, even here. Likely enough, when we stupid awaken, we shall find the queer, tough play a big thing, and even a clear one."

It may be that I am " old and grey and full of sleep," and that what the younger generation is acclaiming is not to them obscurity, though it is so to me. It may be that the things which I think queer and tough are to them crystal-clear. Up to the present the drama, as performed in this country, has been fairly innocent of obscurity. In other words, I find that I still have a pretty good idea of what most plays are about. But I promise you, ladies, that when the day comes in which I find the majority of plays incomprehensible, I shall gather up my pens and my paper and retire from the business of dramatic criticism.

Oct. 14 *Thursday.* Lots of letters about my two Questionnaires, many of their writers insisting that they are only memory tests. I agree. Ivor Brown sent me a charming note from which I cull " What is wanted is not critics more learned than Charles Morgan and A. B. Walkley rolled up into one ball of belles-lettrish omniscience. What is wanted is critics possessing some scholarship (but not too much) and a great love for and knowledge of the living theatre." (I suspect that by " living " theatre Ivor means " provincial ".) Obviously no critic can be the worse for knowing about the influence of Terence on the plays of that tenth-century nun who was called Hrotswitha, or what was Little Tich's name in private life. And I do not think either piece of knowledge necessarily makes its possessor a better critic. That a man can give off-hand the year Jeddah won the Derby, or say how many winners have started at 100 to 1, is no evidence that he can " read " a race. Quite a number of people, complaining that they do not want questionnaires for critics either budding or advanced, have written demanding one for the ordinary playgoer of average cultural intelligence. This puts me in a difficulty because I don't believe the ordinary playgoer has any cultural intelligence. I don't believe that any of the women who clutter up the foyer on first-nights know even whose ghost it was that Hamlet saw! However, I have concocted something for the Ordinary Playgoer, who is presumed to know that Irving reigned at the Lyceum, and Tree at Her (subsequently His) Majesty's Theatre. Four-fifths of the paper deals with theatrical happenings of the last half-century; the remaining fifth comes within the scope of polite theatrical knowledge. I should regard a score of 75 out of a possible 100 as excellent, one of 50 fair, and anything below 40 deplorable.

QUESTIONNAIRE FOR FIRST-NIGHTERS

1. Which of Shakespeare's Kings (*a*) died in an orchard of a fever, (*b*) was poisoned in an orchard, (*c*) resembled his hostess's father while he slept, (*d*) talked about graves and worms and epitaphs, (*e*) would have given his kingdom for a horse, (*f*) went mad? (6 marks.)
2. How did (*a*) Cleopatra, (*b*) Ophelia, (*c*) Juliet, (*d*) Cordelia, (*e*) Desdemona, (*f*) Lady Macbeth, die? (6 marks.)
3. Fill in the blanks. (12 marks.)
   (*a*) What a piece of —— is a man!
   (*b*) The —— of March are come.
   (*c*) How sweet the —— sleeps upon this ——!
   (*d*) He jests at —— that never felt a ——.
   (*e*) Sans ——, sans ——, sans ——, sans ——.
   (*f*) She sat like —— on a monument smiling at ——.
4. Mention two plays by Shaw, Pinero, Drinkwater, Barrie, Galsworthy, Maugham, O'Casey, Priestley, Bridie, Eugene O'Neill, Emlyn Williams, Terence Rattigan. (24 marks.)
5. Mention one play by Tchehov, Rostand, Flecker, Sudermann, Steinbeck, Charles Morgan, Jean-Jacques Bernard, Obey, Synge, Rudolf Besier, R. C. Sherriff, Robert Sherwood. (12 marks.)
6. In what plays by what authors do the following characters occur: (*a*) Lady Wishfort, (*b*) Lady Sneerwell, (*c*) Lady Utterword, (*d*) Miss Prism, (*e*) Sophy Fullgarney, (*f*) Agatha Payne? (12 marks.)

7. Who wrote the music for (*a*) *The Geisha*, (*b*) *The Belle of New York*, (*c*) *The Merry Widow*, (*d*) *Véronique*, (*e*) *The Country Girl*, (*f*) *No, No, Nanette*, (*g*) *Me and My Girl*, (*h*) *The Chocolate Soldier*, (*j*) *The Dollar Princess*, (*k*) *Utopia Limited*, (*l*) *Merrie England*, (*m*) *This Year of Grace* ? (12 marks.)
8. Mention any part with which you associate (*a*) Charles Hawtrey, (*b*) Lewis Waller, (*c*) Edward Terry, (*d*) Fred Terry, (*e*) Wilson Barrett, (*f*) John Barrymore. (6 marks.)
9. What famous actors and actresses co-starred in (*a*) *Still Waters Run Deep*, (*b*) *The Second Mrs Tanqueray*, (*c*) *David Garrick*, (*d*) *Olivia*, (*e*) *Juno and the Paycock*, (*f*) *Richard of Bordeaux* ? (6 marks.)
10. What real person is meant by (*a*) L'Aiglon, (*b*) The Lady with a Lamp, (*c*) The Rose without a Thorn, (*d*) The Anatomist ? (4 marks.)

ANSWERS

1. (*a*) John, (*b*) Hamlet, King of Denmark, (*c*) Duncan, King of Scotland, (*d*) Richard II, (*e*) Richard III, (*f*) Lear. 2. (*a*) Poisoned by an asp, (*b*) drowned, (*c*) stabbed herself, (*d*) hanged, (*e*) smothered, (*f*) we are not told. 3. (*a*) Work, (*b*) Ides, (*c*) moonlight, bank, (*d*) scars, wound, (*e*) teeth, eyes, taste, everything, (*f*) patience, grief. 4. and 5. See *Who's Who in the Theatre*. 6. (*a*) Congreve's *The Way of the World*, (*b*) Sheridan's *The School for Scandal*, (*c*) Shaw's *Heartbreak House*, (*d*) Wilde's *The Importance of Being Earnest*, (*e*) Pinero's *The Gay Lord Quex*, (*f*) Rodney Ackland's *The Old Ladies* (adapted from Hugh Walpole's story). 7. (*a*) Sidney Jones, (*b*) Gustav Kerker, (*c*) Franz Lehar, (*d*) André Messager, (*e*) Lionel Monckton, (*f*) Vincent Youmans, (*g*) Noel Gay, (*h*) Oskar Straus, (*j*) Leo Fall, (*k*) Arthur Sullivan, (*l*) Edward German, (*m*) Noel Coward. 8. See *Who's Who in the Theatre*. 9. (*a*) Mr and Mrs Kendal, (*b*) George Alexander and Mrs Patrick Campbell, (*c*) Charles Wyndham and Mary Moore, (*d*) Henry Irving and Ellen Terry, (*e*) Arthur Sinclair and Sara Allgood, (*f*) John Gielgud and Gwen Ffrangcon-Davies. 10. (*a*) Napoleon's son, the Duc de Reichstadt, (*b*) Florence Nightingale, (*c*) Katheryn Howard, (*d*) Dr Robert Knox.

Oct. 15 *Friday.* Another letter from my little friends " whose names are five sweet symphonies." Except that there are eight of them :

DEAR MR AGATE,

You dis-arm—or should it be dis-leg ?—us, for we are, as you guessed, young dancers. We think you're a brick and we've clearly misunderstood you. Some day when we are a bit older, we hope to emulate Margot and Bobbie and then, if you'll come to see us, we'll dance just for you.

We don't mind your saying you are " crackers," but if we now hear anyone else say it (and people do say it, you know) we'll slosh 'em.

Your devoted

ROSALINDE, ROSEMARY, EDNA, PATRICIA, SYLVIA, ANN, RITA, and DENISE.

P.S. Please give Lady Viking a kiss from us. She sounds charming.

Oct. 17 *Sunday.* Letter awaiting me last night from Brother Mycroft:

14 *John Dalton Street*
Manchester
October 15, 1943

MY DEAR JIMMIE,

Thanks for letter and for *Responsibility.* You ask for my opinion. *Seriously*, forsooth ! Am I ever anything but serious when discussing things that matter ?

You want to be told, first of all, the answer to the question : " Is *Responsibility* a work of art ? " Well, as Joad would say, that depends on your definition of a work of art. My first condition would be that the work must be consistent with itself. It must have a total gesture. It must never step out of its frame, and deny or contradict the limitations imposed by its inherent form. I am not a critic, but I am sure that that was what Humbert Wolfe meant by the " breakdown " in the middle. He confused the issue by calling the metaphysics second-rate. *First-rate* metaphysics would have been just as out of place in a NOVEL.

Did you make up your mind before you started, or, later, started revising, what a novel had to be to be a work of art—or what it had not to be ? Did you care ? Or did you say, " I will invent a new art-form, and be hanged to academic style. I will step out of the frame when I like. I will use the NOVEL form for airing my opinions " ? Whether you made a plan like that or not, that is how the original book appeared, and that is why it failed. It did not fail because you can't write fiction. The parts which are devoted to the creation of character—the supreme qualification for a novelist—were good enough for anybody. I mean, to be written by anybody. Unfortunately you haven't taken Wolfe and Montague to heart, or not wholeheartedly. You will kick against the pricks. Even in your preface you kick. You won't take a hint. Because Montague praises your writing you assume that good writing, as such, is enough to make a good novel, and that the book didn't succeed because "the modern English reader doesn't care about good writing." Then you complain that he is "all for the tale rather than the telling." But the reader is right, because the tale comes first. Your characters must move, react on each other, and live. That is the "tale" you despise. The writing is the means by which you bring these things about, and it must be devoted to that end, and not caper about trying to have a separate existence. Your example taken from the half-page towards the end of the book is the best evidence of your misunderstanding of why the book fails as a novel. For you that passage is a piece of subtle writing to be admired in any setting. To me it is a shining example of bad writing in the setting of a NOVEL, appallingly precious in its appeal to other littérateurs. A hidden allusion like this has *no purpose* except that of showing off, because (1) if the reference is known it adds nothing to your meaning, and (2) if it isn't known it is just an irritation.

To sum up. You have tinkered with the job of revision. You haven't realised what was the matter, or if you did you haven't been ruthless. I am sorry, because there are qualities in the narrative parts which would have made, in my opinion, a first-rate short-length novel. It is both interesting and fascinating, pathetic too in parts. But you can't let the book speak for itself and stand on its own feet. You have nothing to be afraid of. Your writing is not thin or poverty-stricken. It doesn't want loading with extraneous matter. Don't you see that if what you have to say about the people in the book will only run to a short novel, you just can't do anything about it? There are painters of big canvases and small. Size doesn't matter; quality does, essentially. I wish I were a critic to put my feelings into the correct jargon. I can't, but I know I am right in my instinct.

Ever,
GUSTAVE

Here follows a list of the excisions which Mycroft would have made. They run to thirty pages, or one-sixth of the book! I have replied:

Queen Alexandra Mansions, W.C. 2
October 17, 1943

MY DEAR WHISKERS,

As usual, you are right. The trouble is that I have never wanted to be a novelist in your sense. Just as I eat boiled mutton only for the caper sauce, so I read novels only for their trimmings. Surely one would have to be a colossal genius to invent a story worth telling for its own sake ? And even my vanity doesn't run to that. It is not the plots in Balzac which interest me. I have never worried about how many times Lucien de Rubembré got into and out of Vautrin's clutches, but I perfectly remember Esther's last letter of which it is ridiculous to pretend that she ever wrote a line. " Une morte qui demande l'aumône, en voilà du comique ! . . . Allons, il faut savoir se tenir tranquille dans sa tombe." What is this, pray, except Balzac, " showing off " ? You want me to cut the great letter in *Responsibility* because Claude Rodd couldn't have written it. My dear boy, he did write it ! Don't you realise that this letter was written by our brother Edward when he was nineteen ? That I treasured it for twenty years before using it ? That I didn't alter a word or contribute a comma ? I would rather *Responsibility* missed fire and preserved this letter than be a work of art without it.

The essence of my work always has been, and always will be, divagation. I wonder if you know a passage in Walkley's *Pastiche and Prejudice* ? Here is a bit of his essay on *Plays of Talk* :

" What is it gives so peculiar a charm to the criticism of Dryden ? Is it not his discursiveness, his little descriptive embellishments—as, for example, in the *Essay of Dramatic Poesy*, the river trip, the listening for the distant thunder of the Dutch guns ' on that memorable day,' the moonlight on the water, the landing at Somerset Stairs among the crowd of French dancers ? I have said elsewhere how Hazlitt's theatrical criticisms lose in readableness by their strict attention to business, compared with his miscellaneous essays, where he permits himself to wander ' all over the place.' George Henry Lewes's theatrical criticisms can still be read with pleasure for the very reason that they were diversified with deliberate, almost frivolous irrelevancies. And then there was Jules Lemaître with his perpetual ' moi,' which provoked the austere Brunetière to quote Pascal's ' *le moi est haïssable.*' Yet where will you find more enjoyable criticism than Lemaître ? " I had hoped that some day somebody would say this of me.

Obviously you are going to ask—Then why not be an essayist ? The answer is that I have been one. I have written and published seven books of essays which nobody read at the time and which have reappeared in no anthologies apart from my own. I think I must have had a prevision that this was going to be so. But there was never anything to be done about it. Writing better essays wouldn't have helped. Even Walkley's three exquisite volumes didn't sell. I doubt whether Lamb's Essays, written to-day, would find a publisher or readers. As a novelist I suppose I belong to the school of Sterne; where is the plot in *Tristram Shandy*? And what about *Mademoiselle de Maupin*? Gautier's d'Albert, Rosette, Rosalinde, and Théodore are not persons at all. They are merely different ways of spelling "Théophile." All my characters in *Responsibility* are different ways of spelling me. I don't know that I wanted to proclaim this in the new Preface. But I think that I should have let three-quarters of the cat out of the bag instead of only half the animal. I ought to have said that I had deleted only such divagations as displeased me, but that I had stuck to the others like glue.

Ever,

JIMMIE

Oct. 18 *Monday.* From a letter:

Odile's thirty-two fouettés in *Le Lac des Cygnes* are executed to bewitch and dazzle the Prince. Giselle's fouettés express the mental torment she is going through.

How the same twiddle can express both chalk and cheese will ever remain beyond my comprehension. As for Shakespeare, I hold that Troilus, with his "Expectation whirls me round," is the one danceable character.

With reference to my last Quiz somebody writes from South Croydon challenging the statement that "we are not told how Lady Macbeth died." He quotes

> and his fiend-like queen,
> Who, as 'tis thought, by self and violent hands
> Took off her life:

and adds, "You didn't read on far enough." Charming!

Oct. 19 *Tuesday.* Modesty is no part of a critic's equipment. I have no use for the critic who lets you see that he only comes up to the middle button of his subject's waistcoat. There was a time when I thought Jock was inclined to be a little shy, a little Beerbohmish. Now he has put all that behind him. His article on Hazlitt, of which he sends me a proof, is in the grand vein :

> It is one of the many seeming contradictions in Hazlitt's character that besides being a cynic who could say things on his death-bed like " I believe in the theoretical benevolence, and practical malignity of man," he had as fervent a love for humanity in the mass as any human being who ever lived. Liberty was his passion, and poverty that which, perhaps, he hated more than anything. He fought tyranny with a pen that was mightier than a beswordеd army. When the poor cried he wept like Cæsar, then dried his unavailing tears to write an availing pamphlet, soaked in his fury, saturate with his wit. He wrote of Claude and Poussin and Raphael and Titian more eloquently than art critic, before or since, has written about any kind of picture. He is the unsurpassed Sultan of the dramatic critics ; and the practitioners of literary, political, and philosophical criticism to this day all willingly declare him to be the master of their respective crafts. He was as proud as Lucifer—or as Edmund Kean, which is pretty much the same thing. He was saturnine—and yet he was likeable. He was a fascinating human being, made the more so by his dash of diabolism. No writer ever possessed greater integrity, courage, candour, or wit, and no English prose-writer—Shakespeare himself excepted—knew so exactly what he wanted to say and so exactly how to say it.

Oct. 20 *Wednesday.* In response to frenzied demands for more I have compiled for Sunday what Kipling's Beetle would have called " a final exhibition—a last attack—a giddy par-ergon." First I thought of a serious Quiz beginning : " 1. Enumerate the puns in Shakespeare. 2. What theatrical document of the first importance was signed by Napoleon at Moscow in 1812 ? 3. Who wrote (*a*) *Baucis and Philemon* and (*b*) *Philémon et Baucis* ? " And then the jumble of puns, the Charter of the Théâtre Français, together with Swift touched up by Addison, and Gounod helped, or rather hampered, by MM. Barbier and Carré, struck me as a trifle indigestible. Instead I composed this :

QUIZ TO END QUIZZES

1. Who wrote : " Beauty, methinks, seems a requisite qualification in an actress. I can never conceive an hero dying for love of a lady totally destitute of beauty. What

must be the entire perversion of scenical decorum, when we see an actress, that might be the Wapping Landlady without a bolster, pining in the character of Jane Shore, and while unwieldy with fat endeavouring to convince the audience that she is dying with hunger " ?

2. Who wrote the Memoirs of a great French actress " d'après ses correspondances et les rapports de police du temps " ? Who was the actress ?
3. What star of the Comédie Française, obtaining three months' leave of absence on account of her health, travelled the length and breadth of France by carriage, popped over to Guernsey, and gave seventy-four performances in ninety days ?
4. What French actress equipped herself for an American tour with a vocabulary consisting of the words *whiskey-sodas, pale ale, stomach-ache, waterproofs, jockeys, Misses, Mistresses, goddam, thank you, how do you do, Washington, kiss me, cowboy, good night, good-bye* ?
5. In what play is Duse alleged to have been funny ? Who was the author ?
6. Who at one and the same performance played Ophelia in a fair wig and her own dark hair ? And for whose edification ?
7. What great actress stopped a rehearsal and prayed that some knowledge of the rudiments of acting might descend upon her company ?
8. What famous actress said of an actor : " He reminded me of a butcher-boy flashing past, whistling, on the high seat of his cart, or of Phæthon driving the chariot of the sun —pretty much the same thing, I imagine " ? Who was the actor ?
9. What elderly actress, appearing at a charity matinée swathed in pink tulle, prefaced a recitation by asking the audience to imagine that she was a plumber's mate ?
10. What author and actor, afterwards dramatic censor, claimed to be Jack the Ripper ?

ANSWERS

1. Oliver Goldsmith. 2. Edmond de Goncourt. Clairon. 3. Rachel. 4. Aimée Tessandier. 5. *La Locandiera.* Goldoni. 6. Mrs Patrick Campbell. Ellen Terry, who was not amused. 7. Dame Madge Kendal. 8. Ellen Terry. William Terriss. 9. Lady Tree. 10. C. H. Brookfield. As he was walking home from the theatre late one night a drab, emerging from the shadows, threatened that unless he gave her a guinea she would call the police and say that he was Jack the Ripper. Brookfield said, " My poor girl, I am ! " Whereupon she fled.

Oct. 26 *Tuesday.* C. B. Fry gave a luncheon-party at Brown's Hotel to-day. George Brann, the great Sussex batsman, Clifford Bax, Lord Ebbisham, Denzil Batchelor, a clever fat poet now a major at the War Office and still a fascinating talker, and J. A. Six in all, a perfect number. Brilliant stuff about cricket, to which Clifford and I brilliantly listened. Brann told us a story about W. G. at the height of his Indian summer. How the old man went in and started getting fours in his first over. How he suddenly decided to have a go at old Tate. And how the ball went into the clouds and Brann waited for it, and as he waited said to himself, "Two hundred last week against Kent, three hundred yesterday against Middlesex. Golly, if I miss this he'll get five hundred!" How, at the thought, his hands parted, the ball hit him on the chest, and he only gathered it in the neighbourhood of his knees. Was all this harking-back to the past a little melancholy? Perhaps.

Oct. 27 *Wednesday.* Delivered to Jonathan Cape the MS. of *Red Letter Nights*, the sequel to *Brief Chronicles.* Also returned to Hutchinson's the final proofs of *These Were Actors*.

From Jock: "Have had a note from the Government saying that if I like I can be a coal miner!"

Oct. 28 *Thursday.* Sat up late trying to account for Arthur Askey. Shall take my illustrations next Sunday from Euripides, Chaucer, Shakespeare, Webster, Otway, Byron, Hazlitt, Lamb, Delavigne, Boucicault, Montague, and Baden-Powell. I do this half seriously and half for its annoyance value.

Oct. 29 *Friday.* Jock gives me this anonymous communication sent to him c/o *John o' London's Weekly*:

> Tell us about the great TECHNICIANS, who have made possible a full and glowing life for every one. We don't want to read about piddling nonentities like G. A. Sala, Clement Scott, and James Agate.

Nov. 5 *Friday.* No more Rotary Clubs for me. To prepare a speech, travel two hundred miles at my own expense and for no fee, and to be regaled with rabbit pie and cold water—never again, thank you !

Bebe Daniels, in last night's show at the Piccadilly, displayed a good deal of the vitality, gusto, and warm-heartedness of her great predecessor, José Collins. But would José have used a microphone ? Not for all the wealth of Maida Vale ! Why anyone with a good natural voice should prefer to sound like somebody announcing that the 4.30 to Liverpool will start from No. 14 instead of No. 15 platform, passes human comprehension. Max Wall, Richard Hearne, and Jack Stanford, as *Panama Hattie's* three sailors, worked very hard to persuade us that they are adepts at the " screwy," which is the American form of humour. But " screwiness " is not a thing which sits easily on us as a nation. It is true that as I write my gaze rests upon a pair of indignant horses driven by a hoydenish carter with orange hair, lemon-pudding complexion, strawberry-slashed mouth, and grubby paws ending in raspberry nails, wearing an oyster satin blouse and trousers of mulberry corduroy. (I never mix my planes. To protest that this young woman is rendering her country service in a time of need is to transfer the argument away from the plane of manners to that of conduct. I agree, of course, that just as your shop-girl must be allowed her crooner, so your female carter is entitled to wear any get-up she fancies.) But this eccentricity is not, I take it, typical of our national screwiness as a whole. We remain sane, and our clowns show it. Cole Porter's tunes were poorer than ever, there wasn't a line of wit to upset anybody, and the result was a reception which *La Belle Hélène*, *Die Fledermaus*, and *The Mikado* put together would have hardly received.

Nov. 6 *Saturday.* A dinner is to be given to-night to Arthur Christiansen to celebrate his ten-year editorship of the *Daily Express*. Whoever organised this had the extraordinary notion that I might like to prepare a speech and deliver it if the other speakers could be persuaded to sit down in reasonable time. If not, then not. A pity, because I am very fond of Chris, and was looking forward to the dinner. Here is the speech I had already written out:

When I was brainstorming at Chatham, I remember asking the admiral next to whom I sat at dinner whether he knew how to turn his ship round. He replied: "No, sir, I do not know how to turn my ship round. I should be a damned bad admiral if I did. I have officers to remember the things I have forgotten." Similarly I doubt very much whether General Alexander or General Montgomery would know how to make their armies face the other way. Fortunately, they are not likely to be called on for this manœuvre.

As with sailors and soldiers, so with editors. I doubt very much whether Chris could pass an examination on the lower slopes of history, geography, politics, and the arts. Let me begin with *History*. I doubt whether he remembers what nations were opposed at the Battle of Salamis, who were the leaders on each side, and how many sail were engaged. Coming to modern history, I doubt whether he could name this country's Prime Minister at the time of the Battle of Waterloo.

Now for *Geography*. I doubt whether Chris could tell us off-hand whether the Volga runs into the Black Sea, the Caspian Sea, or the Sea of Azov.

In the matter of *Politics* I don't suppose he knows the difference between the Edict of Nantes and the Diet of Worms.

In the matter of the *Arts* I question whether he could write out a complete list of the operas of Verdi, the plays of Ibsen, the films of René Clair, or the novels of Zola. Incidentally, I have a suspicion that his musical, dramatic, film, and literary critics might blot their copy-books if asked to do this.

In the matter of what I should like to call the comprehensive ignorance of a great editor I want to make the point that this is exactly as it should be. The secret of great editorship is intuition. A great editor must be jack of all trades and master of none. If he specialises in anything it will certainly be to the peril, and probably to the detriment, of his paper. He must make friends with the wood as a whole while having a bowing acquaintance with every tree.

Though I take Chris's specialised knowledge to be limited, let me say that he has more than enough of it to spot deficiency in the junior officers he employs to turn his ship round. Try writing rubbish for Chris, and you will pretty soon hear from the quarter-deck, though very politely. Whenever I have tried the easy way I have received a plaintive little note saying, "Do you think, dear James, you could get some book to take the place of Boswell's *Johnson*?" Or, "Is it possible our readers are getting a little tired of those Twelve Great Books which are to form the Nucleus of a Library?"

I daresay it is a long time since the editor of the *Daily Express* read *Sesame and Lilies*. And perhaps he has forgotten the passage in which Ruskin says: "I am not afraid of the word 'sensation,' still less of the thing. It is not less sensation that we want but more." Chris wants the *Daily Express* to be the most sensational paper in England: that is, the paper which has the most of decent feeling and noble passion about the war and the changes to come after the war.

But that is between him and his conscience. What is between him and Lord Beaverbrook is to run the paper so that it keeps its nose in front of any rival nose. To run it smoothly. To keep an eye on a lot of talented and unruly contributors. To insist on order in his schoolroom. In a word, to be the perfect head-keeper of a zoological garden, and maintain order in the menagerie knowing that the King of Beasts is at large in the grounds.

I began at Chatham; let me end at Harwich. I remember asking the admiral how some fifty thousand sailors, who were obviously panting to hear me, proposed to get into a lecture theatre capable of holding only nine hundred. He replied, "We use the ballot system. I have been fortunate enough to obtain a seat in the front row." Realising that I must adapt my conversation to the mentality of this simple gentleman, I said as we walked along the quay, "What is that dingy little craft I see moored alongside?" He replied, "That is the destroyer which brought down the Dornier in the North Sea yesterday." Rushing on my fate, I said, "I think if I were you, admiral, I should give her another lick of paint." He said, "I think if I were you, Mr Agate, I should stick to lecturing."

I think if I were Chris I should stick to editing. He does it so bloody well.

I arranged for a copy of this to be delivered at the Dorchester with instructions to hand it to Chris half-way through the speeches. After which I went to the Café Royal and dined with John Gielgud.

Nov. 7 *Sunday.* At the Club to-day I found a note from a brilliant British film director whom I appear to have praised for keeping a picture low in key. I extract:

> I'm glad to have had the technical sense to see what has escaped most people: the picture gets by because it's *under-played.* How the artists disliked doing it that way you can imagine—temperaments galore. On the whole it can be said that film actors don't need to *act*—they only need to be malleable. But if they are also alive as to the use of the medium *then* you get *real* acting. Otherwise the director does it by putting the face into the right place in the scene. My two leads never even knew what part of the film their scenes appeared in!

All this, of course, is only half true. Nevertheless, I shall make an article out of it, to annoy the Dilysians. Title? *Joy in Aves.* Stalky-ites will know where this comes from; the others don't deserve to be told.

Nov. 8 *Monday.* Hutchinson's have agreed to re-issue *Blessed Are the Rich* and *Gemel in London,* uniform with *Responsi-bility.* I WILL be collected, and if nobody else will do it I shall collect myself! The three slim volumes should look both chaste and seductive in their azure bindings with silver lettering.

Fatras. Our erudite newspapers.

> "Clara Jacobo made her début as Norma in Naples twenty-one years ago, and gave her last performance as Ballo in *Maschera* in Genoa late last year opposite Gigli."
>
> *Evening Standard* (November 8, 1943)

Nov. 9 *Tuesday.* For the first hour of Hemingway's *For Whom the Bell Tolls* I had not the vaguest notion which side all these unwashed brigands belonged to. Dancairo's lot, or Remendado's mob? Somebody wanted to blow up a bridge. Why? Somebody wanted to send a message through to somebody else. What message? The last time I saw Gary Cooper he was a champion at the ball game. What was the Pride of the Yankees doing in a country whose flat spaces would hardly accommodate a billiard table? Why should these bearded and unappetising ruffians harbour Ingrid Bergman, blonde as a glacier? Could it be that like Sonja Henie she was about to skate ? If so, on what ? Why did the dirtiest and most drunken of these scoundrels dither between loyalty and treachery, heroism and cowardice ? What was the point of that elderly Joan of Arc ? And then the fog was momentarily lifted. One of the brigands asked Gary what made him stick his nose in. Gary replied : " Well, brother, it's like this. We Yanks might have let you settle your own domestic disputes among yourselves. But then the Germans and Italians hit on the idea of using your war as a rehearsal for the abominable conflict we know they are about to let loose on mankind. Which was too much for decent Americans. So we are over here to do what we can for the simple peace-loving heart of Spain." After which Gary went on to tell the Republicans that they were the salt of the earth and would no more harm a hair of a nun's head than they would kill a fly. Whereupon Ingrid laid her Nordic curls on part of Gary's enormous chest and said that on the contrary it was the horrible Fascists who had cut off all her hair, and worse. And then, by way of showing what nice-mannered, charming people Republicans are, we were shown a ghastly sequence in which elderly Spanish Fascists were made to pass down a lane of Republicans battering them to death with clubs. After which the fog came down again, and there was a lot more about blowing up the bridge and getting the message through. And the bell tolled for Gary as we knew all along it must, and Ingrid made a lot of fuss as we knew all along she would. The film very good to look at in spite of Technicolor, and the acting the best I have ever seen in a picture. No, I don't mean Gary and Ingrid, who put over the usual Hollywood stuff—very sensitively and all that, but still the old stuff—but the seven or eight hirsute and smelly rogues, including a superb performance by Akim Tamiroff. Judging by what some of the film fellows write this morning about Katina Paxinou, you would think it was the first time they had seen a first-rate actress. Perhaps it is. As Pilar, who is a kind of gipsy Boadicea, she has little to do except look " werry fierce " in the best Nancy Price manner : this isn't and couldn't be on a level with her Electra. All the same, I think whoever prepared the preliminary ' literature ' should have known better than to call this tragédienne " the Lynn Fontanne of Greece." " Why not," murmurs Leo, " the East Lynne Fontanne of Greece ? "

Nov. 10 *Wednesday.* So long as there are rules of orthography and matters are not left to the taste and fancy of the speller, so long will reading be a martyrdom to me. A misspelt word affects my eye just as a wrong note affects my ear. Everybody at the Albert Hall would be horrified if the orchestra began the Fifth Symphony with three G's followed by an E natural. Yet apparently nobody makes any bones about printing Sedan with an acute accent. In Mrs Belloc-Lowndes's delightful *Where Love and Friendship Dwelt* Loti's *Pêcheur d'Islande* is put into the plural, and somebody is made to say "Vient [*sic*] que je t'embrasse!" The result to-night was that I could not read in peace. Surely Déjazet has an accent? Larousse, which I look up, says yes, but I have got to the point when I don't believe Larousse. So I go for confirmation to a letter in my possession written by Déjazet, only to discover that the annoying woman put in or left out accents as it pleased her!

Before *Ego* 6 appears the proofs will have been read by the printer, by the editorial staff at Harrap's, who have a genius for this sort of thing, by me at my brainsickliest, by Leo capriciously, by Jock cannily, by George Mathew devotedly, and by Brother Mycroft at his most Olympian. Nevertheless, I expect to find it teeming—perhaps "teaming"—with mistakes of all kinds. But after my beloved Mrs Belloc-Lowndes anything is possible. And only ten minutes ago I discovered that the *Oxford Dictionary of Quotations* makes Keats write:

> When I have fears that I may cease to be
> Before my pen has glean'd my teeming *train*.

But do these things really matter? Does it worry me that in *Esmond* Thackeray gives the heroine's part in Wycherley's *Love in a Wood* to Mrs Bracegirdle, who never appeared in any of W.'s plays? A rational view might be that accuracy, while important, is not all-important provided there's bigger game afoot. Brother Mycroft would doubtless point out here that it's no good going after big game unless you can shoot straight. Oh dear, oh dear!

Fatras. From a highbrow weekly:

ROOM TO LET. No bath, no c.h.w., but cool, calm atmosphere. Delightful outlook on trees in one of Bloomsbury's most lovely squares. Good fires, sunny, light, airy. Not especially moderate rent. Only reliable tenant accepted. Would prefer tenant away week-ends. Box ——.

Nov. 11 *Thursday.* Delighted with the first copy of *These Were Actors.* Hutchinson's have let me have my way in everything. Elegant type, good paper, bright geranium binding, the dust-cover in Georgian lettering without ornaments, blurb, or advertisements. A cursory reading discovers only one misprint—the omission of a full stop.

Nov. 12 *Friday.* A new complex has declared itself during the last twelve months. This is that one day I shall stand outside Lyons' Corner House with a tray of matches; it is a bitter cold night, and I have not got my bed at Rowton House. With this in view I have been collecting sixpences, which I keep in a cash-box hidden under a loose floor-board. For months, when I have wanted to give a sixpenny tip I have given a two-shilling piece, which means at least one and sometimes three sixpences change. By this means I have accumulated some hundreds, which I fondle in the small hours of the morning, like Gaspar in *Les Cloches de Corneville.* This is not a new neurosis but an old one revived. Forty years ago, when in business in Manchester, I was a prey to the notion that I might have to flee the country, there being no conceivable basis for such necessity. I remember that to cope with this I used to keep a passport and two hundred pounds in sovereigns locked away in a safe. At times I contemplated having a suitcase ready packed. Yet I suppose that I was then, and still am, what by ordinary standards is called sane. About one thing I am absolutely determined. I will never consult a psychoanalyst. They sit about in expensive drawing-rooms wearing hunting-stocks and nursing top-hats. I have seen them do it.

Nov. 15 *Monday.* Part of a letter from Brother Mycroft:

> What do you mean by "neuroses"? The very fact that you think you know all about them suggests to me that they are only "nerves" in the sense that if you had a bit more will-power you could get rid of them. Those are not "neuroses" at all, and are only on the surface. But they

may have an underlying cause which is a true neurosis, the finding and treatment of which might cure everything. Only a psycho-therapeutist can sort it out. But it is no use going to one in the attitude of a dog showing off a bunch of tricks, as a hypochondriac goes to a doctor expecting one nostrum after another to cure different, half-imaginary ailments. A psycho-therapeutist won't be interested in how often you turn off the gas, or whether you can go about alone, or sleep in the dark and so on. But if, having taken stock of yourself, you went to him in real distress, say, about your peace of mind, he would not only be interested, but helpful. But I must stress this, that you must be sincere. One might guess at some such state of mind as this, that in spite of success, adulation, celebrity, you are really miserable, and don't know why—that the peace of mind which is attainable by the humbler is denied to you, and that your most strenuous efforts of stimulation and excitement only result in your requiring more. There is, you know, a quality of living and feeling—a perception of beauty, a satisfaction with life itself, which is outside the arts and lies on a different plane. It has nothing to do with culture. It cannot be bestowed. It is barely glimpsed in the highest art, or any man-made effort. It cannot be shared, or communicated. It is each human being's birthright, an inner revelation sacred to himself. The essence of it is surrender, not achievement ; renouncement, not conquest. Ambition plays no part in it. The capacity to find, in one's own experience, such refuge, is how I should define peace of mind. It may be that your capacity has fallen into disuse. I don't know. I only know that no one can be happy without it. Some people might call it a religious sense. Again I don't know. All this may sound complete rubbish to you, but it is well meant, believe me.

My dear brother is talking about the peace which passeth understanding. What is denied me is the everyday calm enjoyed by the average man.

Dec. 4 *Saturday.* A little speech in honour of Sir Max Beerbohm, principal guest at the Savage Club Annual Dinner :

Devouring Time which blunts the lion's paws has not blunted my admiration for Sir Max Beerbohm. If I am chosen to speak a little tribute to him it is because I had the honour to be one of his successors on the old *Saturday Review*. It was after the last war and there were two of us in the running. Filson Young, who was then the paper's editor, showed me my rival's initial effort. It ended, "Oh Max, what a wag you are!" Filson said, "I will not have English of this sort in my paper. Max is a very great wit. He was never anything so vulgar as a wag."

And now I want to take you back a little. To the year 1898, when, dimly perceiving that the world held more than calico—I was a pushing young salesman in Manchester's grey cloth trade—I started my first newspaper-cutting book. I shall use this, still carefully preserved, to show you that the universal honour in which our guest is held stands, like that of the young gentleman in Tennyson, rooted in dishonour.

My first cutting is the last of those famous Saturday articles signed "G. B. S.":

"The gaiety of nations must not be eclipsed. The long string of beautiful ladies who are at present in the square without, awaiting, under the supervision of two gallant policemen, their turn at my bedside, must be reassured when they protest, as they will, that the light of their life will go out if my dramatic articles cease. To each of them I will present the flower left by her predecessor, and assure her that there are as good fish in the sea as ever came out of it. The younger generation is knocking at the door; and as I open it there steps spritely in the incomparable Max. For the rest, let Max speak for himself, I am off duty for ever, and am going to sleep."

My second cutting is from Max's first article, a week later. It contains the most humiliating, the most abject admissions ever made by a dramatic critic.

"Frankly, I have none of that instinctive love for the theatre which is the first step towards good criticism of drama. I am not fond of the theatre. Dramatic art interests and moves me less than any of the other arts. I am happy among pictures, and have learnt enough to know that I know nothing whatever about painting. Of music I have a genuine, though quite unenlightened love. Literature I love best of all, and I have some knowledge of its technicalities. I can talk intelligently about it. I have my little theories about it. But in drama I take, unfortunately, neither emotional nor intellectual pleasure. I am innocent of any theories on the subject. I shall have to vamp up my first principles as I go along, and they will probably be all wrong and all dull. For I have never acquired any lore in this kind of criticism. I could not test a theory nor quote a line from Hazlitt, Lamb, Lewes, and the rest, whose essays in dramatic criticism I have never read."

All good Savages will remember Macbeth's

> And be these juggling fiends no more believ'd,
> That palter with us in a double sense ;
> That keep the word of promise to our ear,
> And break it to our hope !—

I accuse Sir Max Beerbohm of having paltered in a double sense. I accuse him of breaking his illiterate promise and fulfilling his *Saturday Review* readers' most cultured and erudite expectancies. I turn up his article on Ellen Terry and I read:

" Tragedy, I admit, is the highest form of dramatic art ; and tragic acting is accordingly the highest form of histrionic art."

Now what is this but Lewes's :

" The greatest artist is he who is greatest in the highest reaches of his art."

And this plagiarism, this theft, is the work of a man who boasted, publicly, that he could not quote a line of Hazlitt, Lamb, Lewes, and the rest ! The article goes on :

" Miss Terry is no tragedian : I remember how lovable—what ' a great dear '—Lady Macbeth became through her ; and how unaccountable, and unimpressive, the whole tragedy. But to excel in Shakespearean comedy, as she excels, is to be authentically a great actress."

And in that passage I find my cue. Sir Max Beerbohm was for twelve years authentically a great dramatic critic. And this after denying that he had any of the essential qualifications. Oh, Max, what a wag you were !

Dec. 5 *Sunday.* Conversation in Grape Street :

JOCK. I've come to tell you that I'm away to the Navy in ten days' time. Unless, of course, I refuse to go.

J. A. In which case they'll put you in prison.

JOCK. And Dr Johnson would have been delighted. He would have said : " Here is a man who, rather than be a sailor, has had contrivance enough to get himself into a jail ! "

Dec. 6 *Monday.* A letter from Scotland :

Dec. 2, '43

DEAR MR AGATE,

Having been asked to give an address on Shaw to my colleagues at my Ladies' College I am appalled to find that, to me, he remains an enigma.

At the tender age of sixteen his works have aroused my curiosity and respect, but as for the man, he is beyond my comprehension.

Please, Mr Agate, spare just five minutes of your time in writing his biography for me.

I am,
Yours sincerely,
SYLVIA S——.

Am telling Sylvia to apply to the great man direct. If anybody can cram eighty-odd years on to a postcard it is G. B. S.

Dec. 7 *Tuesday.* " Personally I will pay any reasonable cover charge to look at Miss Beulah Beauregard's shape any time, if it is all I suspect. As far as I can see it is still a very nice shape indeed, if you care for shapes." Shall use this on Sunday à propos of Phyllis Dixey, who, at the Whitehall, conscientiously disrobes and sits around in a number of poses which are very nice poses indeed, if you care for poses.

Dec. 9 *Thursday.* Dreadful evening at the Arts Theatre. *On Life's Sunny Side*, by the Norwegian dramatist Helge Krog. A veranda overlooking a fiord. People talking about love. Somebody alters the disposition of a watering-can. No other action. I play rounds of mental golf at Thorpe Bay, Burnham Beeches, and Lytham, beating young Winsor, who gives me a bisque too many, drawing with young Snow, and losing to young Rawstron on the last green.

A beach, rocks, sunshine. More talkers. It seems that one of the talkers, a gentleman farmer, has taken the equivalent of a Bloomsbury highbrowette to live with him among the turnips. But how can he be sure it's conquest if there is no opposition ? So he invites an old flame of the highbrowette's to run down for a day or two. A variation of Molière's " Vous l'avez voulu, George Dandin. Vous l'avez voulu "? No. Just gab. So I run through as much as I can remember of the genealogies of Dandin's preposterous in-laws, and try to remember whether it was Maturine de Sotenville or Jacqueline de la Prudoterie who refused a royal offer of twenty thousand crowns for the privilege of kissing her finger-tips. In the middle of this the act-drop falls.

Indoors now. The spate continues, and I while away the time thinking of a lecture I delivered to London school-teachers nearly twenty years ago. It is about the lovers in Shakespeare, and takes place at the London School of Economics. I recall how, leaving the theatre, I hear one young woman say to another, " Yes, it was all right. But I wish I'd heard the other lecture." And how I rush to the notice-board and find that my rival's talk has been about " Alternative Systems of Accountancy on Chinese Railways." And I come back to to-night's play. Why must we be always bored with stuff about love ? Why can't this Mr Krog give us something about the peculating directors of funicular railways ? I seem to remember that Ibsen made a pretty good drama about impurities in municipal bath-water.

Dec. 12 *Sunday.* My carefully prepared speech last night at the Water Rats Cabaret and Ball called for some quick revision.

I arrived at the Queensberry Club to find it crowded from floor to ceiling with American and Australian troops, which meant that references to Dan Leno and Arthur Roberts, and even Harry Tate and George Robey, would be lost. However, I got through somehow, and the fact that nobody knew what I was talking about gave, I understand, a tone to the proceedings. Mark played, the First Lord spoke, and all very jolly. I noticed that the speakers looked to a box on the left and began their speeches with " Your Highness." Asking who the Highness might be, I was told it was the Crown Prince of Arabia. Therefore I, too, began " Your Highness." At the end of the speech the M.C. said that the Prince had graciously consented to say a few words. Whereupon the band struck up what appeared to be the Arabian National Anthem, we all stood, and down the stairs came a magnificent specimen of Oriental humanity attended by a woolly Ethiopian who was obviously His Highness's secretary. Splendiferously turban'd and caftan'd, the Prince took the centre of the stage with enormous dignity. And then, at a signal from the M.C., the band struck up a popular dance tune, and the pair fell into a buck and wing dance. This concluded, Bud Flanagan presented each of them with a pound note, and two of Soho's duskier denizens passed out of history. Taking my cue from Damon Runyon, I personally do not think this Crown Prince is any more Arabian than Mr Fred Emney.

Dec. 14 *Tuesday.* Jock joined the Navy to-day, and Fleet Street lost a great deal of its gaiety and charm. Let us hope it is only for a short time. His last quip to me was that, while the prospect is odious, the name of his training ship is enchanting.

Dec. 15 *Wednesday.* Found this on my desk to-night:

Shortly after you left there was a ring at the door, and standing outside I saw two people, a short fat man with a long nose, and a woman who was still shorter and fatter and whose nose was even longer.

THE MAN. You are Mister Ar-*gutt* ?

L. P. No, I'm his secretary.

THE MAN. We would wish to be received by Mister Ar-*gutt*.

L. P. He's not in. Can I do anything for you ?

THE MAN. You allow perhaps that I enter. Allow that I introduce myself. Dr Israel Bauchpresser. (*All bow.*) Allow that I introduce my sister-in-law, Miss Erna Katzengebiss. (*All bow again and L. P. asks them in. He begs them to be seated.*)

DR B. Perhaps you tell Mr Ar-*gutt* what is my complaint. It is that follows. My sister-in-law, Miss Erna Katzengebiss, writes to Mr Ar-*gutt* a letter. She has offered to read to him a play from her, also from me translated into the English. But no answer arrives. I then write to Mr Ar-*gutt* to invite him to write for me an article for my new magazine. Even I give him the subject. But again no answer arrives. Why, if you will tell me, does not an answer arrive ?

L. P. Mr Agate is busy, he cannot answer every letter.

MISS K. Israel, Du vergeudest die Zeit, erzähl' ihm von meinem Stück.

DR B. It is true, I forget. Since this shall be the object of our visit. The piece *Heinrich von Hohenstaufen* will be performed for four times on the next week by our new Society, the German-European Kulturverein. We shall perform at our private theatre in the district of Bron-des-bury. And for my sister-in-law will the finest artists in Germany perform. Rika Pfotz. . . .

MISS K. Beata Polinsky. . . .

DR B. Oskar Rosenschwanz. . . .

Miss K. Gerhardt Blitz, Simon Salamon. . . .

Dr B. You see, the greatest. So here my invitation. Mr Ar-*gutt* shall come to hear the play and shall write about it in the *Sunday Times*.

L. P. I am afraid Mr Agate will do nothing of the kind!

Dr B. He likes not the German plays?

L. P. He loathes them.

Dr B. He likes not the German actors?

L. P. He loathes the German language.

Dr B. But in this country we are guests.

L. P. He hates guests.

Dr B. He will not come?

L. P. I should think it highly improbable.

Dr B. Then we waste the time. Come, Erna. (*To L.P.*) I think you perhaps not understand. We ask not that Mr Ar-*gutt* shall pay. We send him a free seat.

L. P. Even with that inducement I cannot hold out any hope. Good afternoon. (*Once more all bow. And Dr Bauchpresser descends the steps abusing the English bitterly. The last words L. P. can discern are: "Philister . . . Keine Idee von Kunst. . . . Was hat der Napoleon gesagt. . . ."*)

Dec. 16 *Thursday.* George Harrap telephones to say that if I want *Ego* 6 to be published in the spring I must ring down now. I had thought of ending the present, and conceivably last, instalment with a reference to the *Sunday Times* notice of *Brief Chronicles*:

> This book does more than put Mr Agate unremovably in the company of our very greatest dramatic critics along with Hazlitt and Lamb and with one who might have overshadowed them all—to wit, John Keats. It also places him high in the small company of genuinely understanding and inspiring critics of Shakespeare.

I had thought of ending on the note:

> Most people would take this to be a signal for their *Nunc dimittis*. With me it works the other way. I emit a barbaric, Whitmanesque yawp, and cry in my best dog-Latin, *Nunc continuo!*

And now I confess to some doubts as to whether *continuare* is the right verb for me to conjugate. I have before me a booklet entitled *Music and Society*, written by a Mr Eric

Siegmeister and published by the Workers' Music Association. Listen!

> Can it be that we have come to the end of the period of great music? If by " great music " is meant the music that has been great in fulfilling the *bourgeois* function of music, the function of individual exaltation, personal escape, private dreams and emotions, subjective aspirations and release—then unhesitatingly we answer: " Yes! " It is unlikely that there will be many more great works of this kind—at least not in our present society. The vitality of that function of music is passing away with the vitality of the class that called it into being.

If the foregoing is held to be true of drama, then in so far as it falls to me to interpret the achievements of the bourgeois I belong to that class and must pass with it. Meaning that the day is at hand when people will buy their newspapers to read, not me, but some younger man. Very well, then. If I cannot be a draw, I am resolved not to be a drag. On the day that I am convinced that the community is the richer for my silence—I shall shut myself up in my ivory tower. " And, I suppose," laughs some Brave New Reader, " issue belated communiqués about Irving, Bernhardt, and the like? " Yes, dear boy. Except that they had no like.

INDEX OF PERSONS